# Horizons

# Health 6

## Health Inside and Out

## Teacher's Guide

**Organizer / Writer**
Gene Ezell

**Design and Layout**
Leann Kruger

**Major Contributors**
Thea Beebe
Janna Brasser
Jesslyn DeBoer
Connie Gergolas

**Supervising Editor**
Hazel Timmer

**Executive Editor**
Alan Christopherson

 AOP

804 N. 2nd Ave. E.  Rock Rapids, IA 51246-1759  800-622-3070  www.aop.com

*Horizons Health 6* Teacher's Guide
© MMVII by Alpha Omega Publications, Inc.
804 N. 2nd Ave. E., Rock Rapids, IA 51246-1759
All rights reserved.

The framework for this curriculum was provided by:
CHRISTIAN SCHOOLS INTERNATIONAL
3350 East Paris Ave. SE
Grand Rapids, Michigan 49512-3054

*Printed in the United States of America*

ISBN 978-0-7403-1499-5

# CONTENTS

# ACKNOWLEDGMENTS

In the summer of 1989, a new health curriculum for Christian schools was planned. That fall a survey of teachers was conducted in grades K-6. The survey indicated that health was becoming an increasingly significant component of the elementary school curriculum. The survey also revealed that Christian school teachers were eager to have materials containing a clear biblical perspective.

Dr. Gene Ezell, a professor of health education at the University of Tennessee at Chattanooga, developed a content outline and scope and sequence for the *Horizons Health* series. He also was the first author of materials for teacher guides.

Many other individuals helped in the preparation of teacher guides for grades 3–6. The materials were reviewed and field tested in several schools during the 1991-92 academic year. Also providing input, critiques, and suggestions was Ben Boerkoel. Wendy Blankespoor helped to develop the list of resources for units and lessons.

The publications program was directed by Gordon L. Bordewyk. The supervising editor for *Horizons Health* was Hazel Timmer. Judy Bandstra oversaw production of the materials, and Cheryl Strikwerda Randall created the illustrations.

"What's Your Bag?" from *Tribes: A Process for Social Development and Cooperative Learning* by Jeanne Gibbs. Copyright © 1987 by Jeanne Gibbs, Center Source Publications, Santa Rosa, CA 94507; phone 707-577-8233. Used with permission. (Unit 2, Lesson 2)

"Patterns of Inheritance: The Height Game" from *You, Me, and Others,* Grade 5–6, Unit 3: The Chain of Life. Copyright © 1985 March of Dimes. Reprinted by permission of the March of Dimes Birth Defects Foundation. (Unit 2, Lesson 3)

*Michigan Model for Comprehensive School Health Education,* Grade 6, Phase IV. Used by permission of Michigan Department of Public Health. (Unit 2, Lesson 6)

"Jesu, Jesu" by Tom Colvin. Music: Ghana Folk Song, adapted by Tom Colvin. Copyright © 1969 by Hope Publishing Co., Carol Stream, Ill. 60188. All rights reserved. Used with permission. (Unit 3, Lesson 3)

Lesson 19 *Michigan Model for Comprehensive Health Education,* Grade 6, Phase III. Reprinted by permission of the Michigan Department of Public Health. (Unit 4, Lesson 4)

"Seat Belt Survey" from *Three Seconds to Safety.* Copyright © 1982 by the American Seat Belt Council. (Unit 8, Lesson 1)

## Role of the Christian School in Health Education

The primary responsibility for educating children belongs to parents. But in the Christian community parents do not have that responsibility alone—church and school also participate in the task of education. The church nurtures the faith of its young members, leading them to understand the implications of faith for their lives. The Christian school teaches children and young people about God's world, equipping them for lives of service. Deriving its authority to educate from the parents who send their children to the school, the Christian school supports and augments instruction provided in the home by teaching all curriculum subjects from a biblical perspective.

One curriculum subject is properly health education. Historically this subject has had low priority in curriculum planning; however, among educators today there is a growing awareness of the importance of health education in a balanced curriculum. Educators are recognizing that in order to promote the well-rounded development of children, the school must give sufficient attention to the healthful living of children as individuals and as members of families and communities. A sequential and comprehensive health education curriculum, such as the *Horizons Health* series, provides the Christian school with the opportunity to deal with basic life issues from a Christian perspective in a consistent way.

The serious health problems facing the contemporary world—the threat of HIV/AIDS, the widespread use of recreational drugs, the prevalence of teenage pregnancy, the easy access to abortion—underscore the need for a sound, Christian program of health education. More than ever before students need current, accurate information and clear direction on healthful living. Today's health crises dramatically highlight the obligation of home, church, and school to work together to bring the lordship of Christ to bear on the health education of the community's children.

## General Christian Perspective

A Christian perspective on health education begins with the Bible's account of who we are and why we are here. The Bible tells us that we have been created by God in his image. We have been created male and female. We have been created to live in harmony with God, with each other, and with the rest of creation. And we have been assigned the task of caring for God's world.

The Bible has more to tell us. It tells us that because of sin our relationship with God is broken; because of sin we no longer clearly reflect God's image. We live at odds with God and with one another. We don't take care of the created world the way God intended. Even when we try our hardest, we often end up doing the evil we don't want to do (Romans 7:19). And physical death is inevitable.

But that's not the end of our story. In Christ, God has broken the cycle of sin and death. In Christ, God is making us whole. In Christ, God is restoring our relationship to him and to one another. In Christ, we are able to experience the beginning of new life—eternal life— and the hope of a new heaven and earth. We look forward to complete renewal and restoration.

It is this story of redemption history that provides the underlying perspective on health education in the Christian school. When we talk about family life, sexuality, physical fitness, death and dying, and other health topics, it is always in the context of this story.

## Christian Perspective and Health Education

Christians believe that God created each human being as an organic unity. The Genesis 2 account of creation says that the Lord God formed man from the dust, breathed into him the breath of life, "and the man became a living being" (verse 7). The Bible does refer to various aspects of the person—such as the mind, flesh, soul, spirit, or heart—but the stress is on the unity of the whole being. The various aspects of a person—the intellectual, emotional, social, spiritual, and physical—are interdependent. In the New Testament the apostle Paul, writing to Corinthian Christians, supports this point of view. Some Corinthians, influenced by their pagan culture, apparently believed that gluttony, drunkenness, or promiscuous sexual activity did not affect their "spiritual" life. Paul counters by strongly denouncing this attitude (1 Corinthians 6: 12-19).

What is the significance of this Christian view of the person for education? It means that health education cannot be treated as incidental to the curriculum. Rather, it must be an integral part of the curriculum at every level. Physical fitness, nutrition, personal health, emotional health, the functioning of body systems—all strands of the health curriculum— affect the whole child. We must recognize that since healthy living affects us in our totality, health education plays a solid role in developing children and equipping them to serve God in the world.

• • • • • • • • • • • • • • • • • • • • • • •

God has given human beings the task of caring for creation. This task includes being caretakers of ourselves. The *Horizons Health* series helps students fulfill their God-given responsibility in several ways. It teaches them about proper personal and dietary health and encourages them to make good choices in these areas. For example, students learn about the different nutritional value in various foods, how family backgrounds and lifestyles influence eating patterns, and the importance of cleanliness in handling and consuming foods. The series also teaches students about personal safety, helping them to handle emergencies and to take precautions to avoid injury and harm. Another strand of *Horizons Health* deals with body systems, and students come to understand how they are "fearfully and wonderfully made." Still another strand deals with disease. In this area students learn, for example, about the defenses which God has provided for our bodies, and how each person can help prevent the spread of disease. The strand of emotional and mental health leads students to develop an honest and healthy self-image concept and to deal with feelings in wholesome ways. Finally, a curriculum strand dealing with substance use and abuse acquaints students with the risks associated with tobacco, alcohol, and drugs.

The Christian view of a person's responsibility to care for himself or herself in order to honor God runs counter to the prevailing view in North American culture. Our culture says that what we do with our body is an individual matter. Sports and fitness are often used for self-glorification, elevating the body to a higher status than it warrants. At the same time, abuse of the body through addiction, inattention to nutrition, or lack of exercise is also common. In a culture such as this, spelling out how we honor God with healthful living and nurturing Christian attitudes toward ourselves and others are crucial for the Christian community.

• • • • • • • • • • • • • • • • • • • • • • •

The Christian's view of death and dying also differs from the view prevalent in society. Christians recognize disease and death as part of sin's effects on creation. Physical death is inevitable, but for those who have new life in Christ, death is not the last word. However, even though Christ has removed death's ultimate sting, death is still the Christian's enemy (1 Corinthians 15: 26, 55).

One strand of the *Horizons Health* series helps students view death and dying from this Christian perspective. In ways appropriate to the developmental levels of the students, the curriculum deals honestly with topics such as fear of death, inevitability of death, and ways Christians cope with death and dying.

• • • • • • • • • • • • • • • • • • • • • • •

Christians are called to reflect God's love in all their relationships. The social health strand of the health curriculum assists students to develop mature Christian attitudes towards others. They also learn interpersonal skills necessary for getting along with others. Thus students are lead to become contributing members of their communities. To answer our deepest needs, God created us to live in relationship with others.

Christians believe that marriage and family are part of a loving God's design for the human race. God, reflecting on his creation, decided that it was not good for Adam to be alone: "I will make a suitable helper for him" (Genesis 2:18). So God established marriage—and by extension, the family—as a cornerstone of creation. As part of God's creation, marriage was very good. The Bible has such a high view of marriage that it uses marriage as a symbol of the relationship of Christ and the Church.

But marriage and family have not escaped the effects of sin. Sin's results are loneliness, alienation, the breaking of family relationships, and the collapse of marriages. In North American society, these effects of sin are also clearly evident. In fact, for some, marriage and the family simply seem outdated institutions that are no longer useful. And pursuing a course of self-fulfillment is held up by many as the highest goal of life.

Christians believe that in Jesus Christ there is healing for brokenness and power to restore family relationships. He calls us to a life of service and responsibility in the family. And although our efforts are imperfect and our homes are not free of trouble, by God's grace family life can be a source of comfort and joy.

The family life strand of the *Horizons Health* series leads students to appreciate the blessings of family life and to assume responsibilities of family membership. Working through family topics—such as resolving conflicts, the importance of basing family life on God's law, knowing how sexuality affects life, and caring for sexuality in a way pleasing to God—helps students to establish basic Christian life patterns, patterns that will have a far-reaching effect on their lives.

• • • • • • • • • • • • • • • • • • • • • • • •

In summary, the *Horizons Health* curriculum seeks to teach Christian students how the lordship of Christ results in healthful living. For only as students acknowledge their accountability to God and form their lives according to his Word are they able to become all their Creator wants them to become and live lives of thankfulness and service.

# OVERVIEW

## 1. What is Horizons Health?

*Horizons Health* is a comprehensive health education curriculum for grades K-8. The series addresses the mental, emotional, social, and spiritual aspects of health as well as the physical. It helps students take responsibility for their health as individuals and as members of families and communities. It gives them opportunity to develop basic life skills—such as communicating, decision making, and resolving conflicts—in order to prepare them to meet the challenges of daily living. Its Christian perspective leads students to recognize that a healthy lifestyle is a lifestyle of obedience to God.

## 2. How is the curriculum organized?

*Horizons Health* is a flexible curriculum, organized into independent units. The units can be taught in any order, depending on your curriculum needs. Each unit focuses primarily on one or two main strands of the curriculum, with lesser strands integrated where appropriate. These are the eleven strands, which are addressed at each grade level:

Emotional/Mental Health                 Nutrition
Social Health/Interpersonal Skills       Disease Prevention
Family Life/Human Sexuality              Safety and First Aid
Growth and Development                   Substance Use and Abuse
Personal Health                          Consumer Health
Community Health

The scope and sequence chart shows the topics covered in each strand at this grade level and at the other grade levels of the series.

## 3. Do concepts covered in health education overlap with those covered in other content areas?

Because this is a comprehensive health program rather than a single-topic program, overlap unavoidably occurs in certain content areas. Health education, for example, teaches students about how their bodies work and how substance use and abuse, physical fitness, and nutrition can affect body structures and functions; however, structure and function of body systems may currently be taught in science. Schools may wish to integrate areas that overlap.

## 4. What is the personal safety component of Horizons Health?

At grades K-2 the safety unit includes a lesson on stranger education. In addition, at each level from kindergarten through grade 6 there is one lesson in the safety unit on preventing sexual abuse. In age-appropriate ways, each level deals with differentiating appropriate and inappropriate touch, developing self-protection skills, and identifying sources of help in case of abuse.

Since personal safety is a sensitive area, schools should inform parents about the content of these lessons. Clear communication not only creates trust within the community but also ensures that parents will support and reinforce personal safety concepts taught at school.

Before teaching lessons on personal safety, schools should also develop and adopt a protocol for dealing with suspected or reported abuse. Contact the provincial or state department responsible for child protective services to obtain information and copies of relevant laws. Schools interested in obtaining samples of school policy statements on child welfare that include a protocol for dealing with abuse should contact organizations like the Society of Christian Schools in British Columbia, 7600 Glover Road, Langley, British Columbia V2Y 1Y1.

5. **What is the sex education component of Horizons Health?**
Sex education is placed within the broader context of family life and human sexuality, one of the strands of the curriculum. Thus at every level *Horizons Health* deals with concepts relating to human sexuality. The grade 5 unit "Growing and Changing" deals specifically with the onset of puberty and the changes it brings.

6. **Is HIV/AIDS education included in the health program?**
HIV/AIDS education is integrated into the program as part of the disease prevention strand. At grades K-2 there are no HIV/AIDS-specific lessons; however, the broader health issues and concepts addressed at these levels—preventing communicable disease, the relationship between personal choices and health, and our God-given responsibility to honor and care for our body—establish the foundation for understanding HIV/AIDS-specific concepts at higher grades. In grades 3-6 students learn about AIDS and HIV in age-appropriate ways. Grade 5 includes a lesson on sexually transmitted diseases, including HIV/AIDS.

7. **How can schools best implement a comprehensive health education?**
Planning a strategy to implement the program is crucial for the curriculum to be effective. Three main areas to address are these: keeping parents informed and involved, assisting teachers with resources and training in specialized areas, and providing a school environment that supports the program.

First, parents need to be informed and involved. Because some topics covered in health are controversial, good communication is particularly important. Meeting with parents at the beginning of the year to discuss the content and goals of health education and sending letters home to inform parents about what students are learning and doing in *Horizons Health* (particularly in advance of lessons dealing with sensitive issues) are good basic strategies. Involving parents strengthens the program as health concepts learned at school are reinforced at home.

Second, schools need to provide teachers with resources and training. Many health education curricula have compulsory teacher-training sessions because of the special challenges a comprehensive health education program presents. Some health topics have traditionally not been part of the school curriculum in a formal way, and few teachers have had courses in health education. Thus teachers need opportunities through workshops or in-service training to become comfortable in dealing with sensitive areas such as sexual abuse and substance abuse. In addition, they need resources to support the curriculum and to keep current on health issues. Local or provincial/state agencies and volunteer agencies (for example, the American/Canadian Red Cross or American/Canadian Lung Association) are sources of valuable assistance and offer a wealth of resources. In some cases, inviting experts into the classroom may be advisable.

Third, the total school environment should support the health curriculum and reinforce classroom lessons. Students learn in the classroom about eating snacks that are nutritious and "tooth smart," but does the school ask students to take part in an annual candy sale to raise money for the school? Does the school library contain current materials about a wide variety of wellness issues? What does the climate of the school teach about interpersonal relationships, about living in community? Does the school community model what a Christian community should be? Health education cannot end when students step out of the classroom. Schools need to consider what kind of messages the total environment is sending.

# USING HORIZONS HEALTH

The curriculum consists of independent units that can be taught in any order. This flexible design makes it possible for you to choose segments that meet your curriculum needs and your time schedule. The unit summaries found at the beginning of each unit give a quick overview of the unit and help you decide which units or lessons to use.

There are approximately 50 lessons at each of the grade levels. With a time schedule of a 30- to 40-minute session for each lesson, *Horizons Health* requires daily sessions for 12 to 14 weeks (or 17-19 weeks teaching three sessions per week and 25-27 weeks teaching two sessions per week). An interdisciplinary program, health lends itself to integration with other subjects, such as Bible, language arts, music, art, science, and social studies. Suggestions for integration are included throughout the curriculum.

*Horizons Health* provides a carefully planned and comprehensive framework for teaching health education. It is meant to furnish guidelines and suggestions; it is not meant to prescribe each step of each lesson. You are the one to mold and adapt the material and translate it to fit your students and your community.

A student book is an integral part of the curriculum for grades 3-6, providing readings, drawings, illustrations, and other essential materials. Questions at the end of each section in the book check comprehension or stimulate further reflection.

## Teacher Guide Format, 3-6

The units begin with an overview that includes the following components:
- A *Unit Summary* gives an "at-a-glance" list of lessons.
- *Goals* for the unit are outlined.
- The *Background* provides Christian perspective and/or helpful unit information.
- *Vocabulary* lists words students need to know to understand unit health concepts.
- *Unit Resources* offers suggestions of titles of organizations, books, kits, or audiovisuals helpful as teacher or student resources to support the unit as a whole.
- *Lesson Resources* suggests materials for specific lessons. Most of these resources are listed again in the lesson.

The lessons follow this format:
- *Preparation/Materials* lists what things are needed for the lesson and describes necessary preparations.
- *Objectives* for the lesson are outlined.
- *Background* appears in selected lessons, providing specific information on health issues, alerting teachers to sensitive lesson topics, or providing Christian perspective.
- *The Lesson* offers a step-by-step outline. Each lesson ends with a suggestion for closing, providing an opportunity for reflection, self-awareness, summary, or evaluation.
- *Related Activities* provide additional suggestions for student activities, expanding or extending the lesson.

Masters for Teacher Visuals are located in the back of the Teacher's Guide.

## Resources

Multimedia resources can significantly increase the impact of the health curriculum, and numerous suggestions for resources have been included. Few health education resources, however, are written from a Christian perspective. Careful screening is necessary before using resources in the classroom. In some cases, you may decide to use selected sections or perhaps to use the materials but add a critical evaluation.

The listings provide suggestions for resources, but keep in mind that the health field changes rapidly. So although we have included resources that were once available, you will need to re-examine and look online for sources to keep the curriculum up-to-date.

Many community and national volunteer health organizations offer educational materials in their special areas. These materials, which include kits, songs, multimedia presentations, lesson plans, activities, posters, student booklets, or brochures for parents, are often available at minimal cost. Many of the materials produced by these organizations are listed in the Unit or Lesson Resources. A list of national health organizations is included at the end of the Introduction. Because new materials are constantly being produced, contacting these health organizations periodically will help you to tap an ongoing source of valuable resources.

# HEALTH EDUCATION RESOURCES

**SHAPE America**
> 1900 Association Drive
> Reston, VA 20191
> 800-213-7193

**Canadian Association for Health, Physical Education, Recreation, and Dance (CAHPERD)**
> http://www.cahperd.ca/
>> SHAPE America and CAHPERD are national organizations committed to promoting health and fitness through a wide variety of programs and publications.

**Substance Abuse and Mental Health Services Administration**
> 600 Fishers Ln
> Rockville, MD 20857
> 877-SAMHSA-7 (877-726-4727)
> http://www.samhsa.gov/

**National Family Partnership**
> 2490 Coral Way
> Miami, FL 33145
> 888-474-0008

**Office of Disease Prevention and Health Promotion (ODPHP)**
> https://health.gov/
> https://www.healthypeople.gov/
> https://healthfinder.gov/
>> The Office of Disease Prevention and Health Promotion (ODPHP) plays a vital role in keeping the nation healthy. They manage the three websites listed.

**Parents Against Drugs (PAD)**
> 245 Lakeshore Dr.
> Toronto, Ontario
> M8V-2A8
> 416-604-4360
>> Offers current information about drug abuse and a drug awareness.

**National Institute on Drug Abuse**

6001 Executive Boulevard, Room 5213
Bethesda, MD 20892-9561
https://www.drugabuse.gov/

Their mission is to advance science on the causes and consequences of drug use and addiction and to apply that knowledge to improve individual and public health.

**U.S. Department of Health and Human Services**

U.S. Public Health Service
Centers for Disease Control and Prevention, CDC
Adolescent and School Health
https://www.cdc.gov/healthyyouth/
1-800-CDC-INFO (800-232-4636)

Offers resource suggestions and updated information about HIV/AIDS.

# SCOPE AND SEQUENCE

| | Growth and Development | Disease Prevention | Substance Use/Abuse |
|---|---|---|---|
| **K** | • growth awareness • five senses and corresponding body parts • primary/secondary teeth | • germs and disease • preventing spread of germs • effect of smoke on lungs | • defining medicine • rule: only adults give medicine • consulting adult before using any unknown substance • choosing a smoke-free environment |
| **1** | • review of five senses • naming external body parts • joints • four main organs: brain, heart, stomach, lungs • interrelationship of body parts • growth predictions • primary/secondary teeth | • defining communicable/noncommunicable disease • preventing spread of germs • immunizations • health checkups • effect of smoking on lungs | • differentiating drugs and medicines • symbols for hazardous substances • identifying some drugs |
| **2** | • growth awareness • introduction to body systems • function and interdependence of senses • function and basic structure of eyes and ears • visual/hearing impairments | • disease symptoms • defining bacteria and viruses • how germs enter body • effects of nicotine, alcohol, and caffeine on body • identifying eye problems | • identifying common drugs: alcohol, tobacco, and caffeine • products containing caffeine • effect of caffeine on body • how nicotine enters the body • how alcohol affects physical reactions • differentiating prescription and over-the-counter drugs • reasons for using medicine |
| **3** | • overview of body systems: skin, muscular, skeletal, digestive, respiratory, circulatory, nervous, excretory (main parts and interrelationships) • growth and development problems (special populations) | • communicable and chronic diseases • AIDS transmission through blood and hypodermic needles • immunizations, proper food storage, and cleanliness as ways to control disease | • defining terms • proper use vs. misuse of substances • influence of advertising on use of over-the-counter medicines • dosages • labels for information • tolerance and addiction • harmful effects of tobacco, smoking |
| **4** | • miracle of life • hereditary factors • structure and function of blood • the immune system • hair, skin, and nails • structure and function of teeth • digestive system: parts of, process of digestion • cells/tissues/organs/systems • functions and kinds of cells | • care of skin • diseases of digestive system • lack of nutrients and disease • alcoholism • long term/short term effects of smoking • review HIV transmission through blood, needles | • review of terms: drugs, medicines, substance, prescription, OTC • side effects of medications • avoiding misuse of OTCs • harmful effects of tobacco, alcohol, marijuana, cocaine • defining alcoholism • refusal skills |
| **5** | • respiratory system • variations in growth rates • endocrine system • physical, emotional, and social changes of puberty • reproductive system | • main classes of pathogens • chain of infection • some common communicable diseases • preventing respiratory diseases • sexually transmitted diseases, including characteristics, transmission, and prevention of HIV infection | • review of terminology • demonstrating effect of smoking on lungs • refusal skills |
| **6** | • fetal development • stages of life • processes by which cells receive nutrients and oxygen: diffusion, filtration, osmosis • review of main body systems, main parts and functions • hereditary and environmental factors • impairments | • preventing cardiovascular disease • risk factors of cardiovascular disease • diseases of muscular, skeletal, and nervous systems • hereditary and environmental factors in disease • alcoholism and cirrhosis • anorexia and bulimia • AIDS/HIV | • chemical dependency and its effects • steroids • results of substance use • societal pressure to use substances • resisting alcohol advertising • strategies for resisting pressure |
| **7/8** | • characteristics of stages of life • review of interdependence of body systems • changes of puberty • review of reproductive system • impairments • identifying learning styles | • biblical view of disease • lifestyle choices and disease • eating disorders • suntanning • sexually transmitted diseases, including HIV/AIDS • review reducing risk of communicable and acquired diseases • understanding reality of health problems | • alcohol, tobacco, drug abuse (student research) • decision-making and refusal skills |

| | Nutrition | Emotional/Mental Health | Social Health/Interpersonal Skills |
|---|---|---|---|
| **K** | • food for energy and growing • plant and animal food sources • eating a variety of foods | • created unique • differences and similarities • main feelings • situations and feelings • responding to others' feelings | • minding manners • manners and feelings • listening to each other • ways to share • cooperating |
| **1** | • food and body energy • five food groups • eating from all food groups • eating healthy snacks • diet and tooth health | • created unique • alike and different • naming and exploring feelings • body language • dealing with feelings • ways to deal with anger • developing empathy | • purpose of good manners • practicing good manners • active listening steps • sharing • practicing cooperation |
| **2** | • five food groups • limiting extras • daily serving requirements • balanced eating • cleanliness and food handling • eating breakfast • smart snacks for teeth | • identifying individual gifts/interests • blessing others with our gifts • review of main feelings • identifying a variety of feelings • feelings and actions • communicating feelings • developing empathy • saying no and feelings | • communicating with others • developing social skills/manners • showing appreciation • helping others • active listening • selfish/unselfish attitudes • importance of cooperating |
| **3** | • classifying foods • combination foods • define nutrients needed for growth, maintenance, repair of body • limited nutritional value of some foods • healthy snacks • diet and tooth decay | • self-awareness and acceptance • appreciating diversity • identifying and expressing feelings • emotions and body feelings • how feelings affect thoughts and actions • dealing with specific emotions: fear, hurt, anger, being left out • humor and feelings | • developing friendships • factors that affect friendships • kinds of friendships • showing kindness toward others • laughing with, not at • active listening • resolving conflicts |
| **4** | • six major classes of nutrients: fats, carbohydrates, water, minerals, vitamins, protein • function of nutrients • serving size • lack of nutrients and disease • good food, good times | • self-knowledge and knowledge of God • being saints and sinners • individual differences as part of God's plan • using gifts to serve • how others affect self-concept • showing appreciation for others • handling and expressing feelings • avoiding self-putdowns • making decisions | • belonging to groups other than family • showing respect for others • accepting differences • communication skills • working out problems in interpersonal relationships |
| **5** | • review of main nutrients and their sources • vitamins, minerals, and their functions • function of water • individual nutrition requirements • nutrition deficiencies and health • influences on eating patterns | • growing up • identifying individual strengths • range of feelings • developing feelings vocabulary • ways of dealing with emotions • expressing feelings without blaming • overall wellness and emotions • dealing with anger in healthy ways | • wise ways in relationships (Proverbs) • forgiveness and maintaining friendships • respecting others • resolving conflicts • social skills • cooperative skills |
| **6** | • criteria for proper food selection • diet analysis • nutrients: carbohydrates, proteins, fats • reducing salt and sugar • results of unbalanced diet • eating disorders | • new life in Christ • patterns of life: inherited and acquired characteristics • handling ups and downs of feelings • interaction of feelings, thoughts, and actions • identifying and managing stress • recognizing influences • decision making and peer influence | • identifying social support network • factors that build up or break down relationships • erecting barriers: prejudice, discrimination, labeling • communication: basic elements, verbal/nonverbal, active listening • deciding to care about others |
| **7/8** | • proper nutrition and dieting | • identifying self as God's image bearer and God's child • being made new in Christ • self-talk and self-confidence • discovering, accepting, and developing gifts • using gifts to serve God/community • influence of media on self-concept • decision-making values/strategies • setting goals • developing study skills • being assertive • recognizing and expressing feelings | • biblical view of community • types of love • living in community • dealing with internal/peer pressure • using peer pressure positively • friendship • dealing with conflict • communication |

| | Family Life/Human Sexuality | Personal Health | Community Health |
|---|---|---|---|
| **K** | • families—part of God's plan • similarities/differences among families • gender differences • feelings and family • our families and God's family • dealing with death | • good health choices • dressing to stay healthy • exercise and rest • cleanliness and health • care of teeth: brushing and checkups | • health helpers • smoke in environment |
| **1** | • living things reproduce • families—part of God's plan • kinds of families • contributing to family life • family changes • death and Christian hope • Christian families in context of God's family | • making healthy choices • staying fit • eating from all food groups • tooth care: plaque, brushing, checkups, diet • grooming and health | • defining pollution • causes of air pollution • health helpers • immunizations |
| **2** | • families provide basic needs • human sexuality, a gift of God • exploring gender differences/similarities • resolving conflicts • family rules • new beginnings and forgiveness • family heritage and traditions • dealing with death | • good health habits • keeping fit and active • avoiding too much TV • getting enough sleep • eating a balanced diet • eating healthy snacks and breakfast • review of good grooming habits • tooth care: brushing, flossing, snacks | • noise pollution |
| **3** | • God's law of love as the basis of family living • depending on family members • communicating in families • living patterns and culture • life cycle and the family • sexual identity, an integral part of a person • dealing with death | • benefits of fitness • being physically fit; flexibility, endurance, strength • good posture • oral hygiene • eating healthy foods • benefits of sleep | • health agencies • role of community workers in safety |
| **4** | • institution of marriage/family • responsibility and family life • family and the wider community • communicating • death and dying | • components of personal health • building physical fitness • importance of cleanliness • posture • sleep and rest | • effect of contaminated food, water, air |
| **5** | • wellness in family relationships • family's impact on members' development • foundation of marriage • changes during puberty • authority/freedom in family life • coping with change in family life • death and dying | • concept of wellness • review of personal health practices • keeping a healthy balance • inventory of health habits • fitness and overall health • exercise and respiratory endurance | • air pollution • water pollution and health • community health resources |
| **6** | • stages of life/development • courtship, marriage intimacy • beginning of human life • fetal development and birth process • being a Christian family • societal pressures and family life • changes in adolescence and family life • death/dying | • healthy lifestyle • benefits/components of fitness • weight, strength, posture, obesity, losing healthfully • care of skin, eyes, and ears • importance of sleep/rest • oral hygiene • personal cleanliness/disease prevention • setting health goals | • community problems caused by substance abuse • treatment for alcoholism • community health resources |
| **7/8** | • family life • sexuality vs. sex • biblical view of sexuality • myths of sex and sexuality • changes in puberty • chastity and abstinence • healthy male-female relationships • sexual abuse | • healthy lifestyle choices • influence of fashion on ideas of beauty • dieting and health • physical fitness and overall wellness • review components of health fitness • review personal hygiene concepts | • community resources for getting help for substance abuse/other health problems |

|     | Consumer Health | Safety/First Aid |
| --- | --- | --- |
| **K** | | • rules and safety • poison safety • medicine and safety • traffic safety • strangers and safety • fire safety: basic rules • emergency phoning • appropriate/inappropriate touch |
| **1** | • health checkups | • medicine safety • poison safety: basic rules and household poisons • safety and strangers • review of fire safety • car passenger safety • dealing with emergencies • appropriate/inappropriate touch |
| **2** | • aid for visual and hearing impaired | • care of eyes and ears • review of stranger education • intro. to bike safety • review of fire safety • home escape plan • seatbelts • emergency phoning • preventing sexual abuse: appropriate/inappropriate/confusing touch • good and bad secrets |
| **3** | • influence of ads on use of substances • labels as a source of information • reasons for using common health products | • risk-taking • bicycle safety • water safety • electrical appliances • preventing sexual abuse: appropriate/ inappropriate touch, trickery, self-protection, sources of help • action plan for an emergency • first aid: scrapes, nosebleeds, burns, blisters |
| **4** | | • accidents—emotional, decisional factors • review of basic safety rules • playground safety • bicycle safety • fire safety, flame hazards • home alone • preventing sexual abuse: definition, touch continuum, self-protection |
| **5** | • advertising and food choices | • taking responsibility for safety of self and others • basic emergency first aid • rescue breathing • preventing sexual abuse: defining sexual abuse, saying no assertively, sources of help |
| **6** | • getting correct health care | • taking responsibility for safety of self and others • safety in extreme hot or cold weather • safety and natural disasters • review of basic safety rules • home hazard check • defining/preventing sexual abuse: • self-protection, sources of help |
| **7/8** | • evaluating advertisements • media sales techniques | • review of basic safety and first aid • responding in emergencies • preventing sexual abuse • identifying and practicing self-protection skills |

# Unit 1

# Invitation to Health

## Goals

- Students will develop an understanding of the Christian perspective on health.
- Students will be introduced to the content of *Horizons Health*, grade 6.
- Students will work together to build a caring, supportive classroom community.

## Background

This unit gives an overview of the *Horizons Health* curriculum for grade 6. Through discussions and activities, it also seeks to establish a supportive and healthy classroom climate.

Throughout the *Horizons Health* curriculum, students are encouraged to take responsibility for making choices that promote health. But for the curriculum to be successful, you also need to recognize your responsibility as a teacher for maintaining a classroom that fosters good health. Creating a classroom environment that promotes a healthy self-concept, that respects individual differences, and that encourages children to live in God-honoring ways is of great significance in promoting the mental, social, and spiritual health of students. You also need to be alert for signs of individual health problems, and notify the home or enlist appropriate professional help. Classroom teachers make choices daily that influence the health of their students.

## Vocabulary

Plan to integrate the following vocabulary:

| | | |
|---|---|---|
| lifestyle | characteristics | courtesy |

## Unit Resources (Search online for similar resources if these are no longer available.)

Weltmann Begun, Ruth ed. *Ready-To-Use Social Skills Lessons & Activities for Grades 4–6.*
Lessons, activities, and handouts.
https://www.researchpress.com/books/674/ready-use-social-skills-lessons-activities-grades-4-6.
Students learn skills such as sharing, listening, dealing with anger, setting goals, building self-confidence, and dealing with prejudice.

"Free Social Emotional Learning Activities." Centervention.
https://www.centervention.com/social-emotional-learning-activities/.
In this section of the website, there are free lessons, activities, and printables (worksheets) about mindfulness and feelings. Additional books are also listed.
Suitable for K–8.

## Lesson Resources (Search online for similar resources if these are no longer available.)

### Lessons 2–3

"Conflict Resolution Grades 6 to 8." The Nemours Foundation/KidsHealth, 2016.
classroom.kidshealth.org.
The lesson plan links articles, lists discussion questions, and provides activities related to conflict resolution, grades 6–8.

*School Tools*. Western Justice Center.
Schooltools.info.
This website provides lessons and videos about conflict resolution, communication, and other topics. Best suited for middle to high school.

### Lesson 4

"Developing Empathy." Teaching Tolerance.
https://www.tolerance.org/classroom-resources/tolerance-lessons/developing-empathy.
Short Lesson related to bullying and bias with linked PDF materials, grades 6–8.

Ackerman, Courtney. "18 Self-Esteem Worksheets and Activities for Teens and Adults (+PDFs)."
PositivePsychology.com.

# LESSON 1: HEALTH INSIDE AND OUT

## Preparation/Materials
- Notebooks, one per student
- Student books

## Objectives
- Students will define health.
- Students will understand the Christian perspective on health.
- Students will have an overview of grade 6 health topics.

• • • • • • • • • • • • • • • • • • • • • • • • • • • • • • • • • • • • • • • • • • • • • • • • • • • •

## Lesson

1. Tell students to imagine that they are going to get a new pet and, of course, they want their new pet to be healthy. Ask: "How will you determine whether or not the animal is healthy?" Brainstorm a list with the class (include overall appearance, good weight, ways the animal responds to people, appetite, shot record, energy level).

   At the end of the activity, note that there are signs of health in humans just as there are signs of health in animals.

2. Have students complete the sentence "I am healthy when…" Assign them to write three or four different endings to the sentence, each one giving a sign of health. If they have trouble thinking of ideas, suggest that they recall the example from the discussion in Step 1.

3. **Defining health.** Have volunteers share one or more of their sentence endings. Use the discussion to develop a tentative definition of health or a list of characteristic signs of health in human beings.

4. **Student book.** Have the students read "What is Health?" and "Your Choices and Your Health." Discuss the "Think It Over" questions. Focus especially on the various components of complete health: mental/emotional, social, physical, and spiritual (a review of concepts covered at earlier grade levels).

   During the discussion stress the Christian perspective on health: God has given us the responsibility to care for creation—including the responsibility to care for our health. What we do about our health is not an individual matter. We are responsible to God. Use these truths to counter the idea that "it's my body, and I can do whatever I want with it as long as I'm not hurting anyone else."

   1. *Answers will vary, but students should realize the powerful effect of emotions and thoughts on the body. For example, feelings of stress or prolonged anxiety can lead to stomach ulcers and other physical illnesses.*

2. *Answers will vary, but some basic answers would include ideas such as these. Physical health: God is the Creator who makes us stewards of our bodies. Such care enables us to be at our best physically, not for self-glorification, but for reflecting God's image and serving God. Mental health: Our awareness that we are made in God's image gives us a healthy self-concept; knowing that God made us and loves us gives us strength for living; God's law governs our decision making. Social health: Our relationships with others are governed by God's law of love; we forgive others because God in Christ has forgiven us.*

3. *Answers should show awareness of how daily health decisions affect overall health and how establishing good health habits affects health now and in the future.*

4. *Answers will vary.*

5. Refine the class definition of health, or add to the students' list of signs of health, and reorganize the list, classifying items as belonging to mental, social, physical, or spiritual health.

6. Have students turn to the table of contents in the student books for a brief overview of the topics to be covered in *Horizons Health* during the school year.

   - In emotional/mental health, students will be talking about hereditary and acquired characteristics and about stress and exercise and how these affect health. They will also talk about what influences them and how they make decisions.
   - In social health, students will explore how to build good relationships with others and what to do when relationships break down.
   - Students will learn about the body systems, particularly the heart and the cardiovascular system. What causes heart disease? How can fitness help prevent heart disease?
   - In the family life unit, students will talk about the stages of human life and development. They'll also talk about the many changes of adolescence.
   - The unit "Choosing a Healthy Lifestyle" will cover choices that students can make to stay fit.
   - "Drugs and Your Health" will give students the opportunity to learn about the effects of drugs and to practice how to say no to drugs.
   - "Focus on Safety" will teach students what to do to stay safe in different kinds of weather and how to give first aid.

5. **Writing activity.** Distribute the student notebooks, explaining that these notebooks will be used throughout the school year for writing, for keeping articles on various health-related topics, and for other health assignments or activities. (You may want to give the notebooks an appropriate name such as "*Horizons Health*" or "Health Power" notebooks.) Consider having students begin by writing the class definition of health in their notebooks.

Have students reflect on the lesson material by writing in their notebooks on a lesson-related topic or question.

Suggestions:

"What health topics would you like to know more about?"

"Of the health topics mentioned, which interests you the most and why?"

"Why is health an important subject for Christians to learn about?"

"Do you think that God cares whether or not we are healthy? Why or why not?"

6. Have volunteers share their writing with the rest of the class. Then briefly summarize the main ideas of the lesson. Tell students that in the next two lessons they will be thinking about what makes a healthy classroom.

● ● ● ● ● ● ● ● ● ● ● ● ● ● ● ● ● ● ● ● ● ● ● ● ● ● ● ● ● ● ● ● ● ● ● ● ● ● ● ● ● ● ● ● ● ● ● ●

## Related Activities

1. Make posters illustrating characteristics or components of health.

2. Integrate with social studies: Focus on important health issues in countries currently being studied.

3. Health notebook: Assign students to each find one newspaper article that touches on mental, social, physical, or spiritual health. Students can tape the article in their health notebook, and then write a paragraph telling how the article relates to one or more aspects of health.

# LESSON 2: BUILDING COMMUNITY

## Preparation/Materials

• Decide which suggested activities to use, and prepare materials accordingly (see Steps 1 and 3).

## Objectives

• Students will develop an understanding of why cooperation is necessary.

• Students will practice cooperative skills.

## Background

You and the students form a year-long community. Building a community marked by trust, acceptance of individual differences, and cooperation takes attention and effort. The activities and suggestions in this lesson and the next help build community and set the stage for the following affective units of *Horizons Health*.

• • • • • • • • • • • • • • • • • • • • • • • • • • • • • • • • • • • • • • • • • • • • • • •

## Lesson

1. Open the lesson by playing a cooperative game.

   Suggestions:
   • *Where's My Color?* Materials: self-adhesive dots in four different colors. As students sit with eyes closed, place a self-adhesive dot on the forehead of each student. Mix up the colors so that students with the same color dot are not sitting near each other. (Students should be warned not to tell others the color of their dot.) Then have students, without asking any questions or getting hints, try to form groups of the same colored dots. Students will quickly learn that cooperation and nonverbal communication are necessary.

   • *Making Machines.* Students can work in groups to construct machines with movable parts (for example, a blender, a car wash, or a washing machine). Each member of the group should be a part of the machine. Give students a short time to plan their machine and another few minutes to rehearse. Then have each group demonstrate its machine, and have the rest of the class guess what it is.

   Or have the whole class build a machine. Tell students: "We're going to build a machine that we're all part of. When you see a place to fit in, add a sound or a motion, or both. Make sure that you are connected to another part of the machine." (Adapted from *Friendly Classroom for a Small Planet* by Priscilla Prutzman and others [New Society, 1988].)

   • *Message Match.* Each student receives a piece of a message or a single word. Students must go around the classroom and try to match up with other parts to complete the message. If you wish, the activity can be played in three stages:
     – Write a one-sentence message, and then cut it apart into individual words. Students have to combine their words to complete the sentence.

- Write several one-sentence messages. Students have to figure out where their word or piece of message fits the best.
- Have groups of students make messages, using one word for each person in the group. Then mix up the words of all the groups, and, as in previous suggestions, have students piece together the messages. This is easier if starting and ending words are provided on cards. (Adapted from *The Collaborative Classroom* by Susan and Tim Hill [Heinemann, 1990].)

2. Comment on the cooperative skills students used to play the games. Tell students that the cooperative games they just played can help them consider what's important about getting along in a group. Note that school classrooms are "healthy" when students cooperate and help each other. When there is a feeling of cooperation and helpfulness in the classroom, students also feel more comfortable with each other and they enjoy school more. And as Christians we have a more important reason for caring about others—we are to reflect God's love in our relationships.

   Focus on what kind of behaviors are necessary if people are to work together in a group to complete a task. Brainstorm a list and write class members' suggestions on the board. Elicit answers such as the following:
   - listening to each other (eye contact, active listening)
   - being actively involved, being a contributing member of the group
   - being accepting/appreciative of what others say and do (no put-downs)
   - including everyone in the group, giving everyone a role or task
   - working cooperatively to finish group or individual tasks

   As you list each behavior, have students identify and describe the opposite type of behavior. What effect do these behaviors have on the group?

3. Do the following activity to clearly show what is necessary to work cooperatively toward achieving a goal. Divide the class into groups to complete tasks. Some students in each group, however, should be assigned to play the role of noncontributing group members, doing as little as possible to help the group achieve the goal (but not purposely trying to destroy the group's work). All the others are to work as best as they can to complete the activity or task.

   Explain the roles to the class. Then give a piece of paper to each student telling his or her role (for example, *N* for noncontributing and *C* for contributing). Give student groups 10-15 minutes to complete their task.

   Suggested group activities:
   - Making a collage about a topic of choice. Each group must decide how to divide up steps/tasks among members.
   - Creating a group drawing of a desert island. Each group decides what they would want on their desert island, how to picture their island, and how to organize individual drawings, etc.

- Creating cooperative stories. Each person in the group takes a turn contributing to the story. (Making a video might be useful for this activity.)
- Creating skits. Prepare a paper bag for each group that contains a set of objects. Each group must create a skit that incorporates all the objects in the bag.

4. **Discussion.** Talk about the activity. Have the noncontributors tell how they felt about their role. How did the contributors feel about the noncontributors? Consider how lack of cooperation affects the health of the classroom.

5. **Health notebook.** Have students respond to the lesson activities by writing for a couple of minutes in their health notebooks. What did they learn about the way they cooperate with others? Or what things do they enjoy/dislike about working in groups and why?

• • • • • • • • • • • • • • • • • • • • • • • • • • • • • • • • • • • • • • • • • • • • • • • •

## Related Activities

1. Give students continued opportunity to develop and practice cooperative skills. See the lists at the beginning of the unit for suggested resources.

2. Consider cooperative skills used in various areas of business, community, or international life. Invite guest speakers to describe how cooperative skills are necessary to do their jobs.

# LESSON 3: A GOOD PLACE TO BE

## Preparation/Materials
- Optional: poster board for displaying class rules

## Objectives
- Students will consider what makes a healthy classroom environment.
- Students will decide upon classroom norms of behavior.

## Background
Although approaches to classroom discipline vary according to a teacher's style of leadership, all classes will benefit from a set of mutually agreed upon behavior rules. Encourage students to consider how the choices they make influence the climate of the classroom. You may wish to periodically hold a class meeting to review the rules, assess how they are working, and perhaps revise them.

• • • • • • • • • • • • • • • • • • • • • • • • • • • • • • • • • • • • • • • • • • • • • • • • • •

## Lesson

1. Lead the class through a fantasy about a classroom that doesn't have any rules. Engage students' imaginations as you describe a chaotic classroom.

   Alternative option: Play a game, but neglect to tell students one important rule necessary to play it with a group. Discuss the results. Why are rules necessary?

2. Ask: "What kind of a classroom is a good environment?" Explain that in this lesson students will be planning how to make their classroom a place where all enjoy being and learning. Some ideas to include:
   - necessity of respecting others opinions/eliminating put-downs
   - ways to work together
   - place of courtesy in the classroom
   - how to deal with disruptive behavior

3. Divide the class into groups to brainstorm suggestions for classroom norms of behavior. Consider appointing a convener, recorder, and reporter for each group to facilitate the group's work. Encourage the convener to see that each student contributes. After discussing the ideas, each group should rank their suggestions in order of importance or priority.

   Allow about 10 minutes for the activity, and then have reporters read the groups' suggestions to the class.

4. Work in a full-class session to discuss and combine suggestions into a basic set of class norms. Involve the class members as much as possible in organizing and combining suggestions and in deciding which suggestions to adopt, so that students feel that they are coming up with a workable set of norms. As the class decides on a basic norm, write it on the board.

5. Have one or more volunteers write the rules on a piece of poster board to display in the classroom. Add additional rules as necessary in succeeding days and weeks.

   For a more imaginative way of posting the class rules, have student groups or volunteers each write and illustrate a rule on a rectangular piece of poster board. Then use yarn or string to attach the rules, and make a mobile. Or work together to make an "A Good Place to Be" bulletin board that includes the class suggestions.

6. **Closure.** Use questions such as the following to close the lesson and review the Christian perspective:
   "Can you give a reason why one of the rules might be difficult to follow?"
   "What do you think our classroom will be like if we follow the rules?"
   "What rules do you think are connected to loving our neighbor?"
   "What can we do to change the situation when we realize we have been unhelpful or mean?"
   "Being loving to others is hard for everyone. We all do things we're sorry for. How can we learn loving behavior?" (Bring in forgiveness, the Holy Spirit's work in our lives.)
   "How do you think you might be affected by these rules?"

● ● ● ● ● ● ● ● ● ● ● ● ● ● ● ● ● ● ● ● ● ● ● ● ● ● ● ● ● ● ● ● ● ● ● ● ● ● ● ● ● ● ● ● ● ● ● ● ● ● ● ● ● ● ● ●

## Related Activity

- Have students write their response to the lesson in their health notebooks. Consider having them answer one of the questions listed in Step 6.

# LESSON 4: APPRECIATING DIFFERENCES

## Preparation/Materials

- Collect objects for opening activity, a few more than the number of students in the class. Objects should be of one category, each having individual, recognizable variations. Suggested objects: stones, pine cones, leaves, or other natural objects.
- Unit evaluation in student workbook

## Objectives

- Students will identify and appreciate differences among class members.
- Students will practice cooperative classroom behaviors.

• • • • • • • • • • • • • • • • • • • • • • • • • • • • • • • • • • • • • • • • • • • • • •

## Lesson

1. Open the lesson by telling students that they'll be doing an activity that will test their powers of observation.

2. **Activity.** Focus on differences among the objects.
   - Have students choose one of the objects from your collection.
   - Students should each look at their object carefully, noticing its distinguishing features. Suggest that they check for color, size, shape, specific markings, and so on. If you wish, have them name the object.
   - Divide students into small groups. Each student should introduce his or her object to the others in the group. They should point out its distinguishing features.
   - Optional: Collect the objects and put them in one pile (or if the class is very large, in two piles). Then have each student try to find his or her own object in the pile. Suggestion: Have groups do this by turns. If one member of a group has trouble finding the object, the others can help.

3. Briefly talk about the activity. Ask students how they found their particular object. Note the wide variety throughout creation and what it shows about our Creator God. Stress that God also created each human being unique. Note that during the health education course students will be learning to appreciate not only their own unique qualities but also the unique qualities of others. Tell students that in the next activity they'll be thinking about some ways in which individuals are unique.

4. Have students return to the groups formed earlier in the lesson. This time have them brainstorm a list of ways in which human beings are unique. Allow a few minutes for this activity.

5. Ask each group to share one or two ideas from their list, and write on the board a composite list of ways in which humans are unique (include height, color of hair and skin, other special physical features, talents, personality traits, ethnic background).

6. Then have students identify ways in which they are unique. Ask each student to write these on an unsigned piece of paper.

7. Collect the papers. Read all or part of a list, and have the class try to identify the person it describes. If possible, read each person's list.

8. End the lesson with questions such as the following:

   "Is it easy or hard to identify our unique characteristics? Why or why not?"

   "Which characteristics are the hardest to identify? Why do you think this is true?"

   "Why do you think that God created each human being unique?"

   "What difference does it make to know that these unique characteristics are part of God's plan for us?"

   "How are these differences going to affect our classroom?" (Include how much more interesting the class will be because of differences; importance of appreciating these differences; importance of accepting people the way they are.)

9. **Unit evaluation.** Use the worksheets to review and evaluate.

   *Fill in the Blank:*
   *1. Decisions; 2. social health; 3. appreciated/accepted; 4. unique; 5. Physical*

   *Short answers:*
   *1. Correct information is necessary in order to make good decisions about health.*
   *2. Answers will vary. Possible answers include listening to other group members, being accepting of others' work/words, taking an active part in work and discussions, finishing one's assigned task.*
   *3. Physical, social, mental, and spiritual health.*
   *4. Mental health has to do with how a person thinks, feels, deals with problems, and makes decisions.*
   *5. Answers will vary. Probable answers include decisions about diet, exercise, leisure time, sleep, personal health care, relationships with people, relationship to God.*

   *Short essay:*
   *Answers will vary.*

• • • • • • • • • • • • • • • • • • • • • • • • • • • • • • • • • • • • • • • • • • • • • • • • • • •

## Related Activities

1. From the lists of class members' descriptions developed in class, have students create a newsletter that introduces each student. Distribute the lists randomly, and have each student develop his or her descriptive list into a little article for the newsletter.

2. Stimulate global awareness by broadening the lesson to include appreciation of differences of people from other countries.

# Unit 2

# A Person Like You

## Goals

- Students will strengthen their feelings of self-worth.
- Students will take responsibility for improving their mental health.
- Students will choose to deal with stress and their emotions in healthy ways.
- Students will develop an understanding of the decision-making process.

## Background

This unit which focuses on mental health, helps students form a true picture of who they are. It begins where all self-knowledge begins—with knowledge of God and of our relationship to him. To know that we are created by God in his image, that we daily rebel against God, and that God is restoring us and has given us new life in Christ is the beginning of wisdom. "A Person Like You" helps students consider what that new life means for their identity and gives them hope for living.

During this unit students also have the opportunity to learn several basic life skills—coping with feelings and stress and making decisions. Teaching life skills will be most effective if you help students use these skills in a variety of school and classroom situations. Of course, modeling is perhaps the most powerful teaching tool. Show students that you need and use the skills.

In teaching the mental and social health units, one of the most important things you can do for students is to provide a comfortable, supportive classroom environment. Students need an atmosphere which encourages them to explore issues and share knowledge, to build each other up, and help each other.

Christ's kingly rule includes our view of ourselves and it includes our emotions, thoughts, and actions. Teaching this unit gives you a valuable opportunity to help students understand what Christ's kingly rule over all of life means.

## Vocabulary

Plan to integrate the following vocabulary:

| | | | |
|---|---|---|---|
| nucleus | mood swing | acquired characteristics | gene |
| heredity | chromosomes | inherited characteristics | trait |
| emotion | responsibility | positive influence | DNA |
| stress | decision making | negative influence | |

## Unit Resources (Search online for similar resources if these are no longer available.)

"Confidence: A Worksheet." The Nemours Foundation, 2020. teenshealth.org/.
This page provides directions for a multi-step activity (no materials necessary besides paper to write on). This is suitable for all middle school students, not just teens.

"Self-esteem and Body Image." Health Powered Kids by Alina Health, 2015. healthpoweredkids.org.
Short lesson plan for ages 9–14 with printable information for parents.

Koch, Kathy. *Start with the Heart: How to Motivate Your Kids to Be Compassionate, Responsible, and Brave*. Moody Publishers, 2019.

Lyness, D'Arcy. "Self- Esteem." KidsHealth by Nemours, 2018. kidshealth.org.

Morin, Amanda. "Developmental Milestones for Middle-Schoolers." Understood for All Inc., 2020. understood.org.

## Lesson Resources (Search online for similar resources if these are no longer available.)

### Lessons 1–2

Armstrong, William. *Sounder*. New York: Harper, 1969.

Personal stories about youth homelessness can be found through https://www.covenanthouse.org/ and https://endhomelessness.org/.

Hayes, Daniel. *The Trouble with Lemons*. Boston: Godine, 1990.
Tyler struggles with his perception of himself as a "lemon."

Manes, Stephen. *How to Be a Perfect Person in Just Three Days*. New York: Houghton Mifflin, 1982.
Klutzy Milo Crumpley enrolls in a bizarre crash course on how to be a perfect person— only to discover perfection isn't all it's cracked up to be, grades 4–8.

Lambert, Mary. *Family Game Night and Other Catastrophes*. Scholastic, 2017.
Annabell supports her sister as they navigate mental illness, grades 3–7.

Namioka, Lensey. *Yang the Youngest and His Terrible Ear*. Toronto and Boston: Little, Brown, 1992.
A story about the unique experiences of a young Asian immigrant who is trying to establish his own identity within his family, ages 8–12.

O'Dell, Scott. *Black Star, Bright Dawn*. Boston: Houghton Mifflin, 1988.
A story about respect and courage. When her father is injured, Bright Dawn takes his place in the Iditarod with the lead dog, Black Star.

Paterson, Katherine. *Come Sing, Jimmy Jo*. New York: Dutton, 1985.
Eleven-year-old Jimmy Jo from Appalachia struggles to gain confidence in himself and come to terms with his family.

_____ . *The Great Gilly Hopkins*. New York: HarperCollins, 1978.
A story about an ornery, bright girl who is drawn into a circle of love—in spite of herself.

_____ . *Park's Quest*. New York: Dutton, 1988.
A story of Park's search to find out about his father, who was killed in Vietnam. Park learns about family relationships and about his inner self.

_____ . *Who Am I?* Grand Rapids: Eerdmans, 1992.
Katherine Paterson originally wrote this book for the Presbyterian Church (U.S.A.) as part of its fifth and sixth grade church school curriculum. She honestly and engagingly addresses these difficult questions: Where in the world is God? What about me? Where do I belong? Who is my neighbor? What is my purpose?

Torres, Jennifer. *Stef Soto, Taco Queen*. Little, Brown Books for Young Readers, 2017.
A story about the importance of family and identity, grades 3–7.

Sotomayor, Sonia. Just Ask. Philomel Books, 2019.
This book is written for younger ages, but provides insights for older students as well. Justice Sotomayor writes about children with different abilities and conditions.

### Lesson 3

"Life Science." PBS LearningMedia, 2020.
> pbslearningmedia.org.
> This web page has videos, interactives, and articles.
> Resources identify the appropriate grade range.

"Heredity Mix 'n Match." Regents of the University of Colorado, 2013.
> teachengineering.org.
> This activity uses jelly beans to explain heredity.
> There is a video that helps provide directions.

"Pigeon Breeding: Genetics at Work." Teach Genetics by the Genetic Science Learning Center.
> https://learn.genetics.utah.edu/.
> This website provides a variety of activities and information, suitable for students.

*You, Me and Others*. White Plains, N.Y.: March of Dimes.
> A three-part program for elementary school students (K–6), which includes a teacher guide and reproducible masters. The program covers basic concepts of genetics (normal variations and similarities among individuals, principles of heredity, dynamic nature of growth and development). Available from local March of Dimes organization.

### Lessons 4–5

Grimes, Nikki. *The Poetry Zone*.
> https://www.nikkigrimes.com/.
> Books lists and educator guides focused on poetry and multi-cultural literature.

Ho, Minfong. *The Clay Marble*. New York: Farrar, 1991.
> When war breaks out, twelve-year-old Dara and her family are forced to leave their village in Cambodia.

"5 Ways to Know Your Feelings Better." Teens Health from Nemours, 2018.
> teenshealth.org.
> A list of ways to recognize emotions, suitable for any age.

Visit the website for the *Learning Disabilities Association of America* for resources and information.
> ldaamerica.org.
> The resources section and the "New to LD" sections will be most valuable.

*Plain Talk About Dealing With the Angry Child*. Pueblo, Colorado: Consumer Information Center.
> Gives tips for helping a child cope with feelings of anger and aggression.

**Lesson 6**

Rosen, Peg. "10 Ways to Help Your Middle- or High- Schooler Manage Stress." Understood for All Inc.
understood.org.
Information and suggestions for parents/teachers.

*Teachers Guide: Stress (Grades 6 to 8)*. The Nemours Foundation/ KidsHealth, 2016.
kidshealth.org/classroom.
The lesson plan PDF includes articles, discussion questions, and activities.

*Walk in Our Shoes*. California Mental Health Services authority.
walkinourshoes.org.
This website provides information and personal accounts relating to mental health.

**Lessons 7–8**

Note: Many of the resources listed under Lessons 1–2 are also appropriate for Lessons 7–8.

# LESSON 1: ON BECOMING YOU

## Preparation/Materials
- Student workbook activity
- Bibles, one per student
- Student books

## Objectives
- Students will develop an understanding of their new life in Christ.
- Students will feel secure knowing that God loves and cares for them.

## Background
Wholeness and health have their beginnings in our relationship to God. When we are renewed by God and receive new life in Christ, we become God's children. Secure in God's love and promises, we have hope for the future.

• • • • • • • • • • • • • • • • • • • • • • • • • • • • • • • • • • • • • • • • • • • • • • • • • • •

## Lesson (2 sessions)

1. **Student workbook activity.** Begin by having students complete the true/false activity. Make sure that they realize that they will have to give reasons for their answers.

   Use the six true/false statements to draw students into a discussion of the new life we have in Christ and how we receive that life. As students give reasons for marking a statement true or false, encourage others who disagree with them to respond in order to get a lively discussion going.

   - Statement 1—false. The Bible does tell us how we should treat others, but it also tells us who we are and how we should think about ourselves. In fact, the Bible is sometimes called a mirror in which we can see ourselves. Ask: "What does the creation story tell us about ourselves?" Name other biblical stories, and have students tell what we learn about ourselves through them.

   - Discuss statements 2 and 3—both false—together. Stress our inability to "shape up" because of sin (Romans 7:15-19). God created humans in his image, but because of sin that image is fractured. (Ask students to name some ways in which sin affects us; include how it affects our thinking and feeling.) That's why God reaches out to us in Jesus Christ. In Christ, God is restoring his image in us.

     Because of sin, our conscience is dull, so it's not a reliable guide. Following a dulled conscience can get us off the right track. God has given us standards in the Ten Commandments and in Jesus' summary (law of love); however, since we can't live up to the law, God sent Jesus Christ to fulfill God's demands for us.

   - Statement 4—true. Students may not be familiar with the terminology that Paul uses in Ephesians 2:4-6a. Baptism shows that we have been buried with Christ (symbolized by going under the water), and then raised with Christ to new life.

- Statement 5—not a simple true or false. Although we can't earn our salvation by being good and obeying rules, once we have new life in Christ, we *want* to live in a way that pleases God.

- Statement 6—false. This statement expresses a common attitude in North American society that completely ignores our relationship to God and God's call to discipleship.

Close the discussion by centering on the idea of new life in Christ. What are some signs of this new life? In the next step, students will use their Bibles to find out.

2. Have students work in pairs or groups of three to look up the texts on the activity sheet and report to the class what they say about the new life. Tell them to summarize the meaning in 4–5 words. Allow about 5 minutes for the activity.

   Then as each pair or group reports, have all the students fill in the rest of the activity sheet. Read over the list of characteristics of the new life in Christ. Have students add any additional characteristics they can think of (peaceable, full of rejoicing, etc.). Stress that our lives are secure because we are in Christ; the new life in Christ is life that will never die.
   1. *Ephesians 4:32—(a life showing kindness, compassion, forgiveness)*
   2. *Ephesians 5:2—(a life of love)*
   3. *Ephesians 5:8—(a life lived as children of light)*
   4. *Ephesians 5:19—(a life filled with singing hymns)*
   5. *Ephesians 5:20—(a life of thanks to God)*
   6. *Romans 8:6—(mind controlled by God's Spirit)*
   7. *1 John 2:9-10—(person with new life loves brother/neighbor)*
   8. *Romans 6:23—(new life is eternal life)*
   9. *2 Corinthians 4:16—(upbeat life, being renewed inwardly)*
   10. *Galatians 5:22—(marked by fruit of the Spirit)*
   11. *Philippians 4:6—(marked by prayer)*
   12. *Hebrews 12:14—(peaceable and holy life)*

   Note: Consider ending session 1 after finishing the student activity in Step 2.

3. **Student book.** Read and discuss "On Becoming You" and the excerpt from "Who Am I?" by Katherine Paterson. Use the "Think It Over" questions to spark discussion. Focus on the solid reassurance of knowing that our new life in Christ makes us God's children and that nothing can defeat God's love for his children. Also, encourage students to live in hope; after all, the future is filled with promise for God's children.

   1. *Being God's children does not depend on us. Because of what Christ did for us on the cross, we have the right to be called God's children if we repent and accept his gift of salvation, even though we don't always act like God's children.*

2. *It tells us that we are God's children and that God is still changing us, restoring us to God's image in Christ.*

4. **Writing activity.** Consider having students do one of the following writing activities.

   - Write a letter to someone who has never heard of Jesus Christ, explaining what the new life in Christ is. (Students can refer to the descriptions/characteristics from Step 2 to get ideas.)
   - Complete the following sentence with three different endings—"Because I have new life in Christ, I am able to..."
   - Answer this question: "How does it make you feel to know that God wants *you* to be his child and follower?"
   - Choose one of the passages listed on the student activity sheet, read it over several times, and reflect on it. Then write a prayer or a few sentences in response to the passage.

● ● ● ● ● ● ● ● ● ● ● ● ● ● ● ● ● ● ● ● ● ● ● ● ● ● ● ● ● ● ● ● ● ● ● ● ● ● ● ● ● ● ● ● ● ● ● ● ● ● ● ● ● ●

## Related Activities

1. During class devotions or at the close of the lesson, sing a song that ties in with the lesson theme. Two suggestions: Verse 2 of "Baptized with Water" (*Psalter Hymnal,* 269), which speaks of dying and rising with Christ, and "May the Mind of Christ, My Savior" (*Psalter Hymnal,* 291).

2. Use the lesson activities as the basis for a student chapel. Students could create a skit or conversation based on some of the true/false statements. Students could also give choral readings of appropriate Bible passages.

# LESSON 2: WHAT'S YOUR BAG?

## Preparation/Materials

- For activity in Step 2:
  paper bags, one per student
  magazines, scissors, and paste, class supply
  stapler
  optional: Prepare a sample "bag" before
      class    by making a collage of your
          personal interests, likes/dislikes, or
          what types of things represent
          "you."

## Objective

- Students will build a positive self-concept by identifying ways in which they are unique.

. . . . . . . . . . . . . . . . . . . . . . . . . . . . . . . . . . . . . . . . . . . . . . . . . . . . . . . . . . .

## Lesson

1. Write the words "That's my bag" on the board, and briefly talk with the class about the meaning of the phrase—what we like, what we're good at, what is "us." Explain that students are going to think about what their "bag" is and make a collage portraying it. If you have made a personal sample, share your bag with students, giving reasons for some of your choices.

2. Distribute bags, and instruct students to make their bags into a personal collage, using pictures and phrases from magazines. The outside of the bag represents their public image and interests; the inside contains their private or less-shared world.

   Tell students that they may staple their bags shut if they want to ensure privacy for their inside world.

3. Invite students to share the outside of their bags and to offer the rationale for some choices; each member may or may not share a part of the inside world at the time of the activity or at a later date. (You may wish to have students do the sharing in student groups.)

4. Discussion and reflection. Use questions such as the following to stimulate discussion and reflection about the activity:
   "Do you think your bag truly represents yourself?"
   "What did you learn about yourself?"
   "What did you learn about others?"
   "Did members share both parts of their bags? Why?"
   "How do you feel about others in your class (group) now?"

● ● ● ● ● ● ● ● ● ● ● ● ● ● ● ● ● ● ● ● ● ● ● ● ● ● ● ● ● ● ● ● ● ● ● ● ● ● ● ● ● ● ● ● ● ● ● ● ● ● ● ● ● ● ● ● ● ● ● ● ● ● ● ●

## Related Activities

1. Draw self-portraits. Consider having students draw a series of three or four small portraits—one of themselves as babies or toddlers, one at age 5 or 6, one at their present age, and one projecting what they'll look like at high school graduation.

2. Allow students a few minutes to reflect on the lesson activity and to write about it in their health notebooks or journals. Consider using one or two of the Step 4 questions as starters for writing.

3. Have students write warm, appreciative statements about each other. Stress that the statements should be honest and positive—no put-downs.

4. Do an activity that helps students find out about each other and promotes active listening.

Suggestions:

- Make a list for the class of about 6 topics for students to discuss (likes—favorite book, holiday, animal, leisure activity, breakfast food; dislikes—vegetable or other food, TV program, habit of others, school activity, time of day).

- Have each student interview a partner who identifies 3–4 likes and dislikes and explains the reason for the feelings. The interviewer writes down the answers. Then have partners switch roles. Limit the time to 2–3 minutes for each interview.

- Gather the class in a circle, and have students tell one or two (depending on class size) likes or dislikes of their partner. To ensure active listening, have students explain the reason for their partner's opinion.

- Spend a few minutes at the end of the activity drawing conclusions about individuality/differences and similarities (are there any discernible patterns?), using the activity to help create an accepting classroom atmosphere.

# LESSON 3: PATTERNS OF LIFE— INHERITED AND ACQUIRED CHARACTERISTICS

## Preparation/Materials
- For playing the Height Game:
  Ten 3 x 5-inch cards for each student (Mark half of the cards with an *S* for short and half with a *T* for tall.)
  Student workbook activity 1
- Student books
- Student workbook activity 2

## Objectives
- Students will recognize that part of who they are is determined by inherited characteristics.
- Students will understand that their environment also influences and shapes them.

## Background
Much of who we are is determined by our genetic makeup. Our genes determine, for example, the color of our hair and eyes as well as other traits that aren't immediately noticeable. However, our environment also influences us greatly. In fact, sometimes it can be difficult to tell whether heredity or environment is the main factor. Environmental and hereditary factors are often connected in complex ways.

During the discussion of hereditary characteristics, be sensitive to children who are adopted or in foster homes. Be matter of fact in noting that adopted children may not resemble their adoptive parents because rules for development are inherited from biological parents. In order to make the lesson available to all, you may wish to have students do the survey activity on families other than their own. Or it may be possible to do some comparisons of how some adopted children are like their adoptive parents, due to the influence of the environment.

*Note:* Unit 4, Lesson 9, "Having a Disability," includes materials on genetic disorders.

• • • • • • • • • • • • • • • • • • • • • • • • • • • • • • • • • • • • • • • • • • • • • • • • • • • • • • • •

## Lesson (2–3 sessions)
1. Briefly discuss some of the characteristics that are obvious in outward appearance. Ask students about the source of these characteristics. Possible characteristics include eye color, hair color, dimples, or freckles.

2. **Student book.** Begin exploring the topic of heredity by turning in the student books to "Why Are You You Anyway?" and reading the section entitled "Your Heredity: It's in Your Chromosomes." Take time to talk about the illustrations; tie them to the text.

   After reading, check student understanding with factual questions ("What does the cell nucleus do? How does the nucleus know what to do? What does DNA look like? What is it made of? What is the name of a section of DNA that controls one trait?")

   Discuss "Think It Over" questions 1 and 2, found after the section "Your Environment." Question 2 could lead to a brief discussion of "rules of development" for animals.

Birds, for example, grow wings and beaks and feathers and not fur. On the other hand, do all birds look alike? Lead students to realize the truly awesome variation in patterns of development in creation.

1. *Answers should include the idea that each person receives part of his or her chromosomes/genes from each biological parent and these individual instructions form a unique person.*
2. *Species of animals beget the same species. You may also wish to use the example of various inherited characteristics that are evident in a litter of kittens or puppies.*

3. To get students thinking more about specific things that may be inherited, brainstorm a list of some inherited characteristics. Some characteristics to include: shape of body and body parts (hands, feet, face, ears, etc.); hair, eye, and skin color; personality tendencies and abilities; certain illnesses.

Note: You may wish to end the first session at this point.

4. **Student workbook activity 1.** Play the Height Game. The game helps students explore how characteristics such as height (a polygenic characteristic) are inherited from parents in specific patterns. Divide the class into pairs to play the game.

Game instructions:
- Have students turn to Student Activity 1 (the game instructions) in their workbooks.
- Shuffle the index cards (prepared before class), and have each student choose ten cards.
- Next, have student pairs follow the instructions on the activity sheet to discover how genes play a role in determining individual characteristics. Circulate through the classroom to help students who are having difficulties. End the game after students have had the opportunity to produce at least two "children."
- Then instruct partners to work together to answer the questions on the bottom of the activity sheet.

Discuss students' experience with the game and answer the questions.
Answers:
1–3. Answers will vary depending on cards.
4. No. Each is inheriting five of each parent's ten rules, so each child has different rules for development.
5. Shorter than average parents will tend to have shorter than average children—but not always.
6. Yes, because tall parents will tend to have more rules for developing tallness than shortness. But remember that this is not *always* the case.

Points to make in the discussion:
- Inheriting height depends upon many rules of development. Students have used ten in the game, but there are many more in real life development. Some of these rules are more influential than others (dominant and recessive genes).

- Children of the same parents will usually grow up to be of different heights even if they are the same sex. Identical twins have the same rules for development, so they will usually be very close to the same height.
- Tall parents tend to have children who grow up to be tall, and short parents tend to have children who grow up to be short. However, tall parents can have children who are shorter than average, and short parents can have children who are taller than average. If students have difficulty understanding this concept, use the cards to demonstrate how this can happen.

Summarize using the following questions :

"Why are children with the same parents different in height?"

"Are identical twins always the same height? Why or why not?"

"Are all our traits inherited? What determines our other traits?" Note that our environment—the conditions or surroundings in which we live—is also an important influence on us. Tell students that the influence of environment in forming us is the topic of the next session.

5. **Student book.** Turn to the section entitled "Your Environment." Read the section with your class. Use "Think It Over" questions to stimulate a discussion about how environment influences us. Have the students share their responses.

   1. *Each person is unique because he or she has been created in God's images. God has also placed each person in a particular family where he or she grows and develops.*
   2. *A person's environment affects interests by what the person sees, hears, and experiences.*
   3. *A person's environment affects behavior by imitating the behavior of those around him or her.*
   4. *Elicit from students the habits and/or interests that they have that are similar to those of their family. What are different? If the student is having a difficult time answering the question, use the following prompts. What movies, music, or television shows does the student enjoy with his or her family? What activities does the family do together? Are towels or clothing folded in specific ways?*
   5. *Christian parents can influence their children by their words and actions.*

   Consider using the following quotation from W. Somerset Maugham's *The Razor's Edge* to stimulate further discussion on environmental influences: "For men and women are not only themselves; they are also the region in which they were born, the city apartment or farm in which they learned to walk, the games they played as children, the old wives' tales they overheard, the food they ate, the schools they attended, the sports they followed, the poems they read, and the God they believed in." How does each of these items influence us? Elicit from students, for example, how growing up in another area of the country or on another continent might affect what they are like.

6. Talk about the interaction of environmental and hereditary factors. Use the example of height explored in the previous session. "What things besides genes affect your height?" (Diet, exercise, posture.) "Can an extra-nutritious diet make you grow taller than you would normally be?" (No. Although malnutrition can keep someone from attaining full height, good nutrition cannot cause a person to grow taller than he or she would normally be. There is an upper limit determined by the rules for development.)

7. Have students write a fable about environmental influence. Students can create a fable showing positive influences, negative influences, or contrasting negative and positive influences. Another option is to discuss positive and negative influences and to allow students to make their own fables.

8. **Student workbook activity 2.** Have students take home the student survey activity to complete with their family or with the family of a neighbor or relative.

   When the completed surveys are returned to the classroom, elicit from students which items on the survey are about things that are genetically determined and which are things determined by the environment.

• • • • • • • • • • • • • • • • • • • • • • • • • • • • • • • • • • • • • • • • • • • • • • • • • •
## Related Activities

1. Use other resources to explore the pattern of eye color inheritance (or other traits) and the principle of probability. Possible websites/activities are on the resources list.

2. Ask students to measure the heights of all the members of one family. Students can measure their own family or the family of a friend or neighbor. Discuss the height patterns in class: What is the average height of family members? Did tall parents have tall children? Did short parents have short children? Consider graphing the results.

   Extend the activity and have students also compare personality traits/abilities of family members.

3. Health notebook: Have students write about whether they're most like their mother, their father, or some other family member.

# LESSON 4: HANDLING UPS AND DOWNS OF FEELINGS

## Preparation/Materials

- Pictures of people showing various feelings (see Step 1)
- Materials for a Feelings Rainbow poster or mural:

  light-colored paper in four different colors, each cut into the arc of a rainbow (*Note:* arcs have to fit together to make a rainbow and each must be large enough for students to write about 10–15 words on. See Step 3.)

  piece of poster board on which to mount the arcs
- Student books
- Student workbook activity
- Markers or colored pencils, class supply

## Objectives

- Students will review ideas and concepts related to feelings.
- Students will further develop their vocabulary for describing a variety of feelings.
- Students will recognize that having mood swings and a wide variety of feelings is normal.

## Background

What are healthy ways for Christians to deal with emotions? In her book *Healthy Emotions: Helping Children Grow* (Baker, 1987), Mary Vander Goot cautions against two extremes. On one extreme are Christians who promote the idea that good children will have only "nice" feelings. Too often popular Christian literature and art promote this idea by picturing only smiling, sweet children. Vander Goot warns that "if we fall into the habit of thinking that pleasant emotions are good and unpleasant emotions are bad, and if we consequently elect to cover up negative emotions rather than attend to them and grow from them, we lose integrity and become emotionally artificial." Showing sadness, fear, or anger is not un-Christian. However, in reaction to this saccharine approach, other Christians have gone to the opposite extreme, making "an idol of the freedom to express whatever they feel." This approach is dangerously irresponsible. For although an emotion such as anger should not be stifled or denied, randomly expressing anger with no concern for others or no attempt to deal with its cause is also destructive. So then, to deal with emotions in a healthy way we must not only recognize and express the rich variety of human emotions, but we must also learn to control our emotions, to act on them responsibly. Vander Goot puts it this way: "Although our emotions are woven in with our actions, they are counselors to our actions but not their dictators. Our emotions give us a strong sense of our condition; however, we must make insightful and responsible decisions when we act to alter our condition."

To stay emotionally healthy, says Vander Goot, takes maintenance. She singles out three goals to work toward: richness, fit, and control.

The first goal, richness, means being able to express a wide variety of feelings. Many people live impoverished emotional lives. Although there are many reasons for this, sometimes family and societal patterns are the cause. Some families, for example, don't allow open expression of appreciation, affection, or fear; and society frowns upon men expressing fear or sadness and women expressing anger. A narrow emotional life has far-reaching implications because it keeps us from understanding the emotions of others, thus affecting our relationships.

Fit, the second goal, has to do with how emotions connect with events. Emotion needs to be appropriate to an event. And how we emotionally react to various events involves "an element of decision." We have a choice as to how to express our feelings. The goal is to work toward fitting emotions and fitting expressions of emotion.

Control, the third goal, requires a purpose in life, something to give our lives direction. Only in the light of that purpose or commitment are we able to assess our emotional life and work toward reflecting that commitment in our emotions. The goal of control is not to stifle emotions, but to follow up on emotions "wisely so that our feelings, our relationships, our actions, and our perceptions move toward greater and greater integrity."

## Lesson (2–3 sessions)

1. Lead into the lesson by showing the class a few pictures of people and having students identify what they think the people are feeling.

2. Ask the class: "What are feelings?" Use a clustering activity to help students review what they know about feelings and start thinking about what feelings are.

   Write the word *feelings* on the board, and draw a circle around it. Then have students brainstorm their associations with the word, calling out words and phrases. Write their ideas on the board in clusters, organizing them to demonstrate relationships. Include nonverbal expression of feelings, asking leading questions, if necessary, to elicit/review main ideas on the topic.

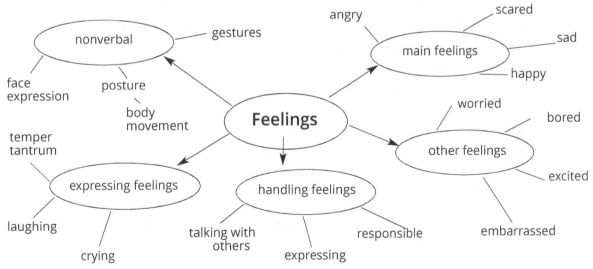

   Close the activity by defining emotions (our inward response to what's going on around us). Be sure students understand that the words *feeling* and *emotion* mean the same thing and can be used interchangeably.

3. Have students work together to make a Feelings Rainbow poster or mural. This activity will help students develop a vocabulary that accurately describes and names feelings.

• Introduce the activity by eliciting from students the four main feeling words: *happy, angry, sad,* and *scared.* Note that other words express different feelings within the broad range of being happy, angry, sad, or scared. Other, more specific words for *anger* include, for example, *furious, irritated, mad.*

What colors do students think of when they think of each of the main feelings? Assign a main feeling word to each of the colored arcs prepared before class.

• Divide the class into groups, and assign each group a color/arc. (If your class is large, you may wish to make two feelings posters.) Each group should write down as many feelings words as they can that fit with their assigned main feeling. Then they should write the words on their arc of the rainbow. Consider making a dictionary available for each group to check on word meanings and spellings.

*Sample feelings words:*
— happy: joyful, excited, pleased, glad, friendly, comfortable, safe, capable, thrilled, relieved, cozy, eager, relaxed, warm
— angry: impatient, frustrated, irritable, jealous, resentful, stuck, furious, annoyed, revengeful, discontented, betrayed
— scared: worried, jittery, anxious, confused, nervous, uncomfortable or uneasy, uptight, tense, embarrassed, terrified
— sad: down, blue, depressed, hurt, disappointed, gloomy, lonely, sorry, empty, full of grief/grieving, left out

Combine the arcs to form a rainbow poster. Add any other words class members may suggest. Briefly comment on how the completed poster gives an idea of the wide range of emotions that people feel. Tell students that recognizing and naming emotions accurately can help us understand our emotions.

Note: This may be a good point at which to end the first session.

4. **Student book.** Turn to the section "Your Feelings," and read and discuss "On the Roller Coaster." Talk about the "Think It Over" questions.

    1. *Her feelings are changing—going up and down. Have students identify the "high" points and "low" points.*
    2. *Answers will vary. In the discussion note that individual temperaments vary, but also note that mood swings are common during adolescence.*

5. Have students jot down a list of the various feelings that Alisha experienced.

6. Call on students to name the feelings. As students share their lists, draw a diagram on the board showing Alisha's ups and downs throughout the day. Also, have students identify why Alisha felt as she did. You may want to differentiate between passing feelings and more serious feelings that stay with us. What are some of Alisha's passing

feelings and what feelings (towards her brother and sister, for example) seem to be more significant?

Being aware of feelings and what causes them is an important step in dealing with them in a healthy way. What does our new life in Christ have to do with the way we handle our feelings?

7. **Student workbook activity.** Ask students to recall the feelings that they experienced in the past day. Have them jot down all the different feelings that they can remember. Is their experience anything like that of Alisha?

Have students turn to the Student Activity in their workbooks and design a mosaic of emotions for one day. Go over the color key, noting that each color represents a given emotion. Have students refer to their list of feelings to choose those that they wish to include on the mosaic. They should color in a block of the mosaic in the appropriate color for each feeling. They should also write the reason for each feeling and the time of day.

8. **Closure.** Have volunteers share some of their feelings. Help students make connections between what happens and their feelings.

- "Which feelings do most class members share?"
- "Are there certain times of the day when most class members seem down? Why might that be?"
- "Why is it helpful to identify our feelings?"

● ● ● ● ● ● ● ● ● ● ● ● ● ● ● ● ● ● ● ● ● ● ● ● ● ● ● ● ● ● ● ● ● ● ● ● ● ● ● ● ● ● ● ● ● ● ● ●

## Related Activities

1. Have students create collages of the different main groups of emotions.

2. Health notebook: Ask class members to write about why they like or dislike having certain feelings. Or have them write about the connection of our uniqueness to our feelings. Does everyone feel the same way in a certain situation?

# LESSON 5: I DID IT BECAUSE...

## Preparation/Materials
- Student books
- Student workbook activity

## Objectives
- Students will develop an understanding of the interaction among feelings, thoughts, and actions.
- Students will be aware of "feelings that lie behind feelings."
- Students will consider healthy ways to deal with unpleasant or difficult feelings.

●●●●●●●●●●●●●●●●●●●●●●●●●●●●●●●●●●●●●●●●●●●●●●●●●●●●●●●●●

## Lesson

1. **Student book.** Read "Feelings are Everywhere" and "Chain Reaction" in the student book.

   Look at the chain reaction cartoon in the student book. Have students study the cartoon and identify the steps in the chain.

   Then read the anecdote telling about a chain reaction, and use the "Think It Over" questions to stimulate discussion.

   1. *Not being asked to play ball.*
   2. *Worse. Have students trace the chain of events from not being invited to play ball to breaking the souvenir.*
   3. *Answers will vary. Lead students to see that being aware of the real cause can help them to better understand their feelings, control how they act, and lead to a healthy resolution of the situation.*

   Using the examples in the book, help students understand that feelings often lie behind feelings. Focus on the interaction of feelings, thoughts, and actions and how we can set off chain reactions. Since once the chain reaction gets started, we often lose track of what sparked the whole thing, it helps to think consciously about what is going on.

2. Ask: "What are some healthy ways to deal with unpleasant or difficult feelings?" Assign student groups to work together to come up with realistic answers to this question. The groups should read and discuss "Working It Out" and then work out Francie's problem with Carla. How should Francie deal with the problem?

   Have each group present its solution to the class, and then have the class decide on the best way to handle the situation.

3. Focus on the role of forgiveness in dealing with anger and hurt. Perhaps give a personal example of how forgiveness gave you the opportunity to make a new start in a relationship and to get rid of resentments or grudges. Stress that although feelings are not right or wrong in themselves, we are responsible for what we do about them, for how we act on them. Without being moralistic, talk about confession and forgiveness and new beginnings that are possible because of our new life in Christ.

   Work the "Think It Over" questions into the discussion.

   1. *Answers will vary. Some possible choices are talking to Carla about the problem, blowing up at Carla, planning revenge, taking the initiative and not waiting for Carla to call or come, burying the anger.*
   2. *Fear may be unpleasant, but it warns us of danger and protects us.*
   3. *Buried feelings don't go away. They damage relationships with others and weigh us down. They are like an untreated disease.*
   4. *Answers will vary.*
   5. *Answers will vary.*

4. **Student workbook activity.** The activity sheet helps students consider concrete ways to deal with difficult situations and to influence their own feelings. Complete the first example as a class.

   Discuss the completed situations/examples. Do students think the changed endings are realistic? Why or why not? If not, what further changes could be made?

• • • • • • • • • • • • • • • • • • • • • • • • • • • • • • • • • • • • • • • • • • • • • • • •

## Related Activities

1. Health notebook: Assign students to find newspaper articles showing the interaction among feelings, thoughts, and actions. Ask students to write a paragraph describing the interaction. You may also wish to have them suggest other or better ways of dealing with feelings.

2. Health notebook: Students can write about people, situations, or things that almost always make them angry. How do they typically express their anger? Has the lesson given them any new insights?

3. Ask students to draw chain reaction cartoons with two different endings.

4. Integrate with language arts, and assign students to finish the story in the student book about Alisha. Or have them write a chain reaction story. Change the emphasis by having them write about a chain of positive feelings instead of negative feelings.

# LESSON 6: HANDLING STRESS

## Preparation/Materials
- Recording of calm, soothing music
- Student books
- Student workbook activity

## Objectives
- Students will identify good stress and bad stress.
- Students will recognize some stressors in their lives.
- Students will consider ways to manage stress.

## Background
For information about stress and how to cope with it see the information sheets following the lesson.

● ● ● ● ● ● ● ● ● ● ● ● ● ● ● ● ● ● ● ● ● ● ● ● ● ● ● ● ● ● ● ● ● ● ● ● ● ● ● ● ● ● ● ● ● ● ● ● ● ● ●

## Lesson (1–2 sessions)

1. Begin by giving students a mildly stressful experience. Play soothing music and ask students how the music makes them feel. Elicit specific emotions from students. Set a relaxed mood. Suddenly, however, pull a switch. Turn off the music, cut the discussion short, and briskly tell students that someone is coming to give them an important test. The test will cover everything that they have learned in the current school year. Following the test, their parents will get a letter about the results.

   After allowing students to experience stress for a short while, tell them you were just giving them the opportunity to experience stress. Give them time to talk about how they felt. Did everyone react the same? (No, because people react differently to stress.)  (This activity is adapted from *Growing Healthy,* Grade 6, Phase V.)

2. **Student book.** Read and discuss the section "Stress and Your Health." Begin by having the students read the cartoon about Valerie and her "headaches." Have the class identify the causes of Valerie's stress. Highlight the definition of stress.

   Explain that as we respond to the world around us, we're busy thinking and feeling and reacting. This, of course, makes demands on us, or gives us stress. Good stress keeps us active and alert. When we are challenged and learn new things, life is interesting. But when stress keeps up or can't be controlled it can become bad stress. Sometimes we call this "distress."

   Discuss the "Think It Over" questions. Save question 3 (about what Valerie can do to deal with her stress) until later in the lesson.

   1. *Exciting events, frightening, upsetting, or uncomfortable situations, things that require difficult decisions, things causing separation, loss, or major change in life, things we worry about, out-of-control feelings.*

2. *Affects appetite, sleep patterns, and feelings; may lead to stomachaches, headaches, and nervousness. People who are under too much stress may overeat or not eat, take out their feelings on others, fight, try to escape by using alcohol or drugs, or act out in various ways. Lead students to understand that these kinds of actions simply lead to more stress.*

3. **Student workbook activity.** Tell students that now they are going to think about what causes stress in their own lives. Have students write down five situations or events that are causing stress in their lives right now. Then have them place a check in each column that applies to the situation or event. Does it take place in the home? School? Involve money? Include a sibling? A friend? Other (enumerate)?

4. Use question 3 about what things Valerie can do to deal with her stress to lead into a brainstorming session about how to handle stress. Consider making this a small group activity.

   Have groups present their ideas to the rest of the class. They should be prepared to tell why and how their suggestions will help a person to control or cope with stress. During discussion use the reference material at the end of the lesson as appropriate.

   Some sample suggestions:
   keeping healthy by eating well, getting enough sleep, and exercising
   stay away from unhealthy foods—caffeine and too much sugar
   try to prevent stress by organizing
   slow down; don't try to do more than you can
   take time to do things you enjoy
   talk to God about things that worry you
   talk to trusted friends and adults about problems or worries
   do something for others—focusing only on your own problems makes them seem
   even bigger

   You may want to identify some negative reactions to stress: blaming others or blaming yourself, overeating, not eating, giving up, fighting, taking your stress out on others.

5. Ask students to go back into their small groups to discuss their Student Activity worksheets. Have them help each other decide on at least two things each person can do to deal with one of their stressful events or situations. They can write their ideas on the back of the activity sheet or in their health notebooks.

6. **Closure.** Ask:
   "Which of these stressful situations are part of growing up?"
   "How do you think knowing that you have new life in Christ can affect your attitude to stressful situations?"

## SOME FACTS ABOUT STRESS: WHAT IT IS AND WHAT TO DO ABOUT IT

### Definitions

First, there are some words that you might want to learn:

a. *Stress or stress reaction:* This is the way our bodies react when extra demands are made on our minds, our feelings, or our bodies. (In everyday language "stress" may be used to mean a stressful event.)

b. *Stressor:* A stressor, or stressful event, might be something difficult that happens in our lives or in our surroundings. It might also be something we feel or think about that makes our minds and bodies work harder than usual.

c. *Tension:* Sometimes our bodies feel stiff, and our muscles are pulled tight. Tension warns us that we are feeling stressed.

d. *Stress spiral:* One stressor can cause another, producing a chain reaction. When stressors accumulate like this, we call the result a stress spiral or a stress chain.

e. *Good stress:* Stress which stretches our capabilities or stress which we can manage and control.

f. *Bad stress or distress:* Stress which goes on and on, or stress which we cannot manage or control.

### General Explanation

Researchers have found that our health is affected by the way in which our feelings, our minds, and our bodies respond to the things that happen to us. When something happens which places extra demands on us, we feel tense because we have to think and work harder. Our minds send alarms to all systems in our bodies so that we can do the extra work. This is called having a stress reaction. Our body systems continue to work harder until things settle down again. After the first alarm, we don't usually notice that we are being stressed—but we are burning up extra energy and feeling some tension whether we notice it or not.

There are many kinds of stressors. Sometimes the stressor is a difficult activity. It may be something that is new to us. Sometimes there is just a high pileup of many little stressors. Sometimes the stressor is something we think about or feel strongly about. Sometimes a stressor is something that comes and goes rather quickly. Sometimes it stays with us, causing ongoing tension and strain.

Some stress is good for us. It keeps us alert; it goes along with learning new things. When we can do something constructive about stress, it keeps life interesting and helps us grow smarter and healthier. But if our feelings, our minds, and our bodies are stressed for a long time, and if we cannot control our stress, it can interfere with what we want to do or become. We may feel upset or just generally down. We are more likely to become sick and to have accidents when we are stressed for too long.

So to be physically and mentally healthy—and to stay that way—it is very important to learn to manage things that happen to us, the ways we think about them, and how we react to them.

## Some Questions and Answers

*What are some example of stressors (stressful events)?*

1. *Things that happen in the environment can trigger stress.*
   a. Frightening or uncomfortable things. For example:
      - A large, barking dog rushes toward you.
      - Someone keeps telling you to hurry up.
      - Someone keeps teasing you.
      - You are on a long hike, and become hungry and cold.
   b. Things which are exciting, but about which you're uncertain or which require many decisions or changes in your life. For example:
      - You win the lottery and have to decide what to do with the money.
      - Another person comes to live with you.
      - You are chosen to be in a class play.
      - You have to kick a field goal in football.
   c. Things which involve separation and loss, or major changes in your life. For example:
      - Someone you care about is hurt or has died.
      - You have to move away from your friends and familiar surroundings.
      - Someone steals something that you care a lot about.

2. *Things you think about can cause stress.*
   a. Things you think about that have recently happened or may have happened long ago. For example:
      - You think over and over how badly you did a job or played a game.
      - You keep thinking about something that made you feel upset and angry a long time ago.
      - You think about getting even with someone.
   b. Things you think about that might happen tomorrow or some other time in the future. For example:
      - You worry whether or not someone will like you.
      - You worry about whether a dog will bark at you on the way to school.
      - You worry that someone may scold or punish you.
      - . You get all excited about your birthday or a special trip coming up.

3. *When your feelings are out of control, they can trigger a stress spiral.*
   a. Feelings which make you get in trouble if you act on them.

For example:
- You feel so happy and proud of something that you aren't considerate and you make others jealous.
- You feel so upset and embarrassed about something that you stop making friends.
- You can't stop feeling responsible because your friend cheated in a game last week.
- You stay so excited after play that you can't settle down to do your school work.

*What Are the Three Stages of Stress Reaction?*

Our bodies adapt to stress in three separate stages: First, there is a stage of *alarm*. We get signals that something is happening; the stressor is there. We may feel surprised or upset. Our bodies prepare us to do something right away! Our glands release hormones to make our hearts beat faster and our lungs work harder. We breathe faster, sugar is released into the bloodstream, our blood pressure goes up, we may perspire more, our digestion slows down and we experience a burst of energy that makes us feel restless. Our bodies are prepared as if we were going to fight or run away. This is the beginning of a stress reaction; it lasts just a short time.

The second stage is *Response: React or Repress.* If we can do something effective about the stressor, our bodies are in this stage for a short time, and no harm is done. If we cannot, we spend a lot of time and energy adapting to the stressor in this stage of resistance. When we are using up more than our usual store of energy to adapt to the stressor, it doesn't matter if we are feeling very good and capable of managing a stressor; too much adaptation produces wear and tear on our minds, our feelings, and our bodies. It can be like driving a car for a long time without taking time out to take care of the car.

The third stage is *exhaustion.* If we have to manage stress for too long, we need time out to regain our adaptive energy. We may feel "tired but happy," exhausted because of a happy event or some good exercise and we can usually recover quite quickly. But the stress may come from too many good changes all at once or a series of hard things to do or to live with; then we are likely to feel depressed, irritable, forgetful, worn out, hopeless, or that nothing we do can go right. In this stage, we are likely to have slow reflexes and poor judgment. This is the time when we are most likely to get into a stress spiral.

*What Can I Do About It?*

Recognize that *only you* can control your own stress reactions! No one else can control your thoughts, feelings, and actions. Your stress is the way you react to events and the way you think and feel about things. Don't waste energy and time blaming others for your stress. Make plans and do something constructive about your stressors.

You can:

a. *Pay attention!* Learn to recognize the signs of stress that are yours alone. Different people react to events in different ways. If you have a pet, a barking dog might not bother you at all; but even a sleeping dog may be very alarming to someone who has been bitten by a dog. There are things that are stressful for you that only you can know about. Pay attention, but don't turn into a worrier about stress.

b. *Practice!* Get in the habit of controlling and managing your own stressors. It's a lifelong job, so why not start today?

c. *Try out different things to do.* Once you have figured out what is wasting your energy, give some of the following hints a try. It may take two or three weeks of trying only one thing to see if it works. Make it a project.

   1. Give your body a break. *Eat properly.* A body that is neither too thin or too fat and that gets what it needs can recover quickly.

      *Get good sleep.* A body that gets enough rest can recover quickly.

      *Exercise.* This is one of the best ways to manage restlessness and strong feelings that won't go away. It's good for your body too.

      *Stay away from extra substances.* Things that make you feel good for a short time are likely to start and maintain a stress spiral. Caffeine, tobacco, extra sugar, and non-prescribed drugs simply spend energy quickly; they don't create new energy.

   2. *Use your brains!* Think ahead, and try to prevent stressors. If you know you have a test, studying is more useful than worrying. Walk yourself through a situation ahead of time to be more prepared when it happens.

   3. *Keep your sense of humor.* Laughter is a good tension breaker. Don't let yourself get tense about your own stress. Just remember that good-natured jokes are fun for everyone; teasing or mean jokes can simply start a new stress spiral.

   4. *Calm down.* When you are too excited, upset, or exhausted to think clearly, take some time out to calm down. Your mind, body, and feelings need a rest when you have been pushing yourself too far too fast. Even in a crisis, it helps to make a brief quiet time for calming down. It is good for your mental health to find some quiet time each day. Sometimes five or six deep, slow breaths can calm you down a lot. Sometimes quiet time or meditation can help. Find your own healthy way.

   5. *Talk it over.* Talk things over with a trusted adult or friend. When you can't figure things out by yourself, you may not have enough information or you might be too bogged down to get new ideas. If possible, choose your listener from among those who have the information or skills you need. Not every problem needs the same helpers.

Sometimes you need someone who knows more about your particular stressor to help you figure things out. Sometimes you just need someone who will listen to you while you think it through.

6. *Get some distance from your stressors.* Try to step back a bit and do something else for a while. If things look hopeless, you may be in the stage of exhaustion, and your problem solving won't go anywhere until you recover a bit. With some time away, your mind may be refreshed, and you may surprise yourself with some good ideas.

7. *Problem solve!* Think constructively about your stressor. Decide what the problem is and what you would like to happen. Think of several different ways to handle it. Think of the consequences of each way. Make a workable plan and try it out.

8. *Be careful about your action plan.* Stress spirals start when you take actions that are irreversible and that only make things worse. Think through the consequences of your solution. Your judgment is bad when you are exhausted. In that condition, don't do anything you can't undo.

9. *Let it go!* Stop reacting to every little thing that might upset you. Your world will never be perfect, and others will always be doing things you wish they would not do. For most of your life, the only person you will be able to control will be yourself. Most of the time, you can only tackle one problem at a time, so you'll have to calm down and let a lot of things pass by.

10. *Stop worrying.* Either make a plan or forget it. This isn't easy, but it can be learned. Try not to dwell on things that have already happened. Ask yourself, "What have I learned from this?" and let it go. If you worry about the future, think of the worst outcome possible. Chances are it won't be that bad, and anyway you can live through it. Make reasonable plans for the worst outcome. Then let it go; it probably won't turn out that badly, but at least you'll be prepared.

11. *Don't try to do too much at one time.* Try one new thing at a time and give up some things that you've outgrown. Trying to do too many new things while still hanging onto all you have been doing will eventually catch up with you.

12. *Always keep some things in your life stable and familiar.* Sometimes we go through periods of change that we have no control over, and one change can lead to another. For example, we move to a new neighborhood; we enter a new school; new people enter our family. If that happens to you, keep as much as possible the same—your clothes, your possessions, your daily routine.

• • • • • • • • • • • • • • • • • • • • • • • • • • • • • • • • • • • • • • • • • • • • • •

## Related Activities

1.  Have students use copies of the Student Activity to survey stress in others. What situations/events are most likely to cause stress? Which factors listed on the sheet most commonly cause stress. Consider graphing the results.

2.  Follow up on students' Step 5 stress-reduction plans. Ask students to try implementing the ideas for a week and then share the results.

# LESSON 7: INFLUENCES THAT MATTER

## Preparation/Materials
- Student workbook activity

## Objectives
- Students will identify things that influence them.
- Students will examine how TV influences them.

• • • • • • • • • • • • • • • • • • • • • • • • • • • • • • • • • • • • • • • • • • • • • • • •

## Lesson

1. Open the lesson with an activity that forces students to make choices. Read sets of options to the class, and have class members move to the right or the left (signal direction) as they make their choices for each option. (Push desks aside to make room, or have students stand in aisles for the activity.) Tell students to choose the option that seems to fit them the best and then to stand with others who have made the same choice.

   A list of suggested options is included, but change or add to the list as necessary for your class.

   **Options:**
   "Do you see yourself as a(n) _____ or a(n) _____?"

   | | | |
   |---|---|---|
   | apple | **or** | orange |
   | lion | | deer |
   | yellow | | blue |
   | mountain | | lake |
   | wall | | door |
   | pizza | | steak |
   | earthquake | | volcano |
   | sun | | moon |
   | pitcher | | catcher |
   | skydiver | | hiker |
   | rose | | dandelion |
   | apartment building | | log cabin |
   | winter snow | | summer rain |
   | submarine | | airplane |

2. Talk about influences on making choices, using questions such as the following:
   "How did you make your decisions?"
   "Were all the choices easy? Were some hard? Why?"
   "Did what others chose have any influence?"
   "What things do you think helped you decide?" (For example, experiences, personality, how friends chose, etc.)

3. Next, divide the class into small groups, and ask each group to present a skit that illustrates one or more influences on choices. Circulate around the room to give assistance and, if necessary, to suggest possible influences to act out. Another option is to assign each group an influence to act out (influence of popular music, parents' wishes, peers, church, community, past experiences, society, God's Word).

4. **Discussion.** After the skits talk about whether the influences are positive, negative, or both. You may also wish to distinguish between external and internal influences.

   Focus the discussion on the power of various influences on our choices. Introduce one or more situations to make the discussion concrete. For example: "Suppose you are in a store and thinking of stealing a (name of object). It's tempting and you really want it, but in the end you leave the store without it. You decide against it. What could have influenced you?" (Fear of being caught, fear of parents' anger if they found out, know it's against the law, conscience balks, friends' reaction, know it's wrong—God's law.)

5. **Student workbook activity.** In this activity students consider one powerful influence on choices in today's world—TV. To give them ideas for filling out the activity sheet, suggest that they think of specific TV shows and how the shows affect them. If some students do not have television or are not allowed to watch it, suggest other forms of media for the exercise.

• • • • • • • • • • • • • • • • • • • • • • • • • • • • • • • • • • • • • • • • • • • • • • • •

## Related Activities

1. Integrate with language arts. Ask students to write poems about seeing themselves as one of the options (apple/orange, lion/deer, yellow/blue, mountain/lake, etc.) in Step 1.

2. Health notebook: Ask class members to find and share articles in newspapers and magazines that illustrate some of the powerful influences in society. Or perhaps they could find articles showing how people in the news were influenced in their choices.

# LESSON 8: DECISION MAKING

## Preparation/Materials

- Student books
- Optional: Write the steps for making a decision on a transparency or on the board (see Step 2).
- Student workbook activity
- Unit evaluation in student workbook
- Optional: Ask a few students to practice the script "Interviews on the Street"

## Objectives

- Students will become aware of the importance of their decisions.
- Students will understand the relationship between Christian faith and decision making.

## Background

As you teach this lesson, avoid emphasizing making "correct" decisions; rather, help students to gain an understanding of what goes into making a decision and of biblical standards to apply to their decisions. And be sure students realize that as surely as we're human and bound to making sinful decisions, God will forgive us over and over again if we confess our sins.

(This lesson has been adapted from *Discovering God's Way,* Parish Life Press, 1984.)

• • • • • • • • • • • • • • • • • • • • • • • • • • • • • • • • • • • • • • • • • • • • • • •

## Lesson

1. **Student book.** In the section "Making Decisions," have students read the script "Interviews on the Street." If you wish, have a few students practice reading it before class.

   Discuss the interview, using the "Think It Over" questions.

   1. *Dr. Yahn relies on instinct; Ms. Bigelow tries to avoid making decisions as much as possible; Sam gathers lots of facts and prays before making decisions.*
   2. *Answers will vary.*
   3. *Answers will vary; one common way is to wait for others to make decisions for them. Ask students for examples. Lead a discussion on the consequences of making a habit of leaving decisions to others.*
   4. *Answers will vary.*

2. Before class write the steps of decision making either on the board or on a transparency, or have class members work together to decide on the steps and write them on the board.

   Suggested steps:
   - Identify the problem. What decision is needed?
   - Think of the possible choices.
   - Gather information. (In order to make an informed decision, a person needs accurate facts. Stress the importance of doing this before making the decision.)

- Think of possible consequences of each choice.
- Make the choice you think is best.
- Take action.
- Evaluate your decision.

3. Lead a discussion on decision making. Ideas to include:
   - After taking action, we should be ready to take responsibility for what we've decided. If we have thought through the decision and acted responsibly, we should be able to defend our decision. What are some guidelines for making choices? (Safety, health, parental opinion and rules, school and community rules/laws, showing respect for self and others, law of love/Word of God.)
   - New life in Christ makes a difference to our decision making. God does not leave us on our own. God has given us his law; God gives us the Holy Spirit. Living close to God helps us make decisions that please him.
   - Why do we make bad decisions? (Lack of experience, information, or discernment; sin.) Stress that God freely forgives when we confess our sins.

4. Have students working in pairs make up situations which present a problem needing a decision. Then have them use the process outlined in Step 2 to make a decision.

   Next, in a full-class session (or, if your class is large, in groups of six or eight) have one of the pair describe the situation and the decision. Then the rest of the class (or the group) interviews the partner, and he or she must defend ("take responsibility for") the decision. (Sometimes this activity is called the "hot seat.")

   Alternative option: each pair makes up a situation (writing it down) that requires a decision; then another pair makes the decision and defends their decision. For another variation, each member of the pair takes turns answering "hot seat" questions.

5. **Student workbook activity.** Assign students to interview one or more adults about how they make decisions, using the questions on the activity sheet. When the interviews are returned, have students share the results.

6. **Unit culminating activities.** Use one of the following suggestions for a unit culminating activity.
   - Make skits modeled after "Interviews on the Street" to perform for other classes. The interviews could be about various topics covered in the unit.
   - Design posters on the unit theme: "A Person Like Me." The posters could include words/phrases and pictures that illustrate how the various topics covered are an important part of shaping each person.

7. **Unit evaluation.** Use the worksheets to review and evaluate.

   *Matching:*
   *1. f;  2. c;  3. h;  4. a;  5. b;  6. d;  7. e;  8. g*

   *Fill in the blanks:*
   *1. heredity; 2. new life; 3. genes/chromosomes; 4. mixed; 5. adrenal glands*

   *Short answers:*
   *1. Answers will vary, but should include the idea that feelings affect how we think and act. Also, unpleasant feelings give signals of problems that need attention.*
   *2. Stress can help us be at our best.  It can prepare us to learn new things and deal with difficult situations.*
   *3. Possible answers include lack of appetite or overeating, change in sleep patterns, stomachaches, headaches, ulcers, nervousness.*
   *4. Feelings may show themselves in other ways: transferring feelings of anger to others or self; effects on the body, such as tiredness, stomachaches, headaches.*
   *5. Answers will vary. Possible answers include expressing/talking about feelings, working to solve the problem that caused the anger, forgiving.*
   *6. Identify the problem, think of possible choices, gather information, consider results of each option, make the decision, evaluate the decision.*
   *7. Answers will vary.  Possible answers include parents, older siblings, God's law or God's Word, popular media, peers.*
   *8. The egg and the sperm each have 23 chromosomes.  When the two join, the fertilized egg, which develops into a baby, has 46 chromosomes that carry the inherited traits.*

   *Short essay:*
   *1. Answers will vary, but should reflect the role of both hereditary and environmental factors.*
   *2. Answers will vary, but should reflect the class discussions in Lessons 1 and 2.*
   *3. Answers will vary. Student answers should recognize that although feelings may come unbidden, often our thoughts and actions prolong unpleasant feelings. In addition, how we react to an event or situation can change our feelings.*

# Unit 3

## People Need People

# Goals

- Students will recognize that good relationships are necessary to health.
- Students will identify ways to build relationships and to avoid erecting barriers.
- Students will examine prejudice, discrimination, and labeling and recognize the pain these practices cause.
- Students will recognize good communication as a powerful tool for building good relationships.
- Students will choose to show caring to and appreciation of others.

# Background

We are social beings, created by God to live in relationship with others. Because of sin, however, our relationships are marked by conflict and brokenness. As a result, we experience alienation and loneliness. Although we would like to think that the growing-up years are relatively free from the pain of broken relationships, if we are honest, we will admit that children experience this suffering, too.

We can help our students by teaching them strategies for negotiating conflicts and ways to promote positive attitudes. Still, as important as knowing strategies and recognizing the effects of attitudes are, these approaches don't get to the source of the problem. Students need to know and experience Christ's power to heal, to restore, and to make new beginnings possible. They need to know what it means to follow Jesus in the way that they relate to others.

# Vocabulary

Plan to integrate the following vocabulary:

| | | | |
|---|---|---|---|
| immediate family | prejudice | discrimination | extended family |
| labeling | minority | relationship | stereotype |
| ethnic group | support network | sender | feedback |
| receiver | barrier | indifference | verbal communication |
| clarify | distractions | nonverbal communication | |

# Unit Resources (Search online for similar resources if these are no longer available.)

"How to Talk to Your Kids About Racism." Nationwide Children's, 2020.
 https://www.nationwidechildrens.org/.

"Resources for Talking About Race, Racism and Racialized Violence with Kids."
 Center for Racial Justice in Education.
 https://centerracialjustice.org/.

Fox, Paula. *The Slave Dancer*. New York: Bradbury Press, 1973.

_____ . *The Village by the Sea*. New York: Orchard Books, 1988.
 When Emma's father has to have an operation, Emma is sent off to live with gruff Aunt Bea. Emma gradually discovers that a person's "outside" and "inside" may be quite different.

"Developing Empathy." Teaching Tolerance.
> https://www.tolerance.org/classroom-resources/tolerance-lessons/developing-empathy.
> Short lesson related to bullying and bias with linked PDF materials, grades 6–8.

Weltmann Begun, Ruth ed. *Ready-To-Use Social Skills Lessons & Activities for Grades 4–6.*
> Lessons, activities, and handouts.
> https://www.researchpress.com/books/674/ready-use-social-skills-lessons-activities-grades-4-6.
> Students learn skills such as sharing, listening, dealing with anger, setting goals, building self-confidence, and dealing with prejudice.

Hamilton, Virginia. *Arilla Sun Down*. New York: Greenwillow Books, 1976.

Kerr, M.E. *What I Really Think of You*. New York: Harper, 1982.

L'Engle, Madeleine. *Meet the Austins*. New York: Dell, 1981.

Woodson, Jacqueline. *Brown Girl Dreaming*. Nancy Paulsen Books, 2014.
> Memoir (free verse poetry) about growing up in the segregated South during the 1960s.

More lesson plans about diversity can be found on teacheringtolerance.org.
> You can search lessons by age group and theme.

*Multicultural Literature for Children and Young Adults*. rev. ed. Milwaukee, Wisconsin: Wisconsin Department of Public Instruction, 1991.
> A selection of books for children and young adults, pre-K–9. These books have multicultural themes and were published in the U.S. and Canada from 1980–1990.
> To order, contact Publication Sales, Wisconsin Department of Public Instruction, Milwaukee, Wisconsin 53293-0179; phone 800-243-8782.

Paterson, Katherine. *Jacob Have I Loved*. New York: Crowell, 1980.
> The story focuses on sibling jealousy and its insidious effect.

Yousafazi, Malala. *I Am Malala (Young Readers Edition)*. Scholastic, 2016.
> This children's addition is suitable for ages 9-11. Malala is an international symbol of peaceful protest, and she tells her story of wanting to change the world.

# Lesson Resources (Search online for similar resources if these are no longer available.)

### Lessons 1–2

Christopher, Matt. *Long Stretch at First Base*. Toronto and Boston: Little, Brown, 1993.
> About playing baseball, personal relationships, and conscience.

Engelfried, Sally. *Half a World Away*. Atheneum, 2014.
> An adoption story that deals with family relationships, emotional changes, and moving to a new country, age 10+.

Hart, Archibald. *Helping Children Survive Divorce*. Thomas Nelson, 1997.

### Lessons 3–4

Doyle, Brian. *Angel Square*. Toronto: Groundwood Books, 1987.
This story is about Tommy, who "takes his life in his hands as he attempts the daily crossing of Angel Square, where children of different religious backgrounds battle it out each day." The trick is to have a friend from each group!
Intended for grades 4 and up

Shetterly, Margot Lee. *Hidden Figures, Young Reader's Edition*. Harper Collins, 2016.
The story of four African American women who helped achieve some of the greatest moments in our space program, grades 3-7.

Fox, Paula. *The Slave Dancer*. New York: Bradbury, 1982.

*Henry's Decision*. Film. New York and Toronto: BFA Educational Media.
A small, shy newcomer replaces an awkward fifth grader as the object of ridicule. The story centers on the problem of acceptance and rejection within peer groups. Length: 26 minutes.

Lai, Thanhha. *Inside Out & Back Again*. HarperCollins, 2011.
The child's view of fleeing Vietnam and struggling with her new life.

Martin, Ann M. *Inside Out*. New York: Scholastic, 1990.
Jonno wants to be part of the "in crowd," but he has an autistic brother. Gradually, Jonno comes to realize how special his brother is.

McKissack, Patricia. *A Friendship For Today*. Scholastic Press, 2007.
A story of friendship and stereotypes during desegregation.

### Lessons 5–7

"Understanding Other People." The Nemours Foundation, 2020.
teenshealth.org.

"8 Tips to Teach Effective Communication Skills." James Stanfield Co, Inc., 2020.
www.stanfield.com/.

### Lesson 8

"6th-8th Grade Fact Sheet & Lesson Plan." National Coalition for the Homeless.
www.nationalhomeless.org/factsheets.
This page also provides other PDFs about homelessness.

Hoose, Phillip. *It's Our World, Too!* Toronto and Boston: Joy Street Books, 1993.
Tells stories of young people from various ethnic backgrounds and ages who have chosen to make a difference. Includes tips on how to write "power" letters, work with media, etc.
Ages 10 and up.

Paterson, Katherine. *The Great Gilly Hopkins.* New York: HarperCollins, 1978.
A story about an ornery, bright girl who is drawn into a circle of love—in spite of herself.

# LESSON 1: YOUR SOCIAL SUPPORT NETWORK

## Preparation/Materials
• Student workbook activity

## Objectives
• Students will recognize the importance of relationships to health and well-being.
• Students will identify a range of relationships.
• Students will identify their support network and recognize its function.

• • • • • • • • • • • • • • • • • • • • • • • • • • • • • • • • • • • • • • • • • • • • • • • • • • • •

## Lesson

1. Write the statement "People need people" on the board. Ask students whether they agree or disagree with the statement and why. In the ensuing discussion, lead students to understand that God created people to live in relationship with others. Being social creatures is part of our "hard wiring." Therefore it's not just "nice" to have others around; it's also necessary for our health and well-being. Describe how being neglected affects babies and small children, retarding their ability to grow and develop normally.

   Explain that in this unit the class is going to look at relationships with others.

2. Have the class identify the categories of people with whom students interact, and write these categories on the board.

   Suggested categories:
   • Family—immediate
   • Family—extended
   • "Like" family (for example, foster parents, long-time neighbors and sitters)
   • Friends
   • Other adults from the wider community (for example, teachers, principal, school nurse, other school staff members, club leader, pastor, family doctor, friends of parents, next door neighbors)

   Briefly discuss each category. Who would be included in each?

3. Ask students to individually write down the categories as headings on a sheet of paper and to list names of people they know that fit under the various headings.

4. Reflect on the lists together. Draw a line similar to the following on the board.

   ←—————————————————————————————————————————→

   Not Close                    Know Pretty Well                    Close

   Explain the continuum to the class. Then ask students to reflect on where the people they listed belong on the continuum. Ask: "Where would immediate family members belong?" Continue questioning about each group of relationships. Help students discover that not all friends are necessarily close friends (you may wish to differentiate here between types of friends—for example, those who are friends because of a common interest such as music or a team sport, or those who share many interests and spend a lot of time together) and that some adults in the school community or from the wider community can be very close. Point out that other adults (such as doctors or nurses) with whom they may not have a close relationship are nonetheless people on whom students depend for important professional services. Encourage awareness of the range of relationships we have and need in life. Also encourage awareness of the richness that this variety of relationships adds to life.

5. Focus on close relationships. Ask the class to brainstorm ways that people in close relationships are important to each other (love and care for each other, provide companionship, help each other, listen to each other, etc.). Lead students to understand that by creating us to be social creatures, God made us dependent on one another. Make the point that part of being healthy is having healthy relationships with others.

6. **Student workbook activity.** Explain the term *support network* (the people on whom we depend), and briefly go over the activity sheet directions with the class. Have students look over the lists made in Step 2. Who are the people on their lists that fit into the various categories in the diagram on the activity sheet? Ask members to write the names in the appropriate circles on the activity sheet. Students' social health has to do with how they relate to the people on their diagram.

7. Reflect on the lesson and the student activity with questions such as the following:
   "Why do people need each other?"
   "What do you think is important about depending on others?"
   "What do you think is important about having others depend on you?"
   "How does it help you to know that there are people you can count on?"
   "How does identifying these people help you?"
   "What difference does it make to know that God created you in such a way that you depend on other people and they depend on you?"
   "What difference does it make to know that God has promised to be with us and that God can always be depended on to keep promises?"

• • • • • • • • • • • • • • • • • • • • • • • • • • • • • • • • • • • • • • • • • • • • • • • • • • •

## Related Activities

1. Integrate with language arts. Name specific situations with which students frequently need help. Then have students write about the person they would turn to and describe what they think the person would do if they asked for help.

2. Create a "People Need People" bulletin board. In the center of the bulletin board, make a collage of pictures of people interacting with each other. Add appropriate pictures/words as the unit progresses to illustrate main lesson ideas.

3. Play popular musical selections dealing with the importance of personal relationships. You may wish to ask students to bring in songs or recordings. What ideas are expressed in the selections? Enjoy and/or critique the selections as appropriate.

# LESSON 2: BUILDING RELATIONSHIPS

## Preparation/Materials

- Optional: Prepare and practice an introductory skit with one or two students (see Step 1).
- For activity in Step 2:
  piece of poster board
  self-stick labels or markers
- Student workbook activity

## Objectives

- Students will understand that sin is the cause of breakdowns in relationships.
- Students will identify actions and attitudes that build up and break down relationships.
- Students will choose to work to build up their relationships.

## Background

In *The Great Divorce,* C.S. Lewis pictures hell as a place where people cannot live in community. As a result, they keep moving farther and farther away from each other. The book gives a frightening but apt description of the damaging effects of sin on human relationships: enthroning one's self results in pushing others away. In contrast, when God is at the center of a person's life and God's love permeates that life, people are able to live with others in harmony and peace. Of course, sin still causes brokenness, but confession and forgiveness make new beginnings possible for believers.

## Lesson

1. Write the headings *Build Up* and *Break Down* on a piece of poster board. Briefly recall the previous lesson's discussion of relationships, and note that in this lesson students will be thinking and talking about what builds up a relationships and what breaks down a relationship.

   Alternative option: Begin the lesson with a short skit illustrating the lesson theme. If the skit demonstrates actions and attitudes that break down relationship, be sure to reenact the skit showing positive actions and attitudes.

2. **Activity.** Have student pairs work together to discover what builds up and what breaks down relationships. Assign each pair to describe at least one way of treating others that they think is essential for building up a relationship and at least one way of treating others that they think is sure to break down a relationship. Consider having the pair write each idea on a self-stick label. Allow 3–5 minutes for pairs to complete the activity. Circulate to help students who are having difficulty.

   Ask pairs to share their ideas, giving each pair the opportunity to offer at least one suggestion in the "build up" and in the "break down" category. Students can place their self-stick labels under the appropriate heading on the newsprint or poster board, or they can write in the suggestions with markers (possibly red for building up and blue for breaking down). Discuss the reasons for the students' choices. Add to the lists as necessary. Be sure to include respecting others (opinions, property, rights), keeping confidences, being honest, and caring about others under the "building up" heading.

3. Reflect on the activity with questions such as the following:

   "What items do you think are the most important on the list of building up and why?"

   "What items do you think are the most important for getting along with (or building relationships with) friends your own age?"

   "What suggestions are important for building relationships with immediate family (or extended family, or adult friends) and why?"

4. Lead a discussion on the basic cause of breakdowns in relationships. Elicit from students the biblical account of Adam and Eve's disobedience. Ask students to identify the results: the breaking of our relationship with God, the killing of Abel by his brother Cain.

   Elicit from students how Christians deal with breakdowns in relationships.
   Ask, for example: "How will the work of the Spirit in our lives affect our relationships with others?" Lead students to understand what the new life in Christ means to our relationships and the role of the Spirit in transforming us.

5. **Student workbook activity.** Have students read the situations and write two endings to each situation—one ending that will help to build up the relationship and one that will surely break down the relationship. Encourage students not to exaggerate but to think of realistic endings.

• • • • • • • • • • • • • • • • • • • • • • • • • • • • • • • • • • • • • • • • • • • • • • • • • •

## Related Activities

1. Integrate with Bible study. Consider having students read passages such as Galatians 5:22–26 dealing with the fruit of the Spirit. How will the work of the Spirit in our lives affect our relationships with others? Or explore the relationships of characters in Bible stories. For example, have students read stories describing the relationship of Saul and David. What caused a breakdown in their initially friendly relationship? Why did David continue to treat Saul with respect?

2. Health notebook: Explore the role of courtesy in relationships. Consider asking students to give characters on certain TV shows courtesy ratings. What message does courtesy—or the lack of courtesy—give? Have students identify ways they can show daily courtesy to each other.

3. Have students make up and perform skits on the lesson theme. You may wish to have them base their skits on the situations described on the Student Activity sheet.

# LESSON 3: ERECTING BARRIERS— PREJUDICE AND DISCRIMINATION

## Preparation/Materials

- Student books
- Student workbook activities 1 and 2
- Optional: Have two students practice reading the conversation in the student book ("Eavesdropping").
- Optional: Make an audio recording of the musical accompaniment (piano or guitar) to the song "Jesu, Jesu."

## Objectives

- Students will be able to describe prejudice and discrimination.
- Students will understand how prejudice blocks relationships, leads to injustice, and violates God's command to love our neighbors.
- Students will consider ways deal with prejudice.

## Background

This lesson zeroes in on one barrier that humans erect in relationships—prejudice. As you consider the topic with students, explore not only the obvious differences that often evoke prejudice and discrimination, but also subtler forms of prejudice that may exist in the classroom community. Note that the next lesson deals specifically with excluding others by labeling. In addition, Unit 4, Lesson 9, deals with excluding or stereotyping those with disabilities.

• • • • • • • • • • • • • • • • • • • • • • • • • • • • • • • • • • • • • • • • • • • • • • • • • • •

## Lesson (2 sessions)

1. **Student book.** Turn to "People Need People," and read and discuss "Eavesdropping," "Prejudice," and "The Next Step—Discrimination." Use the "Think It Over" questions to stimulate discussion on the topic of prejudice and discrimination. Lead students to understand that prejudice and discrimination transgress God's command to "love your neighbor as yourself." Be sure they understand that neighbors include all whom God created. Raise awareness of prejudices and discriminatory behavior present in your community or city—or classroom. Note that an awareness of the problem is the first step in doing something about it.

   1. *Lead students to see how people with disabilities are sometimes treated unfairly and kept from fully integrating in North American society*
   2. *Answers will vary. Help class members to understand why any minority group may be—and often is—the object of discrimination.*
   3. *Discuss the meaning of "love God above all and your neighbor as yourself." Recall the parable of the Good Samaritan.*
   4. *Answers will vary, but make students aware that often our prejudices are hidden— even from ourselves. This may be a good time to raise awareness of specific problems in the community—fair housing, hiring practices, and so on.*

   Discuss how stereotypes can lead to prejudice and discrimination. Stereotypes are fixed ideas we have of other people—usually people of a particular race, ethnic group, or religion. Stereotyping causes us to mistakenly think that all members of the group are alike. Elicit examples of stereotyping from students, or provide a few typical examples (all Asian-American students are good at math and science ; all grandmothers are plump, sweet, and bake apple pie and cookies; all people on welfare are lazy).

2. **Student workbook activity 1.** Focus on ways students can respond to prejudice and discrimination that they see and hear (for example, racial jokes, slurs, and name-calling).

   Divide the class into groups, cut apart the situations described in Student Activity 1, and give each group one of the situations to discuss. You may wish to add or substitute one or two situations that apply specifically to your community.

   When groups are ready, have each group report on its assigned situation. Consider having each group's reporter read the situation to the class and tell the group's ideas about the situation. Give the class opportunity to respond.

3. Teach students the folk song "Jesu, Jesu." Consider providing piano or guitar accompaniment to make this an enjoyable activity. Discuss the lyrics. Use the song with other appropriate lessons.

4. **Student workbook activity 2.** Have students complete the crossword puzzle. Discuss the answers. Identify the various types of differences—ethnic, religious, racial, physical ability—covered. Give or have students give examples of how these differences have led to discrimination.

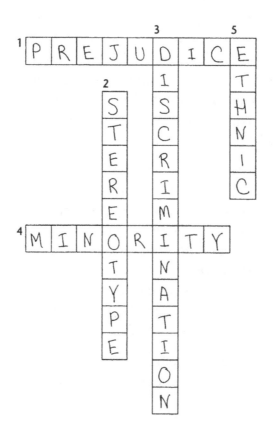

●●●●●●●●●●●●●●●●●●●●●●●●●●●●●●●●●●●●●●●●●●●●●●●●●●●●

## Related Activities

1. Health notebook: Ask students to find newspaper or magazine articles about prejudice and discrimination (online or print). You may wish to have them write a paragraph telling their views on the situation or their ideas for ending the discriminatory practice or rooting out the prejudice described.

2. Have students research and report to the class how Jesus refused to go along with the prejudices of Jewish society. The meeting of Jesus with the Samaritan woman at Jacob's well is an excellent example (John 4). Also see Mark 2:13–17, Mark 10:13–16, and John chapter 9.

3. Demonstrate what it's like to feel discrimination. Give students with brown eyes preferential treatment (allow them to sit where they wish, praise them, give them special privileges, and so on). If time permits, switch roles, so all class members have the opportunity to feel discrimination. Discuss or have students write about what it feels like to be "second class."

# Jesu, Jesu

Ghana Folk Song
Words: Tom Colvin

Chorus

Je - su, Je - su, fill
Je - su, Je - su, fill *(descant)*

us with your love, show us how to serve the

neigh - bors we have from you.

Verses

Neighbors are rich folk and poor, neighbors are black, brown, and white;
These are the ones we should serve; these are the ones we should love;

*to Chorus*

neigh - bors are near - by and far a - way.
all these are neigh - bors to us and you.

Words: Tom Colvin
Music: Ghana folk song adapted by Tom Colvin.

# LESSON 4: LABELING

## Preparation/Materials

- For lesson introduction: some objects with labels (for example, bottle with poison symbol, clothing with designer label, grocery item with well-known brand label and with generic label)
- For labeling activity: self-stick labels, one per student
- Prepare a prejudicial label for each student. Also write on the label how the rest of the class should treat the person. See Step 3 for suggestions.

## Objectives

- Students will identify how they erect barriers and exclude by labeling others.
- Students will recognize labeling as a form of prejudice.
- Students will choose to treat others with respect and love.

## Background

Labeling is one form of prejudice. Labeling shows an uncaring attitude by reducing the other person to an object. Labeling a person on the basis of ignorance, false information, or appearance is a kind of prejudice of which we are all guilty. Probably most of us have also been on the receiving end of labeling. We can remember the pain of being excluded and rejected because we were labeled "different" or in one way or another "not good enough." Most students in your classroom will also have been on both the giving and receiving ends of such labels. Some may be currently struggling with a label problem.

This lesson considers labeling in the light of Matthew 5. In this passage Jesus gives a new law: Love your enemies. It may help students to understand this passage if you make clear that it doesn't mean we have to like everyone and be close friends with everyone. But it does mean that we should have a helping and caring spirit toward all—even our enemies. It sounds impossible, and, of course, we can't do this on our own. But God provides the power and forgives our failures when we confess them. Hold up Jesus' example of caring for others and of refusing to simply write others off with a label. For example, although the Pharisees were quick to label someone a "sinner" and then avoid social contact with that person, Jesus shared meals with tax collectors and sinners.

*Note:* Ideas for this lesson were adapted from the article "What Does Your Label Say?" by Carol Regts in the April/May 1990 issue of *Christian Educators Journal* and from "We All Belong," session 4 of *Discovering God's Way* (Parish Life Press, 1984).

••••••••••••••••••••••••••••••••••••••••••••••••••••••••••••

## Lesson (2 sessions)

1. Introduce the lesson by showing students some objects with labels. Ask: "What's the purpose of labels? What kind of messages do they give? What message does a label with a well-known brand name give? A generic label? A label with a skull and crossbones?
   A designer label?" (Give specific examples of brand names currently popular.)

2. Lead students to understand that people also put "labels" on each other. How do the labels we put on people serve some of the same uses as labels on objects? When we label someone as "unpopular" or a "nerd," what effect does the label have?

3. **Labeling activity.** Consider following these steps.
   - Explain to students that you will put a label on each student's forehead. The labels tell others how to treat them during the discussion or activity that follows. Students should try to discover what their labels say by the way they're treated. Also tell students that for this activity to "work," students should not divulge others' labels or remove their own—even for a quick look (these rules will need strict enforcement). Be sensitive as you assign the labels; some students, for example, might not be able to handle an "ignore me" label.

     Some label suggestions:
     I'm the king/queen. Honor me.
     I'm a beauty. Give me lots of attention.
     I'm stupid. Don't listen to me.
     I'm a jolly joker. Laugh with me.
     I'm a wise guy. Put me down.
     I'm a hero. Praise me.
     I'm a jerk. Ignore me.
     I'm a person with a disability. Feel sorry for me.
     I'm tough. Be afraid of me.

   - Next, have class members interact so that they can discover what their labels are. You may wish to make this a time of free mingling, or you may prefer to have students participate in a structured, group activity. Possible structured activities include discussing a topic on which everybody will have an opinion (for example, "School should be in session on Saturday morning, but not on Wednesday afternoon"), playing games, working together on room clean-up or other simple tasks. Circulate during this period and, if necessary, give students ideas about how to communicate labels. Give students ample time to interact and experience the effect of labeling—a minimum of 15–20 minutes.

   - End the activity by bringing class members together in a circle and giving them the opportunity to say what they think their label is. Ask questions such as the following: "Have you guessed what your label is? How did you guess? How did you feel while you were wearing that label? Would you like to wear that label every day? Why or why not?" Have students take off their labels and read them to the class.

4. **Discussion.** Have a student read Matthew 5:46–48. Ask students to paraphrase the passage and identify what the passage has to do with labeling. How does labeling build walls and break or prevent relationships? Other passages to read: 1 John 3:23–24; 4:19–21.

   Together make up a class goal about avoiding labeling. Ask a volunteer to write out the goal. Then display it in the classroom.

5. **Health notebook.** Assign students to write a paragraph in which they reflect on the labeling activity.

   Suggested writing topics:
   how they were treated while they were wearing the label
   how they felt about the way they were treated or the way they treated others
   how it would affect them to wear one of the activity labels for a long period of time

   Have volunteers share their writing with the class.

• • • • • • • • • • • • • • • • • • • • • • • • • • • • • • • • • • • • • • • • • • • • • • • • •
## Related Activities

1. Focus on stereotypes. Have students collect and place in their health notebooks ads that depict stereotypes. What kind of gender stereotypes are pictured? Other stereotypes to look for—ethnic, racial, occupational.

   Consider writing group skits demonstrating stereotypes. Give the skits for other classes. After the skits, students should explain the negative impact of sterotypes.

2. Health notebook: Assign students to watch specific TV shows and give the shows a prejudice rating. They should be prepared to back up their ratings with specific reasons or examples. Are any characters stereotypes of ethnic groups? Of other groups?

3. Integrate with social studies. What effect has labeling/prejudice had on relationships with other countries? Among main ethnic groups of our country or of any country the class is currently studying?

# LESSON 5: COMMUNICATING AND RELATIONSHIPS

## Preparation/Materials
- Student books
- Make a diagram of geometric shapes and lines for the one-way communication activity (see Step 2).

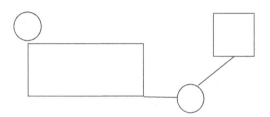

## Objectives
- Students will recognize the importance of clear communication to relationships.
- Students will be able to describe the basic elements of communication.

## Background
Lessons 5–7 of this unit are on communication. This lesson introduces students to the basics of communication, Lesson 6 deals with nonverbal communication, and Lesson 7 gives students the opportunity to practice active listening.

● ● ● ● ● ● ● ● ● ● ● ● ● ● ● ● ● ● ● ● ● ● ● ● ● ● ● ● ● ● ● ● ● ● ● ● ● ● ● ● ● ● ● ● ● ● ● ● ● ● ● ● ● ● ● ● ● ● ● ● ●

## Lesson
1. Briefly review main ideas about building relationships that have been covered so far in the unit. Then explain that the next few lessons are going to be about something that's essential to good relationships—communication.

2. **Activity.** Introduce the topic of communication with a demonstration of one-way communication. Direct class members to take out paper and pencil and follow your instructions (or the instructions of a class member) to complete the drawing of lines and geometric shapes prepared before class. As you give the instructions, don't use any body language (gestures or hand signals), and sit or stand where the class cannot see your face. Don't allow class members to ask you questions or to communicate with each other.

3. Check the student drawings against the original diagram. Reflect on the just-completed activity.
   "Was the communication effective or not? If not, why not?"
   "What was the most frustrating thing about the activity?"
   "Can you recall a similar experience with communication? When?"
   "What do you think would have improved communication"

4. **Student book.** Turn to the section entitled "Communicating and Relationships," and read and discuss "Playing Ping-Pong." Note the diagram that illustrates two-way communication. Compare and contrast the two sender-receiver diagrams, making sure that students understand that when the receiver replies the roles are reversed. What is necessary for good communication?

   Read and discuss "I Thought You Said..."

1. *Sender doesn't use clear language and doesn't communicate what he or she has in mind.*

2. *Answers will vary. In discussion include the importance of sender's using specific and clear language and receiver's checking out the meaning of the message with questions if he or she is unsure.*

5. Use the example of the brother and sister's misunderstanding over using the radio and the "Think It Over" questions to identify both potential problems in communication and good listening and receiving skills. Elicit ideas from the students, and make a list of skills for senders and receivers on the board (or make this a group activity).

   Other ideas to include on skills list:
   Senders: Decide what you wish to say before speaking, pick a good time to speak, use specific rather than vague words, look at the listener, be sure to include all facts, speak clearly, make sure the receiver or listener understands the message (ask questions, ask him or her to repeat the message).
   Receivers or listeners: Pay attention to the speaker, look at the speaker, don't interrupt, respond to show that you're listening, check what you've heard with questions ("Do you mean...?"), ask questions to clarify meaning ("Why is ____ necessary?"), summarize the message.

   As a final step, the sender and receiver should agree on what has been communicated. How would these ideas have prevented the misunderstanding of the brother and sister over the use of the radio?

6. Demonstrate good two-way communication by having a brief conversation with a few individual students. Use skills enumerated in Step 5—asking questions, summarizing, and so on. Give some students the opportunity to do demonstrations also, or give student pairs a few minutes to practice the communication skills.

7. **Closure.** Elicit "I learned" statements from the class to highlight main ideas of the lesson. Be sure to include why good communication is essential in maintaining relationships.

• • • • • • • • • • • • • • • • • • • • • • • • • • • • • • • • • • • • • • • • • • • • • • •

## Related Activities

1. Try a round of the *Telephone Game* to highlight problems in communication. Whisper a sentence (with enough clauses or phrases to make game fairly difficult for sixth grade students) to one person, who whispers it to the next, and so on around a circle of students. The last student says the sentence. Compare the final version with the original. If the class is large, divide into two or three groups, and start the same sentence in each group.

2. Health notebook: Have students collect newspaper or magazine articles which show or deal with different forms of communication (telephone, radio, etc.) Have them write a paragraph about the pros and cons of the form of communication their article is about.

   Or have students write about how people communicate with their pets. What are the similarities with communicating with people? The differences?

# LESSON 6: COMMUNICATING NONVERBALLY

## Preparation/Materials

- Student books
- Cards with names of emotions, one card for each pair of students
- One or more dialogues for demonstrating humming speech written on the board or on a piece of newsprint (see Step 4 for example).
- Optional: pictures showing people relating to others and demonstrating a several ways of communicating nonverbally

## Objectives

- Students will identify ways in which people communicate nonverbally.
- Students will become aware of the importance of nonverbal messages in communication.
- Students will recognize that for clear communication, verbal and nonverbal messages should match.

## Lesson (1–2 sessions)

1. **Student book.** Read and discuss "It's Not Just What You Say." Use the "Think It Over" questions to discuss Charlie Brown's nonverbal communication with Peppermint Patty in the cartoon. Make the point that the message in the sender/receiver diagrams (discussed in the previous lesson) includes the nonverbal as well as the verbal message.

   1. *Peppermint Patty. Charlie Brown*
   2. *Nonverbal—a sigh. It communicates clearly because Peppermint Patty knows what Charlie Brown means by the sigh and she's ready to argue over it.*

   Ask students to turn to "I Can See What You're Saying," and study the pictures showing nonverbal cues. What do they think the people might be saying or feeling? What are the nonverbal cues? Have students jot down their ideas.

   Optional: If students are unfamiliar with the topic of nonverbal communication, you may wish to provide additional pictures in order to cover a wider range of nonverbal cues. Consider numbering the pictures and sending them around the room. Students should write down what they think each picture "says."

   Compare students' responses to the pictures. Although students will have chosen different words, most likely they will pretty much agree on what the people are feeling.

2. Have students identify the cues they received from the pictures about what the people are feeling. Lead them to identify three main categories of cues: body posture, facial expression (including eye contact), and gestures or hand positions. Write these categories on the board. Stress that these cues are all types of *nonverbal communication*. Briefly review the meaning of the term. Write the words nonverbal communication over the headings.

3. Give pairs of students a card with the name of an emotion written on it. Each pair is to act out the emotion for the rest of the class—no words allowed.

   Suggestions for emotions to act out:

   | | | | | |
   |---|---|---|---|---|
   | angry | loving | sad | impatient | joyful |
   | surprised | scared | frustrated | jealous | relieved |
   | embarrassed | excited | bored | irritated | |

   Ask the rest of the class to identify the body language used to communicate the emotion.

4. Identify voice cues as one more nonverbal way to communicate. Have students imitate the following dialogue using a humming speech (with mouth closed and teeth together) to demonstrate:

   | | |
   |---|---|
   | Adult: | It's time to go to bed. |
   | Child: | Right now? Can't I watch this program? |
   | Adult: | No, get ready for bed. |
   | Child: | Just this once? |
   | Adult: | I said no. And I mean it. Now get up and go upstairs. |

   Help students isolate specific ways we communicate vocally—tone of voice (pleasant or unpleasant), pitch, rate of speed, volume.

   Another interesting way to demonstrate voice cues: Make up one or more nonsense sentences (for example: "The droober harths prisickly"), and have students take turns saying the sentence in a way that expresses one of the emotions listed above.

5. **Discussion.** Tell students that although this lesson has focused on communicating with our faces and bodies and voices, usually, of course, we also use words (verbal communication). Reflect on the lesson activities and what they mean for improving communication with others. Consider using the following discussion questions/ideas.

   - "Do you think your family background or the country you're from influences the way you communicate nonverbally?" (Make students aware that people of different backgrounds or cultures may interpret nonverbal cues differently, so being aware of our own background and nonverbal habits is helpful for improving communication. Provide examples or elicit examples from the students. A few examples: (a) showing the bottom of your shoe is considered an insult in Middle Eastern countries and in some Asian countries, (b) making loud noises while eating is a message of appreciation in some Asian cultures, (c) speaking in a loud voice may be considered a mark of interest and self-confidence, and (d) making eye contact with people in authority is considered ill-mannered in some cultures.)

   - "What is another way nonverbal communication can get in the way of communicating clearly?" (When actions and words don't match, we send mixed signals to others. Point out that when signals don't match, people are more apt to believe the nonverbal clues. Nonverbal messages are more apt to be the true message. Example: Someone invites you to join in an activity. You say yes, but your voice isn't enthusiastic and you avoid eye contact. What's the true message? Also give an example of a person saying no, but sending an inconclusive body message.)

- "How can mixed signals lead to breakdowns in relationships?" (Saying one thing and meaning another causes misunderstandings. Directly saying what you mean is the best way to keep relationships open.)

- "How can we send a message of self-confidence in body language?" (Standing straight, speaking firmly, and looking directly at the listener. Have several students demonstrate a self-confident body message.)

6. **Closure.** Summarize the lesson, stressing the importance of matching body language or actions with words to make sure that we communicate clearly.

• • • • • • • • • • • • • • • • • • • • • • • • • • • • • • • • • • • • • • • • • • • • • • • • •

## Related Activities

1. Watch a video for a few minutes with the sound turned off, or assign students to watch part of a TV program with the sound turned off. Have students list the body movements, gestures, and facial expressions that communicate messages to the viewer.

2. Integrate with language arts. Have students write fantasies about a trip to a country in which nonverbal messages are the opposite of many in North America. What amusing or dangerous adventures result? Or have students write about a misunderstanding arising from giving mixed signals.

3. Focus on how we communicate with our hands. Ask students to sit in a circle and take turns pantomiming hand signals. How many hand signals can the class come up with? (Clenched fist, beckoning fingers, hitchhiking sign, clapping, handshake, lifted in greeting, stop sign, folded hands, pointing, "please rise" signal, friendly pat.)

# LESSON 7: ACTIVE LISTENING

## Preparation/Materials

- For talking/listening activity:
  slips of papers with conversation ideas, one for each student (half should be for talkers and the other half for listeners)
  two paper bags, one labeled "Talkers" and the other "Listeners"
- Student workbook activity
- Make up several sentence stems for conversation starters (Step 6) and write them on the board, on a piece of newsprint, or on a transparency.

- For making billboards:
  large, rectangular pieces of butcher paper, newsprint, or poster board
  art materials such as markers or paints

## Objectives

- Students will be able to describe listening and nonlistening (both verbal and nonverbal) behaviors.
- Students will develop active listening skills.

• • • • • • • • • • • • • • • • • • • • • • • • • • • • • • • • • • • • • • • • • • • • • • • •

## Lesson (2 sessions)

1. Start out with two role plays that demonstrate nonlistening. During the first role play, use only nonverbal behaviors. Have a volunteer talk to you about some upcoming school event. While the student is talking show by nonverbal behavior that you're not listening (fuss with objects on desk or clothes, avoid eye contact, etc.). When time is up, ask the student: "Was I listening or not? How did you know that I wasn't listening? How did my actions make you feel?"

   During a second role play with a different student volunteer, demonstrate verbal nonlistening. This time interrupt once or twice with a comment or question that is unrelated to what the student is saying. At the end of the role play, repeat the questions asked of the first student.

   Give the class time to share experiences of not being listened to. How does the experience make us feel?

2. Brainstorm with the class a list of behaviors that block listening (both verbal and non-verbal). Students will probably have some difficulty coming up with verbal nonlistening behaviors. Suggest they think of unsatisfactory conversations they've had with others. How did they know by the reply that the person they were talking to was not listening? (Some verbal nonlistening behaviors: not responding to what was said, changing the subject, answering with information about self, interrupting the speaker, not getting facts straight; nonverbal behaviors: yawning, avoiding eye contact, turning away, fussing with things.) If you wish, have students vote on which behaviors are the most common and/or the most irritating.

Alternative suggestion: Have groups make up lists of nonlistening behaviors, and then in a full-class session make a composite list.

3.  Have students demonstrate and identify nonlistening and listening behaviors with the following activity. On slips of paper write directions for talkers (senders) and listeners (receivers). Place the two types of directions in separate, labeled paper bags. Ask pairs of students to come forward. One student takes a slip of paper from the talkers' bag, and the other a slip from the listeners' bag. Then the students hold a brief conversation, following the written directions.

    Suggestions for talkers:
    > You're telling about a thrilling film you saw last night.
    > You're telling about your family vacation plans.
    > You're describing your favorite food.
    > You're talking about a new pet your parents have promised you.
    > You're talking about an accident you had with your bike.
    > You're explaining the way your bicycle lock works.

    Suggestions for listeners:
    > You're in a hurry to leave and meet another friend.
    > You're too sleepy to listen carefully.
    > You're bored with what the talker has to say.
    > You're eager to tell about your own exciting hiking trip.
    > You're very interested in what the talker has to say.
    > You're sick and have a headache.

    Tell students that in the next session they'll be focusing on good listening.

## Session 2

4.  Recall the diagrams of sender/message/receiver in the student book. Stress that one common breakdown in communication occurs when the receiver doesn't listen to the message. Recall the comparison of two-way communication to playing Ping-Pong. Note that the person waiting for the ball to land on his or her side must be alert and active. The receiver must be aware of what's going on and be ready to respond.

5.  **Student workbook activity.** Have students complete the activity on active listening. Go over various habits or skills listed. Ask students: "Which of the points are about paying attention to the sender or speaker? Which are about concentrating on what the speaker is saying? Which are about responding to the message?" Have students identify ways to respond that show the speaker that we are listening.

    Brainstorm a list of words that describe the behavior of someone who's listening (alert, active, concentrating, interested, paying attention, tuning in, open, trying to understand, thinking, encouraging).

Give students a short time to reflect on their own listening habits. Which skills do they need to improve?

6. Divide students into groups of three to practice active listening. Students should count off to form triads (they'll need to remember their number for the activity). In each triad, person 1 chooses one or two sentence stems and talks about them; person 2 responds with active listening responses, verbal and nonverbal; person 3 observes and at the end of the conversation restates the message to check on speaker's meaning. Direct students to switch roles and discuss another topic.

Reflect on the activity with questions such as the following:
"What was the hardest thing about the listening exercise?
"How did it feel to be carefully listened to?
"When do you think it would be important to repeat what the speaker has said? Why?"
"What poor listening habits did you notice?"
"How do you think our imagination helps in active listening?" (Helps us to enter into the other person's situation.)
"How does listening to others show that we care about them?"

7. Culminating activity on communication. Have students design billboards to advertise an idea about the importance of communication to relationships or about ways to improve communication. Provide large sheets of paper and art materials for the activity. Encourage students to think of a slogan or a picture or symbol to express the idea they want to get across. (Examples: "Interrupting Is Disrupting"; "Thanks for Listening"; "Tell me. I'm Listening.") If you wish, make this a group activity with each group working together to design and make a billboard. Display the completed billboards.

• • • • • • • • • • • • • • • • • • • • • • • • • • • • • • • • • • • • • • • • • • • • •

## Related Activities

1. Health notebook: Have students reflect on the lessons on communication with "I learned" statements. You may wish to review their statements and use them for reteaching.

2. Health notebook: Ask students to write a short entry on their own listening habits. Also ask them to set individual goals for improving listening. What habit or habits need changing?

3. Set goals for improving listening in the classroom. What is the best class listening habit? Which habit or habits need changing?

Consider asking a volunteer to write out the class goals and post them for a period of time. Periodically check up on progress.

4. Focus on the importance of eye contact. Consider having students take a poll of their encounters with 5–10 people. Then have them rate the degree of eye contact with each: poor, fair, or good.

5. Spend time practicing particularly difficult types of communication, for example, expressing apologies or talking over disagreements.

# LESSON 8: DECIDING TO CARE ABOUT OTHERS

## Preparation/Materials
- Student books
- For Step 3 activity:
  poster board, one piece per student
  markers or other art materials as needed
- Unit evaluation in student workbook
- Optional: Lesson 3 audio recording of musical accompaniment for song "Jesu, Jesu"

## Objectives
- Students will compare and contrast attitudes of indifference and caring.
- Students will develop their understanding of caring as a Christian attitude. Students will make affirming statements to other class members.
- Students will decide, with God's help, to care about others.

## Background
In this last session of the unit, students will examine the attitude of indifference to others, and will consider why this is an unchristian attitude in the light of God's love for us. As you teach this lesson, help students to understand that with God's help we can decide to become caring Christians.

## Lesson

1. **Student book.** Begin by having three students read the dialogue "What's It to You?"

   Use the "Think It Over" questions to spark a discussion. In answering question 1, focus on Lee's attitude of indifference. Write the word *indifference* on the board, and ask students what it means. Compare and contrast the attitude of indifference with a caring attitude. Make clear that a caring attitude expresses itself in actions. What actions express Kara's caring attitude toward Michelle? Consider working with the class to list ways we show that we care about others.

   1. *Shawna: lacks empathy for Michelle, eager to be part of in-crowd; Lee: uninvolved, uncaring; Kara: caring, full of empathy for Michelle, accepting of differences.*
   2. *It raises the question of what it means to you when others are being treated unfairly or cruelly or being picked on.*
   3. *Answers will vary. Elicit from students the difficulty of standing up for the one who is outside of the group for one reason or another.*

2. Focus on how we can express appreciation of others. Stress that people are greatly influenced by what others say about them and by how others treat them. Refer to the conversation in the student book. Ask: "What kind of picture did Jon give Michelle of herself?" One way to care for each other is to build each other up by showing respect and appreciation.

3. Making affirming statements. Give students the opportunity to make affirming statements about each other. Guide students in the type of comments to make—specific

and concrete rather than general and vague, and "I" statements rather than "you" statements. For example: "I enjoy your friendly smile" rather than "You're nice."

Distribute one piece of poster board to each student. Direct class members to make a frame around the edge that includes their name. They can write their name in different colors to form a frame, or they can create another border design and write their name in large letters on the top or bottom of the poster. Then have students circulate with their posters or pass their posters around. Each student writes one affirming remark within the "framed" poster of each class member. Give the posters a catchy name such as "Poster Pats" or "Poster Pals."

*Note:* caution students against misplaced "humor" and negative remarks or put-downs.

4. Closing lesson questions:
   "How is indifference the opposite of caring?"
   "Why do you think expressing our appreciation of others is a good thing to do?"
   "How can we influence others by expressing our appreciation?"
   "What effect do you think a caring attitude has on our relationships?"
   "Why is it difficult to care about others? What gets in the way?"
   "How can we become the caring persons we want to be?"

5. Consider closing the unit by singing the song "Jesu, Jesu." Another song suggestion is "Make Me a Channel of Your Peace" (*Psalter Hymnal*, 545).

6. **Unit evaluation.** Use the worksheets to review and evaluate.

   *Matching:*
   *1. b; 2. g; 3. d; 4. h; 5. i; 6. a; 7. c; 8. f; 9. e*

   *Fill in the blanks:*
   *1. respect; 2. prejudiced; 3. mixed; 4. Labeling; 5. social; 6. eye contact*

   *Short answers:*
   1. *Answers will vary. Examples: Redheads are hot-tempered; all children are noisy.*
   2. *Possible answers include communicating with body posture, gestures, facial expression, eye contact, and tone of voice.*
   3. *Saying one thing and meaning another often leads to misunderstandings. People usually believe the nonverbal message.*
   4. *Possible answers include interrupting the speaker, not responding to what was said, changing the subject, avoiding eye contact, turning away.*
   5. *Possible answers include what we experience, what others say, popular media, what we need to make ourselves feel important.*

   *Short essay:*
   1. *Answers will vary.*
   2. *Answers will vary but should reflect the class discussions in Lessons 2 and 8.*

• • • • • • • • • • • • • • • • • • • • • • • • • • • • • • • • • • • • • • • • • • • • • • • • • •

## Related Activities

1.  Have students write letters to someone in their support network to express appreciation. The letter could be to a family doctor who has been close, to a church school teacher or club leader who has spent time organizing activities and providing snacks, or to a neighbor who has always been hospitable.

2.  As a culminating activity, do an appropriate unit project. Sixth grade students could help younger students with class work or perhaps take part in a community project (cleaning up litter, cutting grass or shoveling snow for someone who needs help, or a similar project).

3.  Health notebook: Give students opportunity to write their response to the affirming statements on the posters. How do the posters make them feel about themselves?

# Unit 4

# Bodyworks

## Goals

- Students will develop an understanding of the importance of smoothly functioning body systems.
- Students will develop an understanding of persons with diseases and disabilities.
- Students will recognize the relationship of lifestyle to cardiovascular disease.
- Students will assume greater responsibility for caring for the body God has given them.

## Background

In *Beyond Doubt* (Christian Reformed Board of Publications, 1980), Cornelius Plantinga tells an anecdote about Whittaker Chambers, a dedicated atheist. One day when Chambers was watching his child as she sat in her high chair, "he found himself staring with fascination at his daughter's tiny, intricate ear. It seemed to him a marvel. Only a *planner* could have planned that ear." This experience "set Chambers on the road to belief."

The human body is truly amazing. And it's very smart. In fact, it's brilliant. It performs to a large extent "on its own." The heart beats, lungs breathe, stomach digests, kidneys purify—all without our even thinking about it. When we study the human body—its parts, processes, growth and development, we cannot help but wonder at the complexity of its design. But our study should lead us to marvel not only at the body, but also at the God who created it.

God has given us life, and that life is mysteriously and inextricably linked to a body so complex that we will never completely understand it. Our fitting response is awe and wonder and praise to God, the Creator. "I will praise you," said the psalmist, "because I am fearfully and wonderfully made; your works are wonderful, I know that full well" (Psalm 139:14).

Our study in this unit also deals with diseases and with disabilities. If we're honest, we'll have to admit that some people have been set on the road to unbelief because of the suffering that diseases and disabilities bring. How can an all-wise, all-knowing, all-powerful, and loving God allow diseases and disabilities?

This painful question is best answered by looking at Jesus. Jesus healed the diseases and disabilities of those who came to him. The Gospels are full of these accounts. Matthew, for example, writes that many followed Jesus "and he healed all their sick" (12:15). Jesus shows us that God wants us to be healthy. Disease—and death—are an intrusion in God's creation. What's more, by giving us a preview of what life will be like in the new creation, Jesus gives us hope for the future. Disease and death don't have the last word.

## Vocabulary

Plan to integrate the following vocabulary:

| | | | |
|---|---|---|---|
| plaque | platelets | plasma | communicable disease |
| cardiovascular | oxygen | phagocytes | noncommunicable disease |
| carbon dioxide | hemoglobin | antibodies | atherosclerosis |
| stroke | lymphocytes | health agency | high blood pressure |
| valve | white blood cells | red blood cells | |

Names of parts of eight body systems (see individual lessons)

## Unit Resources (Search online for similar resources if these are no longer available.)

*KidsHealth from Nemours*. The Nemours Foundation. https://kidshealth.org/.
Website that has a page for parents, kids, and teens. Information, activities, and videos about a variety of topics.

"Anatomy Home Learning." Innerbody Research.
https://www.innerbody.com/htm/body.html
Interactive human anatomy systems, multi-media and text. Suitable for a variety of ages.

Brand, Paul, and Phillip Yancey. *Fearfully and Wonderfully Made*. Grand Rapids, Michigan: Zondervan, 1987.
This resource may provide ideas for class devotions and Bible study that tie in with lessons on the human body.

Anatomy coloring pages can be downloaded from https://coloringhome.com/ and https://www.coloringnature.org/.

Kitteredge, Mary. *The Human Body: An Overview*. The Healthy Body Series. New York: Chelsea House, 1989.
Intended for grades 6–12.

Stark, Fred. Gray's Anatomy: *A Fact-Filled Coloring Book*. Philadelphia: Running Press, 1990.
This portfolio has 60 detailed drawings with descriptive text and a ready-to-color poster. Also included is information on how the body grows, heals, changes; why eyes blink, the stomach rumbles, and the heart beats; and details on the tiniest bones and largest muscles.

## Lesson Resources (Search online for similar resources if these are no longer available.)

### Lessons 1–2

"The Human Body Project." Scholastic.
https://www.scholastic.com/teachers/unit-plans/teaching-content/human-body-project/.
Unit plan with three lesson plans and 8 reproducibles, grades 3–5.

*American Lung Association*.
Lung.org.

Bryce, Emma. "How your muscular system works." Ted Conferences, LLC.
ed.ted.com.

Butler, Enda. "Oxygen's surprisingly complex journey through your body." Ted Conferences, LLC. ed.ted.com.

Grant, Lesley. *Discover Bones: Explore the Science of Skeletons*. A Royal Ontario Museum Book. Reading, Massachusettes: Addison-Wesley, 1991.
This high-interest student resource takes a look at bones, covering their structure and function as well as such topics as growth, animal skeletons, and archaeology.

Bennett, Howard. *The Fantastic Body: What Makes You Tick & How You Get Sick.* Rodale Kids, 2017.

Cole, Joanna and Bruce Degen. *The Magic School Bus Explores the Senses*. Scholastic, 1999.

*The Human Body! (Knowledge Encyclopedias).* DK Children, 2017.

**Lessons 3–5**
Webb, Sarah. "Blood Does a Body Good." Science News for Students.
https://www.sciencenewsforstudents.org/.
This article, written for students, includes reading questions and a word find.

"The Circulatory System." PBS & WGBH Educational Foundation, 2020.
pbslearningmedia.org.
The lesson plan includes a video, activities, and worksheets, grades 6-8.

"Heart and Circulatory System." The Nemours Foundation, 2020.
kidshealth.org.

**Lessons 6–8**
Canavan, Roger. *You Wouldn't Want to Live Without Bacteria!* Franklin Watts, 2015.

"Unit 1: CDC Basics." Division of Population Health, National Center for Chronic Disease Prevention and Health Promotion, 2020.
https://www.cdc.gov/healthyschools/bam/cdc_basics.htm.
This unit includes a variety of resources, including activities, PDFs, and source links.

Hermes, Patricia. *You Shouldn't Have to Say Goodbye*. Richmond Hill, Ont.: Scholastic, 1984.
A 13-year-old girl has to learn to accept that her mother is dying of cancer.

"Unit 4: Health Conditions and Diseases." Division of Population Health, National Center for Chronic Disease Prevention and Health Promotion, 2019.
https://www.cdc.gov/healthyschools/bam/cdc_basics.htm.
This unit includes a variety of resources related to health conditions (like asthma and diabetes) and vaccine-preventable diseases.

*Science Journal for Kids and Teens*. Science Journal for Kids.
https://sciencejournalforkids.org/.
Peer-reviewed science research adapted for students.
Search by grade level and topic (Health and Medicine for this unit).

"The History and Science of Cancer." PBS & WGBH Educational Foundation, 2020.
pbslearningmedia.org.
This page links multiple lesson plans about cancer and cells (videos and activities for each).

Bryce, Emma. "How does the immune system work?" Ted Conferences, LLC.
ed.ted.com.

"Learn How to Control Asthma." National Center for Environmental Health, 2019.
https://www.cdc.gov/asthma/children.htm.
This web page has information and fact sheets about asthma for kids.

**Lessons 9–10**

"Unit 5: Disabilities and Birth Defects." Division of Population Health, National Center for Chronic Disease Prevention, 2019.
https://www.cdc.gov/healthyschools/bam/cdc_basics.htm.
This unit includes a variety of resources related to disabilities, impairments, and disorders.

Martin, Ann M. *Inside Out*. New York: Scholastic, 1990.
Jonno wants to be part of the "in crowd," but he has an autistic brother. Gradually, Jonno comes to realize how special his brother is.

"Understanding Disabilities." Teaching tolerance.
https://www.tolerance.org/classroom-resources.
A research-based activity for grades 6-12.

Taylor, Theodore. *Tuck Triumphant*. New York: Doubleday, 1991.
In this sequel to *The Trouble with Tuck*, Helen has a newly adopted brother, Chok-Do, who is deaf and without speech.

# LESSON 1: BODY AWARENESS

## Preparation/Materials

- Arrange for the activities in Step 1 as necessary, and obtain these materials:
  stopwatch, at least one
  needle and thread, buttons, and scrap material
  meter sticks or pieces of string one meter long
  Student workbook activity 1
  Optional: volunteers to help with measuring and recording at each station
- Student workbook activity 2

## Objectives

- Students will identify differences in abilities.
- Students will develop their understanding of the different abilities and limitations of each person.

## Background

As we go through this unit, we will see many ways that all people are alike. But we will also notice ways in which people are different. For example, we all have muscles and bones, but we do not all have the same ability to use those muscles and bones. Some people may have special ability to use muscles to run fast, to jump high, or to do delicate handwork. Recognizing these differences helps students appreciate their own abilities and be more accepting of their own limitations and those others. Becoming aware of some animal "records" also provides an interesting perspective on human abilities.

As the students prepare to do the lesson activities, talk about how they can make everyone feel good about participating. Note that if our focus is to live a Christ-like life, we want to become encouragers of others, not mockers.

•••••••••••••••••••••••••••••••••••••••••••••••••••

## Lesson

1. **Student workbook activity 1.** Set up a series of activities for the class to do. The smoothest way to do the activities will be to set up stations in the gym and have groups of students move from one station to the next. Have necessary materials for measuring or doing the activity at each station.

   The suggested activities measure abilities and characteristics:
   how long students can hold their breath
   how tall students are
   how far students can jump
   how long it takes to sew on a button
   how fast they can run a 15 m. race (in gym or outside)
   how high students can jump or climb on a rope (if possible)

   Consider following these steps:

   - Introduce the activities to the class, and explain how they are to be conducted. Talk about how students can help and encourage each other.

   - Have students turn to Student workbook activity 1. Explain how students are to record the results of each activity.

- Have students go to the gym or school playground to do the various activities and record results.

2. **Student workbook activity 2.** Have students turn to the second activity sheet and follow along as you talk about the fantastic abilities of certain animals. You may wish to speculate about why these animals need these abilities and how they use them.

   Ask students to compare their "records" with the listed animal records. Discuss the "fairness" of using these comparisons. Broaden the discussion to include the "fairness" of comparisons among abilities of people. Talk about the abilities/limitations that we all have. Working as a class, come up with ideas on how to be accepting of each other.

3. **Health notebook.** Have students write their responses to some aspect of the lesson. For example, students can write about how their activity results make them feel and why.

• • • • • • • • • • • • • • • • • • • • • • • • • • • • • • • • • • • • • • • • • • • • •

## Related Activities

1. Generate math problems based on the measurements from Student Activity 1. Student pairs can make up problems for other class members to solve.

2. Integrate with language arts, and write fantasies based on the "For the Record" handout. Encourage students to be creative. For example, ask students to imagine what it would be like to have the abilities of one of the animal record holders or how an animal holding one record (for example, the red kangaroo) might be able to outwit an animal holding another record (for example, the cheetah).

# LESSON 2: BODY SYSTEMS

## Preparation/Materials

- Student books
- For student presentations on body systems: art materials (poster board, construction paper, markers)
- Student workbook activities 1–8
- For *Body Systems Jeopardy* game:
  note cards
  *Body Systems Jeopardy* question cards in the Teacher Resource section
  a corkboard to display the question cards
  Cut apart the sets of questions and answers. Tape each set (one question and answer) to one side of a note card. On the other side write the point value of the question (assign higher point values for harder questions). Tack the question cards on the corkboard and hang it in a central location.
  Optional: overhead projector to display transparencies of body systems (masters are in the Teacher Resources section)

## Objective

- Students will review the functions and main parts of eight body systems.

## Background

This lesson uses student presentations and a game to review eight main body systems (the reproductive system will be reviewed in Unit 5). Knowing about body systems raises student awareness of the intricacy of the body and of the importance of each system. It also prepares students to understand how their lifestyle choices affect each system—and their health.

Note that Student Activity 9 provides some questions for playing the game *Body Systems Jeopardy.* You may wish, however, to have students make up questions/answers and create game cards or to add questions yourself that reflect class discussion.

To make the game more difficult but also more educational, add another step to the jeopardy game. Display enlarged versions of the blacklines of body systems (or put transparencies of the body systems on the overhead). Whenever a team supplies a correct answer, it can win five bonus points if a team member is able to correctly point out on a drawing of the body system the organ, tissue, or body part described in the question/answer. Each time a team tries for extra points, a different member of the team must go to the chart—until every group member has had a turn.

• • • • • • • • • • • • • • • • • • • • • • • • • • • • • • • • • • • • • • • • • • • • • • • • • • • • •

## Lesson (3–4 sessions)

1. **Student workbook activities 1–8.** Review body systems with student group presentations. Consider following these steps.

   *Note:* In an individual setting, the student may label each of the workbook activity sheets as the teacher presents the material. Use the Student Book as a reference.

   - Divide the class into groups, and assign each group one of the following body systems: skeletal system, muscular system, digestive system, respiratory system, circulatory system, urinary system, nervous system, and endocrine system. Tell each group to prepare a presentation to the class about its assigned body system. The presentation should include the main parts of the system and what the system does in the body.

- **Student book.** Have the class turn to "Bodyworks." Read and discuss the introduction, reviewing body structure—cell, tissue, organs, systems. Briefly page through the material on body systems, and have groups locate their assigned system. Student groups can use the book material as a basis for the presentation about their system.

  If you have other student resources on body systems available, briefly explain the content of each and how it may be useful.

- Have students prepare their presentations. Encourage students to be creative. Groups may wish to act out certain functions, and/or make cards with names of the system's main parts. Using an overhead projector may also be helpful.

  Circulate in the classroom to give suggestions and provide help to students as necessary.

- Have groups give their presentations to the class. Before each presentation have students find the student workbook activity of the body system being discussed. Class members should fill in their worksheets as the group goes over the various parts of the body system.

  At the end of the presentations you may wish to clarify certain points or add any important information that was omitted. Students can also refer to student books to complete the body systems worksheets if necessary. Use the "Think It Over" questions for review/discussion.

  1. *cranium (skull) protects brain and delicate parts of the ears, rib cage protects heart and lungs, vertebrae protect nerves running from the brain down the back*
  2. *skeletal system, muscular system*
  3. *nervous system, endocrine system*
  4. *liver, large intestine, sweat glands, lungs*
  5. *Wastes would build up in the blood, contaminating it.*
  6. *The spinal cord links the brain to the lower parts of the body. If the spinal cord was damaged, messages couldn't get from the brain to the leg muscles.*

2. For further review, play *Body Systems Jeopardy.*

   - Divide the class into two teams. Assign students to be timekeeper, scorekeeper, and encourager.
   - Show students the corkboard with the question cards, and explain the rules of the game.

   Rules:
   (a) The team that has the turn begins by choosing a category (one of the body systems) and point value of desired question.
   (b) The teacher takes that card from the pocket chart and reads the statement about the body system.

(c) The team has a specified period of time to formulate a question that fits with the answer. If the team knows the right question, they get the card and the number of points written on it. (Note that the response must be in the form of a question to be accepted.) If the team does not respond in time, the other team may try to answer the question. If the first team gives the wrong answer, the second team may try to answer the question.

(d) The team that gives the correct answer gets another turn. It may continue to play until a wrong answer is given. (Adjust the way the game is played to fit your classroom situation. You may wish to have teams take turns choosing categories and questions, or you may wish to shorten the response time.)

(e) When all the cards have been used or time has run out, count the points.

3. Close the lesson by talking about ways of taking care of various body systems. Although caring for the body is discussed in some detail in later units, this is a good opportunity to stress the importance of a healthy lifestyle—getting enough sleep, getting exercise, and eating healthy food. You may wish to tell students that the cells of the brain, spinal cord, and nerves, unlike skin and blood cells, cannot be replaced. Stress the importance of wearing safety equipment to protect these parts of the body—particularly the brain. Have students name sports or activities in which wearing a helmet is an important protection for the brain.

• • • • • • • • • • • • • • • • • • • • • • • • • • • • • • • • • • • • • • • • • • • • • •

## Related Activities

1. As a review activity, have each student trace the outline of his or her body on a large piece of paper. Have them cut out the body shape and then draw in main parts of various body systems.

2. Use the diagrams and questions from *Body Systems Jeopardy* to construct a test on the lesson material.

3. Focus on the muscular and skeletal systems. Have groups of students use magnifying lenses to examine some meat and bones (chicken legs work well). They can use a pin or needle to pull the raw meat apart. Have them write down their observations.

4. Show students how water can be cleaned by filtering using filter paper and dirty water. Note that this way of cleaning water is similar to the way kidneys filter waste from the blood. Talk about the importance of water in the body to keep this process going.

5. Dissect frogs to examine a frog's body systems. (Frogs and dissection guides are available from biological supply houses.)

6. Have students find pictures of objects that have functions analogous to parts of the body (computer/brain, balloons/lungs, garden hose/esophagus, gasoline pump/heart). Place the pictures in the appropriate place on a body shape. This idea could be used for individual posters or for a bulletin board display.

# LESSON 3: CLOSE-UP OF YOUR CIRCULATORY SYSTEM

## Preparation/Materials

- Student books
- Prepare the "take a walk through the heart" activity. See Step 3 for options and needed materials.
- Student workbook activity
- Invite a health professional (for example, school nurse, representative of local Heart Association, or pediatrician) to explain what blood pressure is and how to measure it.
- Blood pressure equipment (Note: To take students' blood pressure, pediatric equipment is necessary)

## Objectives

- Students will be able to describe how blood moves through the heart and travels to the cells.
- Students will identify the main parts of the heart and circulatory system.
- Students will understand how to measure blood pressure and heart rate and the relation of these measurements to health.

## Background

Diseases of the circulatory system—cardiovascular diseases—are one of the major health problems of North Americans. This unit highlights the circulatory system—how it works and how to keep it healthy. Cardiovascular diseases such as high blood pressure, strokes, and heart attacks are specifically covered in Lesson 7.

## Lesson (4–5 sessions)

1. Interview with a heart. Have students create a "person-on-the-street" type interview with a heart, writing the interview in script form. The interview should cover the basic information about the heart contained in the student book ("Your Blood Vessels," "Your Heart and How It Works," and "Your Heart Rate"). You may wish to have students work as pairs or small groups on this assignment, reading and studying the student book material together, choosing facts to include in the interview, and then writing the interview.

   Read the following sample opening of an interview to give students ideas for getting started:

   Interviewer: Hello everybody. Jane Happymouth here. Welcome to today's edition of *Inside Information.* We've got a great show lined up. Today's guest has some fascinating things to tell us, and I'm sure he's going to be a really big hit. He's someone none of us could live without, so let's all give a big round of applause to our guest for today—the Heart!

   Welcome to *Inside Information,* Heart. Glad you could make it. How are you feeling today?

   Heart: I feel great. But, of course, I'm a young heart and very strong. I still have millions and millions of beats ahead of me.

Interviewer: Millions? Wow! But tell us, Heart, why do we need you in our bodies?

Heart: That's a good question...

(This excerpt is taken from "Module 1: How Your Heart Works" from the American Heart Association's kit *Getting to Know Your Heart.*)

Have students share the completed interviews with other class members. Student pairs may enjoy reading the interviews, one student taking the role of interviewer and the other the role of the heart.

2. **Student book.** Page through "Close-up of Your Circulatory System" to review any facts that may have been omitted in the student interviews. Examine the drawings and diagrams of the heart, and discuss the "Think It Over" questions.

   1. *Arteries: Blood leaving the heart travels through arteries.  This blood is bright red because it has just been loaded with oxygen in the lungs.  The walls of arteries are thick and muscular so that they can stretch and widen to accommodate spurts of blood.  Veins: Carry blood, bluish-red in color and loaded with carbon dioxide, away from the cells and back to the heart.  Blood in veins moves with little force, so walls of veins are thinner.  Veins also need valves to keep blood flowing in one direction.*
   2. *Student answers should include the idea that the tiny capillaries are necessary to reach every part of the body and service cells.*
   3. *To keep blood flowing in one direction.*

   Consider including the following facts about the circulatory system in the discussion:
   - Blood travels from the heart to the brain and back in 10 seconds.
   - Blood travels from the heart to big toe and back in 20 seconds.
   - Blood travels very fast through the large arteries—about a foot a second.
   - Veins carrying blood back to the heart are equipped with pocket-like valves that are able to flap open and trap blood that starts to flow the wrong way.
   - Each heartbeat squirts about one-half cup of blood through heart valves.

3. Take a walk through the heart. Construct, or have students construct, an outline of heart large enough to walk through.

   Suggested formats/activities:
   - Using masking tape or string or rope taped to the floor, make an outline of a heart on the classroom floor. Or draw a large heart on poster board or butcher paper (to make the heart large enough, you may have to use several large pieces and tape them together). If you are using color, make the right side of the heart blue to show oxygen-poor blood, and make the left side red to show the oxygen-rich blood coming from the lungs.

   Then walk through the heart to show the flow of the blood. Also name parts of the heart, and have students stand on the correct places in the heart. Another option is to make cards with the names of various heart structures/parts. Students must name the part on their card, explain its function, and stand on the part in the heart outline.

• Design a miniature putting course in the shape of a heart. (If the weather is suitable, make the course on the playground.) Use garden hoses or colored (blue and red) bender board. A flag/marker at each hole can give the name of the structure of the heart. Students can putt balls through the heart. Consider using foam balls for golf balls and yardsticks for putters. (We are indebted to the American Heart Association for this activity.)

4. **Student workbook activity.** Have students trace the flow of blood through the heart using blue and red colored pencils. Then have them label the structures of the heart.

*Note:* Depending on the activities chosen, Steps 1–4 will take 3–4 sessions. Consider devoting one session to cover the material in Steps 5–8 on heart rate and blood pressure.

5. Prepare for the visit of the health professional by helping students recall what they know about blood pressure and preparing some questions to ask the visitor.

6. Have the health professional explain what blood pressure measures, why it is an important measure of health, and why pressure varies from person to person.

Use pediatric equipment to take the blood pressure of two or three students. Give the range of readings to show that individual blood pressures may vary.

If time, equipment, and volunteer help permits, consider taking the blood pressure of all students. If any students have elevated blood pressure, give the information to the school nurse or home for follow-up.

7. Have students determine their heart rate. To show that the heart beats at different rates, consider having students take their pulse while lying down, sitting up, and immediately after exercising. They can count the number of pulse beats in 30 seconds and then multiply that number by 2.

Note that the heart rates just measured depended on body position and amount of activity. Ask: "Why do you think body position affects heart or pulse rate?"

Elicit from students other factors that affect the heart rate. Factors include level of activity, weight, age (rate is higher in children), sex (boys' rate is lower than girls'), eating (rate goes up by a few beats for almost two hours after eating), time of day (the pulse keeps going up during the day and may be 6–20 beats higher by late afternoon than right after getting up in the morning), strong feelings (speed up the pulse rate), smoking and other drugs (make the heart work harder than normal).

Explain that a heart that is fit puts out more blood with each beat and therefore doesn't have to work as hard.

8. You may wish to assign students to take their pulse at various times in the day and after various activities for a three-day period. Students can also take the pulse rates of different family members for comparison. Are any of the factors identified in Step 7 influencing their pulse rates? Students can record the results in their health notebooks.

9. **Student book.** Assign students to read "Your Heart Rate" and "Blood Pressure" and answer the "Think It Over" questions.

    1. *The rate or force with which the blood pushes against the artery walls.*
    2. *The highest number measures the pressure when the heart is pumping; the lower number measures pressure when the heart is relaxing between beats.*

• • • • • • • • • • • • • • • • • • • • • • • • • • • • • • • • • • • • • • • • • • • • •

## Related Activities

1. Health notebooks: Have students collect and share articles having to do with the circulatory system. For example, articles about heart transplants and other medical news and views.

2. Contact local organizations for films, discussion posters, and other educational materials about the heart and the circulatory system. In Canada contact the Canadian Heart and Stroke Association; in the United States contact the American Heart Association.

3. Demonstrate the difference between the way blood flows through arteries and through veins. Obtain a baster or ear syringe and a container of water. Fill the baster with water. Squeeze the bulb and push out the water with force to give an idea of how blood moves through arteries; simply tip the baster and let the water flow out to show how blood flows through veins.

4. Show students how heart valves work. *Getting to Know Your Heart,* which is a kit for grades 4-6 available through the American Heart Association, contains a siphon with a valve to demonstrate this.

5. Make and solve math problems based on heart rate figures. For example, taking 72 as the resting pulse rate of an average adult and 42 as the resting pulse of well-conditioned adult, figure how many heartbeats a fit person saves in a minute. How many will he or she save in an hour? In a day? A year? Figuring that with one heartbeat a fit person can save the .3 fraction of a second it takes for an extra heartbeat, how many seconds, minutes, hours, or days of work are saved in a year? (Idea adapted from *Heartbeat* by Charles T. Kuntzleman [Fitness Finders, 1984]).

6. Study the information on pulse rates collected in Step 7 of the lesson to try to detect patterns in rates (for example, patterns related to gender or age.)

# LESSON 4: DISSECTING A HEART

## Preparation/Materials

**Note:** Should you wish to have the students do this optional activity, supplies are available at the following website: **www.homesciencetools.com**

*   For dissecting:
    "Dissecting a Heart" instruction sheet in Teacher Resources, one per student group

    dissecting kits, one per student group

    five-inch straws, one for each heart

    paper towels, dampened with water, about six per group

    newspaper or aluminum pie tins, one per group

    sharp scissors or scalpel, one per group (in addition to the one in the dissecting kit)

    Animal hearts to dissect, one per student group and one for teacher demonstration. Fresh heart must be ordered ahead from a butcher or from a slaughterhouse or meat packing plant (check listings in the yellow pages of the telephone book). Pig or lamb hearts are preferred; calf hearts are acceptable. *Note:* If frozen hearts are purchased, allow a half day to thaw.

*   Arrange for parents or other adults to assist student groups. If assistants are not available, do one dissection (teacher demonstration) in a full-class session.
*   If possible, obtain (possibly borrow this from a medical doctor) a heart model to use as a visual aid during dissection or possibly use a drawing of the heart (such as a completed Lesson 3 Student Activity)
*   Optional: Obtain one beef and one chicken heart to compare size.

## Objective

*   Students will further explore the structure of the heart by dissecting an animal heart.

## Background

The student activity is adapted from the Michigan Model, Grade 6, Phase III.

•••••••••••••••••••••••••••••••••••••••••••••••••••••••••••••••

## Lesson

1.  Review the previous lesson. Discuss any questions students may have on the structure and function of the parts of the heart. Refer to the diagrams in the student book as necessary for clarification.

2.  Demonstrate the dissection of an animal heart. Use the procedure outlined in the "Dissecting a Heart" handout. If you prefer, ask a science teacher, school nurse, or other knowledgeable adult to do the dissecting.

3. Divide the class into small groups of four or five students. The groups should be small enough so that each student has the opportunity to handle the heart. Distribute to each group the Student Activity handout, "Heart Dissection Procedure," and have students dissect their own specimens following the procedure outlined.

    1. *Answers will vary.*
    2. *It will feel slippery.*
    3. *Answers will vary.*
    4. *No, because the heart has stopped pumping.*
    5. *These veins and arteries are tough and stretchable and resemble a garden hose.*
    6. *The pericardium is very thick, strong, and transparent. It looks very much like transparent plastic wrap.*
    12. *The left side of the heart pumps blood to all parts of the body; it must work harder than the right side. The harder muscles work the bigger they get.*
    13. *The mitral valve strands are usually stronger and thicker.*
    15. *To provide the heart with the oxygen and nutrients it needs.*

4. **Closure:** "Today we have explored an actual heart to understand more completely the structure of the heart. In dissecting the heart, we saw and felt the left side (pumps blood to all parts of the body) and the right side of the heart (pumps blood to the lungs). We saw that both sides of the heart have an upper chamber (to receive blood) and a lower chamber (from which the blood is pushed out). The major function of the heart muscle tissue is to pump blood throughout our body. The heart muscle is an involuntary muscle that works 24 hours a day."

● ● ● ● ● ● ● ● ● ● ● ● ● ● ● ● ● ● ● ● ● ● ● ● ● ● ● ● ● ● ● ● ● ● ● ● ● ● ● ● ● ● ● ● ● ● ● ● ●

## Related Activities

- Health notebook: Have students write about their heart dissecting experience. What did they learn? What was the most interesting new fact they learned or the most interesting part of the experience? What was the least interesting or perhaps disgusting part of the experience?

# LESSON 5: LOOKING INSIDE YOUR BLOOD

## Preparation/Materials

- Student books
- For examining blood:
  microscope(s)
  slides of blood
  If the school does not own these materials, try to borrow them from a local health organization or laboratory.
- Invite a health professional to assist with this lesson. (One suggestion: Contact a local medical lab or blood bank. These organizations may be able to also provide both slides and microscopes for this session.
- Student workbook activity

## Objective

- Students will identify basic components of blood and the functions of these components.

## Background

"The pale yellow fluid called plasma makes up about 55 percent of whole blood. About 92 percent of plasma is water with dissolved nutrients, mineral salts, and waste products. The remaining 7 or 8 percent is composed of proteins. The proteins are of three types. Albumin helps to keep blood pressure normal by regulating the amount of water in plasma. Globulin contains antibodies, which are chemical substances that are effective against specific diseases. Fibrinogen works with platelets in the clotting process. (Plasma from which fibrinogen has been removed is called serum.) Plasma carries food to the tissues and transports cell wastes and heat. It is vital also in giving blood sufficient volume to maintain blood pressure."

The rest of the blood contains the red blood cells, white blood cells, and platelets. Red blood cells are shaped like tiny disks. Both sides of red blood cells are concave, which increases their oxygen-absorbing area. The red pigment in blood cells is called hemoglobin. When hemoglobin combines with oxygen, it becomes bright scarlet. "The life span of a red cell is short ...about 30 to 120 days. Then it breaks up. The spleen, a small organ near the liver, filters out much of the red-corpuscle remains. New red blood cells come from bone marrow at a rate of 2 million or more per second.... There are between 25 and 30 trillion red blood corpuscles in an average-size person."

The white blood cells destroy invading disease bacteria. "Certain kinds of white cells are produced in the bone marrow. Others are formed in the lymph nodes. They are present in the blood in a ratio of about 1 to 600 red cells... White blood cells move and change their shape. This ability enables them to move through tiny pores in the capillary walls and to travel through the tissue fluid. They travel to the center of infection and surround it. The bone marrow speeds up production, pouring an enormous number of white cells into the blood. This explains why the white-cell count rises rapidly during a serious infection."

"Blood platelets are smaller and less numerous than red cells. They total about 1½ trillion. Platelets are essential in the clotting of blood. The life of a platelet is only three or four days. They are removed from the blood by the spleen, the liver, and the lymph nodes."

(Quoted/adapted from *Modern Health* by James Otto and others [Holt Rinehart, 1980].)

*Note:* HIV infection is covered in Unit 5, Lesson 5. If you invite a health professional, you may wish to cover HIV transmission in this lesson.

• • • • • • • • • • • • • • • • • • • • • • • • • • • • • • • • • • • • • • • • • • • • • • • • • • • • •

## Lesson

1. Ask: "What is blood made of? What is in your blood?" Elicit responses from students to find out what students know about blood.

   What information is lacking? Encourage the class to think about what they know about the body systems—in particular, about the circulatory system—and come up with a list of good questions. Have students look for the answers to the questions during this session. If unanswered questions remain at the end of the lesson, have students research the answers.

2. **Student book.** If you intend to do the activity in Step 3, tell students that reading and discussing the book material will help them understand what they will see when they look at blood with a microscope.

   Read and discuss "Looking Inside Your Blood." During discussion use information as appropriate from the background material.

3. Using microscopes, examine slides of blood. Try to include slides of both diseased and healthy cells for comparison. If possible, have a health professional lead the activity and explain the slides to students.

   If enough microscopes are available for small student groups to each have the use of one, consider having student groups discuss and then draw what they see.

   Allow time for full-group discussion. Also use this opportunity to address any questions about blood that are still unanswered.

4. **Student workbook activity.** Have students complete the activity sheet by making up a clue for each word in the puzzle. You may wish to allow the class to refer to student books.

5. **Closure.** Ask summary questions. Also lead students to understand that this lesson's content is a basic starting point for learning about blood: The life-sustaining substance that flows through the circulatory system is amazingly complex—and still another pointer to the mind of its Maker.

• • • • • • • • • • • • • • • • • • • • • • • • • • • • • • • • • • • • • • • • • • • • • • • • • • • • •

## Related Activities

1. Interested students may wish to research the Rh factor in blood.

2. Have interested students research and report on the body's lymph network. What is its role in the immune system? What other important tasks does the lymph system have in the body?

3. Discuss blood as a central Christian symbol. What special significance does blood have in the Old Testament? In the New Testament? Or consider what "magical" properties are assigned to blood in various cultures and religions.

4. Obtain a copy of the form that blood donors must fill out, and examine the questions with the class. Why is each question necessary?

# LESSON 6: CAUSES OF NONCOMMUNICABLE DISEASE

## Preparation/Materials
- Student books

## Objectives
- Students will identify and be able to describe the Christian perspective on disease.
- Students will recognize that both environmental and hereditary factors cause noncommunicable disease.

• • • • • • • • • • • • • • • • • • • • • • • • • • • • • • • • • • • • • • • • • • • • • • • • •

## Lesson

1. Tell students that the remainder of the unit deals with diseases that attack the various body systems and keep them from working the way they should.

   Use a whole-class clustering activity to get students thinking about the topic of disease and to tap their prior knowledge about disease. Write the word *disease* on the board, and draw a circle around it. Then ask students to brainstorm words or phrases that come to mind when they think about diseases. Use circles and arrows to show the relationship between concepts (see Unit 2, Lesson 4 for an example of clustering). Two basic words to include in the clustering diagram are *communicable* and *noncommunicable*.

2. **Student book.** Read and discuss "Why? Why? Why?" and "Causes of Disease," the first two sections under the heading "Your Body Systems and Disease." During discussion of communicable diseases, help students recall basic facts about communicable disease covered at previous levels (use the "for reference" material below as appropriate). Also elicit from the class names of additional noncommunicable diseases (hemophilia, cardiovascular diseases, various types of cancers, allergies, lupus, diabetes). Discuss the "Think It Over" questions.

   1. *Answers will vary. Help students to understand that disease is an intrusion in God's creation and that God wants us to be whole and well. Jesus loved and cared for people, but Jesus was also demonstrating God's will for us and giving a foretaste of what life will be like in the new creation.*
   2. *Lack of good health care and sanitation make communicable diseases more likely in developing countries. Some types of noncommunicable diseases may not be as common in these countries because diets are low in fat and sugar. Besides, without modem appliances, people do more hard physical work.*
   3. *Heredity and environment; environment can raise the risk provided by heredity.*

   Bacteria and viruses are the most common pathogens causing communicable diseases.

Bacteria are in the air, water, ground, and in the human body. Most of them are not harmful, and some are helpful and even important to life; however, when harmful bacteria grow and multiply (and they can multiply very quickly), they give off poisons that can make us sick. Diseases caused by bacteria include leprosy, pneumonia, tuberculosis, and strep throat.

Viruses, a group of pathogens even smaller than bacteria, are the cause of most communicable diseases. Viruses are usually found only in animals, plants, and humans (the host). When viruses enter the human body, they invade body cells. Once inside the cells, viruses act as a kind of fifth column and use the cells' energy to rapidly reproduce themselves. Finally, viruses burst out of a cell (which dies in the process), and go on to invade other cells. If the virus reproduces in large numbers and damages many cells, a person becomes sick. Each virus causes only one disease. Diseases caused by viruses include polio, rabies, measles, mumps, chicken pox, flu, and the common cold.

Other types of pathogens causing infectious diseases are protozoa and fungi. Protozoa are one-celled animals. Some types of protozoa live in soil, in salt water, in fresh water—and in people. Some protozoa can cause diseases such as malaria and African sleeping sickness. Fungi, which are actually a type of plant, live in the human skin and may cause diseases such as athlete's foot.

Some main ways communicable diseases are spread: through the air (for example, by pathogens put into the air by coughing and sneezing); through water (from bacteria or protozoa in water); through food (for example, by not washing fresh foods carefully, not cooking or storing foods properly); through direct contact with infected people (for example, shaking hands, kissing, touching infected body sores, sexual contact); through indirect contact (handling objects used or touched by an infected person); through wound infections; and through insects (flies and cockroaches by landing on food). HIV is transmitted through infected body fluids but not by casual contact with people who are infected.

The body's first line of defense against communicable diseases is the body's outer covering of skin, mucous membranes in body openings, tears, and stomach acids. The body's white blood cells—phagocytes—are the second line of defense. Antibodies produced by other white cells—lymphocytes—are the next line of defense.

3. **Health notebook.** Ask students to identify one environmental risk factor and write a paragraph on how that factor can cause or increase the risk of noncommunicable disease. (Students should not duplicate student book examples.) You may also wish to have students specify whether individuals can control or avoid the risk described.

   If possible, have students identify the environmental risks on their own or in discussion with a partner. If this is difficult for the class, brainstorm some risk factors as a class (for example, diet and other lifestyle factors, use of drugs, air and water pollution).

   Find ways for class members to share their paragraphs and ideas.

● ● ● ● ● ● ● ● ● ● ● ● ● ● ● ● ● ● ● ● ● ● ● ● ● ● ● ● ● ● ● ● ● ● ● ● ● ● ● ● ● ● ● ● ● ● ● ● ● ● ● ● ● ● ●

## Related Activities

1. Health notebook: Ask students to cull articles about diseases from current newspapers and magazines. Have them identify whether the disease discussed in each article is communicable or noncommunicable. If noncommunicable, what factors increase risk of the disease? Are there known ways of preventing the disease?

   Or, consider asking students to find articles on new ways of treating or preventing diseases. Discuss student findings.

2. Integrate with social studies. Have students research which communicable diseases are common in other countries. How are the diseases spread?

3. Review the causes of communicable diseases and ways to prevent them from spreading.

4. Make a chart listing communicable diseases and indicating which have vaccines for prevention. Include specific information about recommended doses/time schedules. Students can contact local health organizations to obtain the information.

# LESSON 7: CARDIOVASCULAR DISEASES

## Preparation/Materials

- Student books
- Student workbook activity
- Optional: Obtain pictures or slides showing the progression of cardiovascular diseases (see Lesson Resources).

## Objectives

- Students will identify common cardiovascular diseases and their causes.
- Students will be able to describe how to care for the cardiovascular system.
- Students will take responsibility for caring for their own cardiovascular system.

## Lesson

1. Write the words *cardiovascular diseases* on the board, and ask students what kind of diseases these are (diseases of the heart and blood vessels). Explain that this group of diseases is one of the major causes of death in North America. Ask students to provide possible reasons why cardiovascular diseases are so prevalent in North America. Also ask them to identify the specific names of some cardiovascular diseases. Accept all responses, and tell students that they will be finding out about cardiovascular diseases and what they can do to avoid getting these diseases.

2. **Student workbook activity.** Ask students to read "Cardiovascular Diseases" and "What You Can Do." They should use the information in the student book to complete the Student Activity worksheet. Two answers are provided on the chart; students should fill in the rest of the chart.

3. **Discussion.** Go over the completed activity sheets, and discuss the "Think It Over" questions.

    1. *Plaque is a waxy substance that consists of fat and cholesterol. When plaque builds up in the arteries, it blocks the easy flow of blood, so the heart has to pump harder to push blood through the arteries. This is called atherosclerosis.*
    2. *Atherosclerosis causes the arteries to narrow, so the heart has to pump harder to force blood through. This raises blood pressure.*
    3. *Possible answers include being a nonsmoker; cutting down on fat and cholesterol in your diet; getting enough exercise; controlling stress.*

Study the pictures of blocked arteries in the student book. Also display any photographs you have obtained of a diseased heart or of the progression of cardiovascular disease.

You may wish to discuss why these diseases, which are such a major health problem today, were not as prevalent in earlier years (less stressful lifestyle, more physical work, shorter life span).

Have students describe activities in which they participate that will help them keep their heart and blood vessels healthy.

4. **Closure.** "Today we have talked about cardiovascular diseases, a group of diseases that affect the heart and blood vessels. We learned that we can help keep our cardiovascular system healthy by being nonsmokers, cutting down on fats in the food we eat, getting enough exercise, and learning to control stress."

## Related Activities

1. Obtain statistics (from local health organizations) on the number of deaths due to heart attacks and other cardiovascular diseases in Canada or the U.S. Obtain information from the past ten years so that students can discover trends. Consider having students make graphs for deaths from heart attacks and strokes.

2. Have interested students research current treatment for various cardiovascular diseases.

3. Make posters illustrating ways to keep the cardiovascular system healthy.

# LESSON 8: THE DISEASE I HAVE...

## Preparation/Materials
- Encyclopedias and other student resources for researching diseases.
- Student workbook activity

## Objectives
- Students will identify a number of noncommunicable diseases and disorders that affect the body.
- Students will recognize specific effects some noncommunicable diseases and disorders have on the body.
- Students will develop an understanding of what it's like to have these diseases or disorders.

## Background
This lesson plan suggests that each student make a report on one noncommunicable disease or disorder. If you make topic assignments well before this lesson, students will be able to contact appropriate health agencies or medical offices for pamphlets and fact sheets, and be ready to give their reports.

To add interest and to keep reports from being abstract and technical, students should imagine that they actually have the disease or disorder. They should prepare their presentation from the viewpoint of a person who has the disease.

An alternative lesson plan is to have students working in groups research a disease and give a report. Assign each group a disease (try to have diseases of various body systems represented). Perhaps each member of the group could find the answers to two of the Student Activity questions.

Both this and the next lesson deal with sensitive material. Encourage attitudes that are respectful. But as you help students develop empathy, also lead them to recognize that diseases and disabilities do not define people.

• • • • • • • • • • • • • • • • • • • • • • • • • • • • • • • • • • • • • • • • • • • • • • • • • • • • • • •

## Lesson (2–3 sessions)

1. Tell students that for this lesson's assignment each student will "have" a disease or disorder. Students will do research to find out about their disease, and then they'll describe for the rest of the class what it's like to have the disease.

2. Making the reports.

   - Assign students a noncommunicable disease or disorder to research and report on. Some students may be interested in reporting on a particular disease or disorder because they know someone who has it.

     Here are suggested diseases to assign:
     allergies
     ALS (amyotrophic lateral sclerosis)
     rheumatoid arthritis

asthma
beriberi
chronic bronchitis
cirrhosis
diabetes mellitus
glaucoma
emphysema
high blood pressure/hypertension
kwashiorkor
leukemia
lung cancer
lupus
multiple sclerosis
osteoporosis
Parkinson's disease
rickets
stomach or duodenal ulcers
Tay-Sachs disease

- **Student workbook activity.** Have students turn to the activity and use the questions as a guide in gathering information. Go over the questions with the class. Add any additional questions you wish students to answer.

  Encourage students to be creative in their research and presentations. Stress that reports need not be long, but they should include basic facts about the assigned diseases.

- If students have not been given the report assignment in advance of the lesson, allow time for class members to prepare their reports.

- Have each student give his or her report. Instruct other class members to listen for ways that each disease is similar and different from theirs.

3. **Closure.** Elicit from class members how "having" diseases has helped them better understand the lives of people who actually do have these diseases.

# LESSON 9: HAVING A DISABILITY

## Preparation/Materials

- For activity in Step 2:
  masking tape
  blindfolds
  very dark sunglasses
  plastic wrap
  string or clothesline rope
  cane, walker, crutches, wheelchair—if
       available
- A set of cards describing various situations,
  one per student group (see Step 5)

## Objectives

- Students will develop an understanding of
  people who have disabilities.
- Students will become aware of and learn to
  fully include those with disabilities in school
  and church life.

## Background

   *Disability* is a general term used for a
functional limitation that interferes with a
person's ability to, for example, walk, lift, hear,
or learn. It may refer to a physical, sensory, or
mental condition. A congenital disability is a
disability that has been present since birth (a
congenital disability is not necessarily
hereditary). A developmental disability is any
mental and/or physical disability that has an
onset before age 22 and may continue
indefinitely (from *Guidelines for Reporting and
Writing About People With Disabilities* [The
Research & Training Center on Independent
Living, 1990]).

## Lesson (2 sessions)

1. Recall the thoughts and feelings that were presented during the discussion of diseases.
   Tell students that this lesson is about people with disabilities. (You may wish to make
   the distinction between diseases and the disabilities that may result from diseases.
   For example, a person who had polio may have a disability as a result.)

   Have students give some examples of disabilities (deafness, blindness, low vision or
   visual impairment, Down syndrome, dwarfism, speech disorders, a person without
   speech, quadriplegia, paraplegia). What might have caused the disability?

2. Explain that class members will have the opportunity to experience, in a very limited
   way, what it is like to have a disability. Assist students as necessary to simulate having
   disabilities.

   Suggested simulations:
   - Tape the thumb of the dominant hand to the palm.
   - Blindfold some students (they should not be able to see at all).
   - Cover just the eyes of some students with plastic wrap (their vision should be
     indistinct).
   - Give very dark sunglasses to some students to wear. Instruct them not to remove
     the glasses without permission.

- Tie one arm to the chest or waist.
- Assign use of the cane, walker, crutches, or wheelchair you have procured.

3. Have students continue their routine classroom activities, or plan some special activities such as the following for students to do.

- Ask students to take out a sheet of paper and write their names on the upper right corner.
- Ask some students to deliver a note to the office.
- Take the class for a walk outside with instructions to observe small plant life.
- Play a few active games.
- Do activities that make students aware of physical obstacles that create barriers (narrow aisles, doorknobs hard to grasp or too high, drinking fountains too high, placement of light switches, inadequate lighting, and so on).

4. **Health notebook.** Give students the opportunity to write their thoughts and feelings about their experience while it is still fresh in their minds. Volunteers may wish to share their responses.

5. **Discussion.** Talk with students about how it felt to have to cope with a disability. Use questions such as the following:

"What were some difficulties or obstacles you encountered?"

"What changes in the environment would be necessary or helpful so that you could interact more freely with others and take a more active part in school/classroom activities?"

"What attitude would you like others to have toward you?" (Use this as an occasion to discuss some common attitudes/actions people often have towards those with disabilities: feeling pity, being afraid to talk and interact or to make friends, asking rude questions, treating people with one disability as though they have multiple disabilities—for example treating those who are blind as though they are also deaf.)

"In what ways do you think you would like others to help? (How would you react to someone trying to help you with something you can do yourself? What if you really need help and no one offers to help you?)"

"How can we focus on the abilities rather than the limitations of people with disabilities?"

"Do you think there is a specifically Christian attitude toward people with disabilities? If not, why not? If so, describe what the attitude is."

6. **Closure.** "During these last few sessions we have tried to understand what it is like to have certain diseases or disabilities. What are some things you think you've learned through your experiences?"

## Related Activities

1. Obtain educational materials or possibly a classroom speaker through a local organization that acts as an advocate or support group for people with disabilities.

2. Integrate with language arts, and have students develop their writings from Step 4 into essays, narratives, or poetry.

3. Ask students to design products that meet physical needs of people with specific disabilities. The Anderson Design Association, for example, has created the Helper, a cane that can retrieve objects from high or low spots using gripper jaws. Other innovative designs include a walk-in bathtub with a door, and kitchen utensils with oversized, textured handles.

4. Invite a representative of a local church to talk to the class about what efforts the church makes to be inclusive and to meet the special needs of people with health problems.

   To prepare for the session, consider introducing various situations for student groups to discuss. (For example, a church member who is injured in car accident and needs round-the-clock care. The family doesn't have the resources to provide this. What can the church do?)

5. Have students research what Christian organizations or institutions there are in the wider community to help people with special health needs.

6. Make available student resources—biographies, autobiographies, and novels—about people with impairments (*see* Lesson Resources for suggested titles). Do the books stress the main character's abilities or limitations?

7. Show a film or online video about the life of a person who has disabilities.

8. Integrate with Bible studies. Have students locate and read Bible stories that deal with diseases or disabilities. What connections do they make between the stories and their experience? Or read about the beginning of the Church in the opening chapters of Acts. In what ways did the early Christians help each other?

# LESSON 10: GETTING HELP— COMMUNITY RESOURCES

## Preparation/Materials
- Student workbook activity
- Make a list of health agencies in the area for students to investigate. Consider including agencies such as the following:
  Red Cross
  American Heart Association
  Cancer Society
  Diabetes Association
  Lung Association
  Professional medical or dental associations
  State and community health agencies
  Health care clinics and hospitals
- Unit evaluation in student workbook

- Optional: Create other role plays/cards about diseases related to the heart and circulatory system.

## Objectives
- Students will identify reliable sources of information and care for health needs.
- Students will learn how to find available resources for people with health needs.

## Background
Federal, provincial or state, and local government agencies provide a wide variety of health services to the public. In addition, there are national professional and voluntary agencies that are concerned with specific health problems or services. The first two lesson steps were adapted from Michigan Model, Grade 6: Phase IV.

## Lesson

1. Have a brief discussion about the need for help with health problems. To make the discussion more concrete, use problems of the circulatory system as an example.

   - "What are some ways people can get information about problems of the heart and circulatory system?" (From family and friends, family doctor, reading articles and books and watching TV programs, from health agencies.)
   - "How could you get help in an emergency—if a member of the family has chest pains, for example?" (Use the local emergency number to call for help; call doctor.)

2. **Student workbook activity.** Have students do role plays about getting reliable help and care for high blood pressure.

   Students may cut out the role play cards. Assign the role play directions to four volunteers and explain what each is to do. Tell students to act as they think the person would act in a real-life situation. Allow them a short time to prepare and then have them do the role plays. You or another student can play the other character in each role play.

   Conduct a short critique after the play. Ask if any important points were left out. Ask what might be different had the disease been a heart attack or stroke. You may wish to have students do other role plays if time allows.

3. Have the class find out about various health agencies and the services they offer. Students can interview a representative of the agency in person or by telephone.

   - Provide a list with names of agencies/organizations and their telephone numbers.
   - Have pairs of students work together to find out about one organization, or divide up the list among student groups.
   - Work together with the class to generate a list of appropriate questions to use in the interview.

     Some sample questions:
     "What kind or organization are you—a government agency? A volunteer agency?
     "What kind of people do you help? What are the services you offer?"
     "Where do you get money to operate?"
     "How does a person go about getting help from you?"
     "Are there other organizations that you are connected with?"
     "How many people get help from your agency each year?"
     "How many people work for your agency?"

     Also discuss appropriate interview conduct. Perhaps ask a few students to role play initiating and ending a conversation.

   - Give students opportunity to share the results of their interviews. Students can do this orally or write up summaries of their conversations. Another option is to have students compile a class booklet or brochure telling about the area's health services.

4. **Unit evaluation.** Use the worksheet to review and evaluate the unit. You may also wish to refer to the portion of the student book dealing with the body systems and the heart for further review or evaluation.

   *Short answers:*
   1. *supports the body and carries its weight; protects body organs—heart and brain; stores minerals; makes red blood cells in marrow*
   2. *makes the body able to move and stand upright; needed to help other body systems work*
   3. *skeletal muscles, smooth muscles, and cardiac muscles*
   4. *changes food into nutrients that the cells need*
   5. *mouth, small intestine, large intestine, stomach, esophagus*
   6. *takes in oxygen and gets rid of carbon dioxide*
   7. *nose, trachea, lungs, bronchial tubes, alveoli, bronchioles*
   8. *transports oxygen and nutrients to cells; helps control body temperature; transports waste materials to exit points*
   9. *heart, arteries, veins, capillaries*
   10. *cleans blood; removes liquid wastes from body*
   11. *kidneys, ureters, bladder, urethra*
   12. *controls body's activities; carries messages to and from the brain*

13. *brain, spinal cord, nerves*
14. *produces hormones that control different body functions*
15. *glands, for example: thyroid, parathyroid, ovaries, testes*

*Fill in the blanks:*
*1. wall of muscle; 2. noncommunicable; 3. heart rate; 4. tissues; 5. valves; 6. antibody;*
*7. Plaque; 8. Blood pressure; 9. plasma, platelets, red blood cells, white blood cells;*
*10. antibodies; 11. cardiovascular; 12. disease germs*

*Short answers:*
1. *They snap shut to keep the blood flowing in the same direction.*
2. *Because the blood is low in oxygen.*
3. *Answers will vary.*
4. *To help make blood clot in case of a wound.*
5. *The immune system*
6. *Heredity and environment.*
7. *A heart attack typically occurs when the supply of blood to the heart is cut off due to a blocked artery/atherosclerosis.*
8. *Plaque builds up in the arteries near the heart, making these blood vessels narrower. The buildup inhibits the flow of blood, and the heart has to constantly exert more pressure than normal to push blood through the blood vessels.*
9. *Possible answers include avoiding smoking, being physically fit, limiting amount of fat- and cholesterol-rich foods in diet, controlling stress.*

*Short essay:*
*Answers will vary. Many noncommunicable diseases are caused by a combination of hereditary and environmental factors. Hereditary factors cannot be controlled. Although some environmental factors can be controlled, others, such as pollution of the environment, are not easily controlled.*

## Related Activities

1. Consider how recreational facilities contribute to community health. Have students prepare a list of community recreational facilities and the services or opportunities they provide.

2. Have class members write editorials about the need for a specific community health organization.

3. Invite a representative from your local health department to speak to your class about its programs and responsibilities.

4. Raise awareness of global issues. Research the work of the World Health Organization (WHO), which was founded by the United Nations in 1948. What programs does it offer? What are the main issues or problems it faces?

5. Ask class members to create posters for the classroom about the health organizations they researched. Each poster could focus on one or two main services the organization offers.

# Unit 5

## Family Life

Lesson 1:   The Stages of Life

Lesson 2:   Adolescence—A Time in Between*

Lesson 3:   An Intercourse on Intercourse (Optional)*

Lesson 4:   Where Do Babies Come From? (2 Sessions)*

Lesson 5:   Risky Business*

Lesson 6:   Growing Up and Reaching Out (2 Sessions)

Lesson 7:   Where Do You Come From?

Lesson 8:   The Christian Family—Within and Without

Lesson 9:   For They Shall Be Comforted (1–2 Sessions)

*NOTE:  The material in these lessons should be presented to boys and girls in separate classes, *only after* notifying parents of the topic and content in advance and receiving written permission. Visuals and selected student activity sheets for these lessons have been placed at the back of this Teacher's Guide as reproducible masters.

## Goals

- Students will review and expand on their understanding of the family life themes of *Horizons Health*.
- Students will develop an appreciation for their own sexuality.
- Students will learn healthy, Christian expressions of their sexuality.
- Students will marvel at the gifts of life, family, and friends.
- Students will develop a greater appreciation of God as a Father who cares deeply for his family.

## Background

This unit takes a comprehensive look at family life. Building on previous lessons in *Horizons Health*, this unit offers the sixth grade student a Christian preparation for adult family life. Topics covered here include the biblical basis for marriage and family; the joy of sexual intercourse within marriage; the miraculous events of conception, fetal development, and birth; the principles of love practiced by a Christian family at home and in the community; the role of friends; and the hope of Christians in the face of death. The unit provides perspectives that will help you act as a joyful witness to God's infinite wisdom and boundless love.

You may feel some discomfort or reluctance to deal with the sensitive topics of this unit, but it is crucial to discuss these matters within the context of our responsibility as Christians and to affirm that sex and sexuality are good gifts from God. Too often Christians convey the impression—and students are quick to pick this up—that basic bodily functions and the pleasure of sex and sexuality are bad or distasteful.

During this unit be aware that some students may have had sexual experience. In fact, some may be experiencing sexual abuse. (Don't discount this possibility. Reliable sources show that the incidence of sexual abuse in Christian homes is similar to that of the population in general.) Guard against judgmental statements that may increase their pain or feelings of guilt. Approach the biblical norms as God's way of protecting human relationships and of making the sexual relationship something special and beautiful. God's commands are meant to keep us from being hurt and from hurting others.

Unit 8, the safety unit, contains a lesson on the topic of preventing sexual abuse. You may wish to integrate that lesson into this unit.

Of course, informing parents about the content of this unit is particularly important. Some schools hold meetings at the beginning of the school year to review the content and goals of health education with parents; in addition, however, it is wise to send parents a letter to inform them of the specific topics to be covered in the unit. This gives parents the opportunity to reinforce the health concepts learned at school.

## Vocabulary

Plan to integrate the following vocabulary:

| | | | | |
|---|---|---|---|---|
| adolescence | intercourse | embryo | uterus | nocturnal emissions |
| sperm | ovum/ova | cesarean | cervix | reproductive organs |
| depression | puberty | fertilization | semen | faithfulness |
| placenta | intimacy | ARC | labor | nuclear family |
| grief | acceptance | menstruation | fetus | implantation |
| pregnancy | umbilical cord | amniotic fluid | hospice | extended family |
| denial | conception | bargaining | support groups | |

Acquired Immune Deficiency Syndrome (AIDS)

Sexually transmitted disease (STD)    Human Immunodeficiency Virus (HIV)

## Unit Resources (Search online for similar resources if these are no longer available.)

Byars, Betsy. *The Animal, the Vegetable, and John D. Jones*. New York: Delacorte, 1982.

Chase, Emily Parke. Help! *My Family's Messed Up*. Kregel Publications, 2008.
A Christian view of family struggles, adoption, addiction, and other topics.

Cooney, Caroline B. *Family Reunion*. New York: Bantam, 1989.
Shelly is nervous when her blended New York family plans a visit to her cousins in Iowa. She's always thought of them as The Perfects, and she doesn't know whether to be relieved or disappointed to find that her aunt's family isn't so perfect after all.

Dobson, James. *Preparing for Adolescence*. Ventura, Calif.: Regal, 1989.
A student activity workbook.

Moss, Jeff. *The Butterfly Jar*. New York: Bantam Books, 1989.

_____ . *The Other Side of the Door*. New York: Bantam Books, 1991.
Both of these collections include lively poems about family life. Suggested poems: "Moving," "Sara Messenger's Mother," "The Picture," "The Tree," "Weddings," and "My Mom Sings."

Nilsson, Lennart (photographs), Mirjam Furuhjelm, Exel Ingleman-Sundberg, and Claes Wirsen. *A Child Is Born*. New York: Delacorte Press, 1976.
Intrauterine photographs show progress of human development from conception to birth. Discusses states of pregnancy from parents' point of view.
There are revised versions of the book as well as similar texts.

Taylor, Sydney. *All-of-a-Kind Family*. Reprint. New York: Dell, 1980.
Intended for grades 3–6. A study guide by Beatrice Davis (Novel-Ties Series) is also available from Learning Links, 2300 Marcus Ave., New Hyde Park, New York 11042; phone 800-724-2616.

## Lesson Resources (Search online for similar resources if these are no longer available.)

**Lesson 1**

Fleischman, Paul. *The Borning Room*. New York: HarperCollins, 1991.
> A story of four generations of Ohioans whose most important events—births and deaths—take place in their home's "borning room."

**Lesson 2**

Cole, Joanna. *Asking About Sex*. New York: Beech Tree, 1988.
> Uses a question-and-answer format to present information about sexuality to pre-teens.

Dunham, Kelli. *The Girls Body Book: Fifth Edition*. Applesauce Press, 2019.
> Book for grades 4-7.

*Learning About Sex: A Series for the Christian Family*. Rev. edition. St. Louis, Mo.: Concordia, 1988.
> The entire series is available through christianbook.com.
> Written from a distinctively Christian perspective, this sex education series has a variety of individual books.

Todnem, Scott. *Growing Up Great!: The Ultimate Puberty Book for Boys*. Rockridge Press, 2019.

Madaras, Lynda. *What's Happening to My Body?—Girls*. New York: Newmarket Press, 1986.
> This volume addresses female students and looks at both the female and male body during puberty.

**Lessons 3–4**

Christensen, Larry. *The Wonderful Way That Babies Are Made*. Minneapolis: Bethany House, 1982.
> Addresses the topic of reproduction with illustrations and explanations.
> Large print material is for ages 3–8; paragraphs in smaller print provide additional material for children ages 9–14.

**Lessons 7–8**

Berry, Joy. *Every Kid's Guide to Handling Fights With Brothers or Sisters*. Chicago: Childrens Press, 1987.
> Ten reasons why siblings fight, why fighting is harmful, and four steps for avoiding fights with your brothers or sisters.

Gardner, John Reynolds. *Stone Fox*. New York: HarperTrophy, 1992.
> Wyoming is the setting for this story of a sled-dog race and the relationship between a boy and his grandfather. For ages 7–11.

Hamilton, Virginia. *Cousins*. New York: Putnam, 1990.
> A novel about five very different cousins that teaches about betrayal and the power of family.

Hermes, Patricia. *You Shouldn't Have to Say Goodbye*. Richmond Hill, Ontario: Scholastic, 1984.
> A 13-year-old girl has to learn to accept that her mother is dying of cancer.

L'Engle, Madeleine. *Meet the Austins*. New York: Dell, 1981.

MacLachlan, Patricia. *The Facts and Fictions of Minna Pratt*. New York: HarperCollins, 1988.
> Eleven-year-old Minna wishes that her family was more like that of her friend Lucas, and Lucas wishes that his family was more like Minna's.

Namioka, Lensey. *Yang the Youngest and His Terrible Ear*. Toronto and Boston: Little, Brown, 1992.
A story about the unique experiences of a young Asian immigrant who is trying to establish his own identity within his family. For ages 8–12.

O'Dell, Scott. *Black Star, Bright Dawn*. Boston: Houghton Mifflin, 1988.
A story about respect and courage. When her father is injured, Bright Dawn takes his place in the Iditarod with the lead dog, Black Star.

Paterson, Katherine. *Jacob Have I Loved*. New York: Crowell, 1980.
The story focuses on sibling jealousy and its insidious effect.

_____ . *Park's Quest*. New York: Dutton, 1988.
A story of Park's search to find out about his father, who was killed in Vietnam. He learns about family relationships and about his inner self.

Peck, Robert Newton. *A Day No Pigs Would Die*. New York: Knopf, 1973.

Taylor, Theodore. *Tuck Triumphant*. New York: Doubleday, 1991.
In this sequel to *The Trouble with Tuck*, Helen has a new adopted brother, Chok-Do, who is deaf and without speech.

Jackson, Kate. "Free Family Tree Lesson Plans for Kids and Teens." Family History Daily. https://familyhistorydaily.com/.

**Lesson 9**

Bauer, Marion Dane. *On My Honor*. Boston: Clarion, 1986.
Joel and Tony go swimming in a forbidden, treacherous river. Tony drowns and Joel confronts his guilt.

Craven, Margaret. *I Heard the Owl Call My Name*. New York: Doubleday, 1973.
A young adult novel about a priest who must learn how to live in order to learn how to die.

Kübler-Ross, Elisabeth. *Death: The Final Stage of Growth*. Englewood Cliffs, NJ: Prentice-Hall, 1975.

Lewis, C.S. *The Last Battle*. New York: Macmillan, 1956.

Paterson, Katherine. *Bridge to Terabithia*. New York: HarperCollins, 1977.

# LESSON 1: THE STAGES OF LIFE

## Preparation/Materials
- Student books
- Student workbook activity
- Prepare a question box for student use during the unit.

## Objectives
- Students will develop an understanding of the different stages of life.
- Students will deepen their understanding of the difference that Christian faith makes to every stage of life.

## Background

Consider having a question box in the classroom for unsigned student questions. Handling questions in this way gives students the opportunity to ask questions that they do not feel free to ask in a whole-class session. It also gives you time to screen questions and to prepare answers to difficult or sensitive questions. You may want to refer some particularly sensitive or difficult questions to parents, a physician, or another knowledgeable person.

It is a good idea to set some basic guidelines before students submit questions. Consider telling students in advance that you will make the final decision about what questions are appropriate for class discussion. Make clear that even if you choose not to discuss a question in whole-class session, it doesn't mean that the question is bad. Perhaps you do not consider the question to be of general interest, or perhaps you are not be prepared to lead a class discussion on that specific topic.

Although students may use slang terms rather than correct terminology in their questions, be sure to provide students with correct terminology in your answers. De Spelder and Strickland (*Family Life Education, Grades 4, 5, 6*) suggest telling the class, "'In this class I will be trying to balance two conflicting goals: I want to teach the proper vocabulary for body parts and functions, and I want to communicate so that you can understand. Sometimes you may not know the correct (acceptable) word for something you have a question about. Use whatever word you know to ask the question, and I will answer using the correct word.'"

According to De Spelder and Strickland, student questions generally fall into three broad categories: (1) requests for information; (2) "Am I normal?" and (3) permission-seeking questions. It may help you to keep these categories in mind as you sort questions and prepare answers.

## Lesson

1. Open the unit with a whole-class clustering activity on the idea of *family*. (See Unit 2, Lesson 4 for an example of clustering.) Some possible associations/clusters include the following: family relationships, family responsibilities, gender roles, family activities, family traditions. Introduce one cluster on stages in family life, and have students brainstorm word associations. Use the activity as a lead-in to the student book reading on stages in family life.

2. **Student book.** Have students turn to the heading "Family Life," and read and discuss "The Story of a Lifetime." Study the diagram showing the stages of a lifetime, and answer the "Think It Over" questions.

1. *Answers will vary. In discussion lead students to identify some characteristics of each stage that are unique and satisfying.*
2. *Answers will vary. Lead a discussion on the difference that living in hope makes in every stage.*
3. *Resurrection. Christ's resurrection body gives a preview of what our resurrection bodies will be. You may wish to read John 20:10–27 which describes three of Jesus' post-resurrection appearances.*

3. **Student workbook activity.** Have students answer the questions on the worksheets. Discuss responses in pairs, groups, or as a class. Is there a certain age that many students have negative feelings about? What colors their perceptions of certain stages of life? Are the popular media an important influence? What about role models?

   If time permits, have students turn over their activity sheets and write about what they like the least about being a child and what they think they will like the least about each of the other stages. Again, address responses and identify some reasons for them.

4. Introduce the question box. Tell students that they can put their unsigned questions about family life into the box at any time during the unit, and you will answer them. In addition, explain that there will be opportunities in some lessons for the whole class to submit questions.

5. **Closure.** Make the point that God has a purpose for the life of each person. All the different threads of a person's life—family members, friends, experiences—are woven into the fabric of God's purpose. Stress that God is with us through every stage, guiding us and turning evil into good.

• • • • • • • • • • • • • • • • • • • • • • • • • • • • • • • • • • • • • • • • • • • • • •

## Related Activities

1. Integrate with language arts. Assign students to write narratives based on their responses to the Student Activity questions (for example, based on a memorable childhood experience). Some students may wish to write poems expressing feelings about the stages of life.

2. Ask class members to interview people of different ages to discover what their opinions are about the various stages of life. Compare the results of the interviews. Is there consensus, or do opinions of individuals in the same stage vary widely?

3. Explore stereotypes in the media about people in the various stages of life. Do these stereotypes have some basis in fact? How do the stereotypes influence how we treat people? Recall the influences identified in Unit 3 Lesson 3 on prejudice and discrimination.

4. Have class members read and discuss biographies and autobiographies.

5. Integrate with art. Explore how various artists have pictured family life or different stages of life.

# LESSON 2: ADOLESCENCE—A TIME IN BETWEEN

## Preparation/Materials
- Student books
- Student workbook activity (*Note:* an additional optional student activity is included in Teacher Resources)
- Teacher Visual. Enlarge the visual or make a transparency of it.
- Optional: overhead projector

## Objectives
- Students will learn about the physical changes that take place during puberty.
- Students will appreciate their body as the unique and good creation of God.
- Students will develop a positive attitude of anticipation toward the changes of puberty.

## Background
An open, comfortable classroom is particularly essential for this unit on human sexuality and the changes of puberty. These topics are inherently interesting to upper elementary students, but students are often embarrassed by discussions of the topics. In some families these topics may be considered so private that parents avoid discussing them. Students will betray their feelings of embarrassment by nervous giggles and quick glances at friends. It's helpful to openly recognize these feelings at the outset, telling the class that some embarrassment is normal. As the unit progresses, class members will probably feel more comfortable.

Alternatively, teachers may wish to present this material in segregated classes so that discussion will be more open and relaxed.

Whichever instructional method is used, parents should be notified in advance of the content of the lesson.

• • • • • • • • • • • • • • • • • • • • • • • • • • • • • • • • • • • • • • • • • • • • • • • • •

## Lesson
1. Begin with a general discussion of adolescence as a time filled with "in-betweens." Students in grade 6 are either coming to the end of their elementary years or just starting middle school. They are becoming more independent from their parents, but they still need their parents to fill many of their physical and emotional needs. They may be starting to take on jobs outside of the home (babysitting, paper routes, lawn care), but they are far from being able to support themselves. At times they may take responsibility for themselves and act in grown-up ways, but at other times they may want others to take responsibility for them.

   Point out that everyone goes through this in-between time in a different way because each person is unique. Recall the lesson from Unit 1 in which students each had similar objects that they could tell apart by special markings. In the same way, God knows each of us and loves us as we are.

2. Shift the discussion to the topic of the physical changes of puberty. Note that these developments take place at different times and at different rates in each individual. On the average, girls develop earlier than boys. Make the point that even before there are any outside signs of development, changes are going on inside—hormones are being released and preparing the body for change.

- Begin by reviewing basic changes that are common to both boys and girls during puberty. List the changes on the board, overhead, or a handout.

*Changes experienced by females and males:*
— A rapid (and often sudden) increase in height takes place.
— The voice changes. (This is usually more dramatic in boys than in girls. As the rest of the body grows, so does the voice box. Males' voices are deeper than females' because the male voice box is larger. Change in voice is usually gradual, but it may occur suddenly.)
— Perspiration increases. (Note the need for daily washing and deodorants or antiperspirants.)
— Skin secretes more oil as sweat glands become more active. Acne may become a problem.
— Hormone production increases. (Boys and girls may have more frequent changes in mood. Hormones may also trigger an increased interest in the opposite sex.)
— Faces alter. (Faces change quite a bit—boys' more than girls'. The nose and jaw especially change.)
— Feelings of independence may increase.

- Review the following steps of change in females and males. Use the charts of the Teacher Visual to show the broad, normal age ranges at which the different physical changes of puberty can occur in boys and girls.

*Changes in girls:*
— Hips widen. (Pelvis is wider than in boys to allow room for a baby to be born.)
— Growth spurt takes place. (Girls usually first experience growth spurt in head, hands, and feet.)
— Breasts begin to develop. (This may be a gradual growth over 3-4 years. One breast may grow faster than another. Both large and small breasts will produce milk when a woman has babies, so size does not affect function.)
— Pubic hair appears.
— Menstruation begins.
— Other body hair (underarm, legs, forearm) appears.
— Pubic hair coarsens.
— Breasts are fully developed.

*Changes in boys:*
— Testes grow. (The testes, or testicles, are two small organs in the scrotum. Eventually sperm cells are made in the testes.
— Pubic hair appears.
— Growth spurt takes place. (Boys usually first experience growth spurt in arms, legs, and muscles.)
— Pubic hair coarsens.

— Penis develops. Scrotum and testes continue to grow. (Development of testes and scrotum are usually the first sign of puberty. Penis growth coincides with growth in height about a year later. Both large and small penises will eventually release semen, so size does not affect function.)
— Shoulders and chest become broader.
— Voice changes, becoming deeper. Also body and facial hair appear.
— Sperm production begins.
— Other body hair (chest, legs, forearms) appears.

3. **Student book.** Read and discuss "Adolescence: An In-Between Time." Discuss the "Think It Over" questions.

    1. *Students may include moodiness, worrying, experiencing stronger emotions.*
    2. *Lead students to understand that physical changes themselves may lead to worry or upset feelings. In addition, hormonal changes also affect feelings.*
    3. *In discussion help students to understand the superficiality of standards of beauty held up in the media.*

4. **Optional student activity.** Reproduce and distribute the "Changes of Puberty" worksheet found in Teacher Resources. You may wish to use the activity as a quiz or as a review to be completed in groups. Consider having students rewrite the false statements to make them true. *Note:* You should tell parents about these activity sheets when you inform them of the unit content.

5. **Student workbook activity.** This activity sheet is intended to help students initiate a conversation with parents about puberty. Encourage students to find a good time to have the talk. *Note:* You should tell parents about these activity sheets when you inform them of the unit content.

6. **Question box.** Tell students that the next lesson will be on the reproductive systems and on sexual intercourse. Note that you would like to make the session relevant to their concerns and help them to fill in gaps in their knowledge. Ask class members to each submit at least one question (unsigned) for you to answer in the next session. (If students don't have questions, they can submit a blank piece of paper.) Use student questions to prepare for the next class session. *Note:* It is advisable to have written permission from parents before presenting the material in the next lesson. Prepare permission slips to send home with students.

• • • • • • • • • • • • • • • • • • • • • • • • • • • • • • • • • • • • • • • • • • • • • • • • • •

## Related Activity

• Health notebooks: Ask students to bring in two pictures of themselves, one recent photo and one several years old. Students should mount the pictures on a sheet of paper and identify the age when each was taken. Then they should write a description of the physical changes that have taken place in the time between the two photos.

# LESSON 3: AN INTERCOURSE ON INTERCOURSE

*NOTE:* This is an optional lesson and the material should be presented to boys and girls in separate classes, ***only after*** notifying parents of the topic and content in advance and receiving written permission.

## Preparation/Materials
*   Transparencies of both Student Activities 1 and 2 (in Teacher Resources)
*   Overhead projector

## Objectives
*   Students will review the human reproductive system (covered in grade 5).
*   Students will learn that sexual intercourse is a way for married couples to physically communicate their love for each other and to have children.
*   Students will understand the biblical norm for sexual intercourse.
*   Students will learn that sexual intercourse may result in pregnancy or sexually transmitted diseases.

## Background
At birth females have about 400,000 immature egg cells or ova in their ovaries. During puberty the ovaries produce and release hormones that begin the menstrual cycle. Each month an ovum begins to mature in the ovary. At the same time the uterus begins to build its lining (endometrium) to prepare to nourish a fertilized egg. The mature ovum, which is released from the ovary, travels through the fallopian tube to the uterus. If the egg is not fertilized, it moves through the uterus and vagina and on out of the body. The uterus then sloughs off the unneeded lining, which also gradually passes through the vagina and on out of the body.

The male testes are the counterpart of the female ovaries. They produce both sperm and the male hormone testosterone. The testes are continuously forming sperm in their tiny, thread-like, coiled tubules. From puberty to old age the testes produce sperm—500 million or more each day. Although the temperature of the human body is around 98.6° (37° C), sperm develop best at a temperature three to four degrees lower than that. That's why the testes are located outside the body in the scrotum. The scrotum is equipped with special muscles to draw the testes closer to the body or to lower them away and in this way control their temperature.

Sperm, which can only be observed through a microscope, are so tiny that over 100 million sperm can swim in one small drop of fluid. In the head of each sperm is a set of 23 chromosomes containing genes that can pass on characteristics to a child. Sperm gradually move from the tiny tubules in each testis to a larger tube called the epididymis, lying over the back of the testis (uncoiled the epididymis would be about 20 ft./6 m. long). Here the sperm cells grow and mature. During this time, weaker sperm die and are absorbed into the tube lining.

The remaining sperm move into the sperm duct (vas deferens), which leads up into the body to a seminal vesicle, a gland which produces a chemical that gives the sperm energy and activates the sperm's tail. Next, the prostate gland releases fluids that mix with the sperm, forming a mixture called semen.

In addition, two small glands (Cowper's glands) release a clear, sticky liquid that lines the urethra, the tube through which the sperm leave the body. This clear liquid is an alkaline substance that appears to protect the sperm by neutralizing acidity in the urethra.

During intercourse, hundreds of millions of sperm cells are deposited in the vagina, close to the cervix. From there they swim up through the uterus and into the uterine or fallopian tubes.

About 100 sperm make it as far as these tubes. If an ovum is in one of the tubes, the sperm cluster around it. Conception/fertilization occurs when one sperm joins with the ovum to make one cell. (Adapted from *Learning About Sex: A Contemporary Guide for Young Adults*, by Gary F. Kelly [Barron's, 1986].)

## Lesson

1.  Recall that in the previous lesson students talked about how puberty changes the body. The primary change is that sex organs grow and develop and start making sex cells that make it possible to have babies. Explain these terms: *reproduction, reproductive organs, reproductive system.*

    Briefly review the male and female reproductive systems. Using the overhead, label the parts of the reproductive system. If desired, reproduce and distribute Student Activities 1 and 2 from the masters in the back of this Teacher's Guide and have students fill in those worksheets at the same time. Briefly state the function of each part named (elicit the information from students as much as possible).

    Consider also reviewing the menstrual cycle of the female (covered in grade 5):
    *   Egg leaves the ovary (occasionally two or more eggs are released at the same time)
    *   Fallopian tube catches the egg and pulls it into the tube.
    *   Egg moves along the fallopian tube for four to six days.
    *   Egg comes nearer to the uterus. The lining of the uterus (endometrium) begins to build up/thicken. Fertilization (which occurs when male sperm joins the female egg) may take place. (Fertilization/conception is discussed in the next lesson.)
    *   Egg enters the uterus. Uterine lining thickens.
    *   The egg is not fertilized, and the lining gradually leaves the body through the vagina.

2.  Explain and discuss sexual intercourse. Answer questions students have submitted, and/or use the questions and answers provided here. If students have been reluctant to ask questions, you may wish to elicit more questions or prepare additional questions and answers yourself. An excellent resource is *Sexuality and the Young Christian* by Joanne DeJonge, which deals with topics such as birth control, masturbation, homosexuality, and circumcision.

    *   "What is sexual intercourse?"
        *Intercourse* is a word that means communication. It can be used to describe dealings or communications between persons or groups. The word *intercourse* also describes a physical act between two people.

In *sexual* intercourse a husband and wife put their bodies very close together. They may begin by kissing, stroking each other, and touching each other (foreplay). The man's penis becomes firm and erect. The woman's vagina becomes sensitive and moist. When both partners are ready, the man will move his penis inside the woman's vagina until semen is released. The climax of sexual excitement for both men and women is called orgasm.

- "What is the purpose of intercourse?"

  God created humans as sexual beings, and sexual intercourse is a good gift of God. One purpose of sexual intercourse is to have children (procreation). Another purpose is to communicate love. In sexual intercourse husband and wife communicate, or share their deep feelings for each other. That's why another term for sexual intercourse is *making love.* The Bible says that in sexual intercourse husband and wife become one.

- "How can sexual intercourse begin a baby?"

  When a man and a woman make love, the man's sperm may join with (fertilize) one of the woman's eggs. The woman's body releases an egg about once a month. If an egg is present and comes in contact with a sperm, a baby will begin to grow. When a woman has a baby growing in her uterus, she is pregnant.

- "Why is sexual intercourse outside of marriage wrong?"

  When a man and woman have sexual intercourse, they give themselves to each other in a very special way. When intercourse is misused, people can hurt each other very badly. So God has given guidelines in the Bible about how to conduct our sexual lives.

  First of all, God tells us that sex is for married couples. It is a sin to give ourselves to each other sexually if we are not married.

  At marriage a man and woman promise to be faithful to each other for life. Having sex outside of marriage breaks the marriage relationship. The break deeply hurts both marriage partners.

  Another important reason sexual intercourse belongs in marriage is that if the woman becomes pregnant, marriage is a secure environment in which to care for and raise a child.

  Sex outside of marriage can also expose the partners to many kinds of diseases (covered in next lesson).

- "Why do you think people joke about sexual intercourse or talk about it with disrespect?"

  Sometimes people joke about sex because they are uncomfortable talking about it. Joking is a way to relieve embarrassment. Talking about sex in disrespectful ways may result from not recognizing that sex is a gift from God. (Elicit students' ideas. Consider how we can react when others talk about sex in demeaning ways. Include the topic of pornography in this discussion.)

3. Focus on the qualities of a good marriage. Make the point that while sexual attraction is important to a good marriage, a good marriage needs many other important things. Ask: "What do you think makes a good marriage?" Some ideas to include are love, loyalty, trust, honesty, kindness, mutual respect, courtesy, faith in God. Develop a list of ideas.

4. Have students list on a piece of paper some topics they would like to discuss further with a parent. Encourage them to initiate a talk with a parent, using the list as a starting point.

● ● ● ● ● ● ● ● ● ● ● ● ● ● ● ● ● ● ● ● ● ● ● ● ● ● ● ● ● ● ● ● ● ● ● ● ● ● ● ● ● ● ● ● ● ● ● ● ● ● ● ● ● ● ● ●

## Related Activities

1. Set up a class parenting project. While many students may enjoy babysitting or child care at this age, few recognize the implications of the full-time responsibilities of parenthood. Assigning partners or individuals the task of "parenting" an egg or sack of flour for a few days or a week can simulate the experience.

   Set up a list of responsibilities for whatever inanimate object you choose to assign as the "baby." Nurseries and childcare for pay (a penny an hour) may be established. You may want to indicate some definite "dont's" that would result in harm to the "baby."

   Have the students keep a journal of what they did to provide for their "baby" during the week. Cap the activity with a discussion of the challenges of parenting.

2. Assign students to research various topics related to marriage. Topics could include the following:
   - marriage vows (new, old, the ones their parents used)
   - differences in the marriages of different generations (my grandparents' marriage, my parents' marriage, and the marriage I might have someday)
   - finding good resources for help when a marriage has problems
   - the importance of community support.

3. Integrate with social studies. What is the nature of the marriage relationship in other countries/cultures? Are marriages arranged, or do young people choose their partner?

4. Integrate with Bible study. Examine and discuss Bible passages dealing with marriage (Genesis 2:21–25; Matthew 22:30, Mark 10:7–10, 1 Corinthians 7:23, 39–40).

# LESSON 4: WHERE DO BABIES COME FROM?

## Preparation/Materials

- Teacher Visual
- Student resources on fetal development
- Drawing and writing supplies
- For simulating amniotic sac:
    a marble
    a sturdy, large balloon
- Fill the balloon with water until it is about 2" in diameter. Place the marble in the balloon. Tie the balloon's neck.
- Student books

## Objectives

- Students will review the process of egg fertilization and implantation in the uterine wall.
- Students will recognize the functions of the placenta, the umbilical cord, and the amniotic fluid.
- Students will develop understanding of the process of both fetal growth and development and of birth.
- Students will develop a sense of reverence and wonder for the gift of life and the miracle of birth.
- Optional: Obtain a copy of *A Child is Born* by Lennart Nilsson (Dell, 1989).

## Background

The embryonic development in the womb progresses as follows.

### First month

The embryo begins to develop a heart, liver, and digestive system. It is being nourished and is getting rid of wastes through the placenta and the umbilical cord (the vascular structures that connect the growing infant to the wall of the uterus). By the end of one month the embryo's heart starts beating. The entire embryo is approximately ⅛ inch (½ cm) in length.

### Second month

By the end of eight weeks, the arms and legs of the fetus have begun to form. All the major internal organs have developed. Facial features—eyes, ears, nose, and mouth—become more defined. Brain development is well under way. The fetus reacts to in utero stimulus, demonstrating that it has developed its sense of feeling. By this time the fetus has grown to nearly two inches (5 cm) in length.

### Third month

By the third month, the fetus is growing rapidly, adding a few millimeters of length each day. Facial features are becoming distinct. Fingers, toes, ears, and eyelids are formed. The first hair appears. Skeletal development begins. Eyelids have formed over the eye. (Eyelids will remain closed until the seventh month.) By now the fetus weighs about one ounce (28 g) and is three inches (8 cm) long.

### Fourth month

All of the organs are formed, and now the baby must simply grow in size. By the fourth month, it becomes more active and may begin to push its arms or legs against the sac in which it floats. Fingernails are developing. Prenatal photography shows some fetuses at this stage sucking their thumb. At this stage a baby may be more than six inches (15 cm) long and weigh more than ¼ pound (114 g).

### Fifth month

The heartbeat of the fetus is now audible with a doctor's stethoscope. Movements are stronger and more easily felt. The baby has grown to about 10 inches (25 cm) in length and weighs approximately ½ pound (227 g).

## Sixth month

The mother's abdomen continues to enlarge, and the baby's movements become more vigorous. The baby's skin appears red and wrinkled. Weight is about 1½ pounds (680 g), and length is about 12 inches (30 cm).

## Seventh month

The baby's eyes may occasionally be open for short periods of time. If born at this time, the infant would be considered a premature baby and require special care. Weight is approximately 2½ pounds (1.13 kg), and length is about 15 inches (38 cm).

## Eighth month

The baby is now almost fully grown. Movements or "kicks" are strong enough to be visible from the outside. The skin is no longer quite as wrinkled. The baby usually moves to the head-down position, the birth position. Weight is around 4 pounds (1.81 kg), and length is approximately 16½ inches (42 cm).

## Ninth month

The baby has now reached the size and maturity to be able to live outside the mother's body. Its head is covered with hair. The baby also settles down lower into the abdomen. By now it weighs around 6–7 pounds (2.7 to 3.2 kg), and is 20 inches (50 cm) or more in length.

Observing the miraculous development of a baby inspires awe and wonder. In this lesson lead your students to praise God's wisdom and love.

• • • • • • • • • • • • • • • • • • • • • • • • • • • • • • • • • • • • • • • • • • • • • • • •

## Lesson (2 sessions)

1. **Student book.** Study the pictures of fertilization and development of a baby. Read and discuss the accompanying text and answer the "Think It Over" questions.

   1. *The blood of the mother carries nutrients and oxygen to the baby. The blood moves into the placenta, and from there nutrients and oxygen pass through the thin walls of blood vessels in the placenta into blood vessels in the umbilical cord and on to nourish the baby. Note that the blood of mother and baby do not mix.*
   2. *The beginning of new life is so amazing that it truly is a miracle. Focus on the mystery of life and on our dependence on God who is the Giver of Life.*

   If you have obtained a copy of *A Child Is Born*, show the marvelous photographs of the process of fetal growth and development to augment the text (or make it available for students to peruse during free time).

   Consider incorporating the following material at appropriate points in the discussion.

   Recall that one ovum is produced by the female per month. In the 48 hours after it is released from the ovary, it is "ripe" for fertilization. Sperm may remain viable after being released into the female for about the same amount of time.

   The sperm propel themselves with whip-like motions of their tail. They travel through the cervix, the uterus, and the fallopian tubes. While many sperm may be released, only one will penetrate and fertilize the egg. The sperm's genetic code will determine the gender of the child.

The fertilized egg continues its journey through the fallopian tube to the uterus, where it embeds itself in the lining of the uterine wall. By this time the single cell of the original ovum has already been transformed into a cluster of multiple cells. (The cells have also already begun to specialize.)

Recall that the uterine lining (endometrium) begins to thicken to prepare for the egg. If the egg is not fertilized, the lining gradually leaves the body through the vagina. This sloughing off of the uterine lining is called menstruation.

Explain that the fetus will remain in the mother's uterus for the next nine months (about 280 days). Some of the cells will develop into the placenta (which will supply the baby with nutrition and oxygen and remove wastes).

The fetus lives within and is protected by the amniotic sac. This is a bag filled with fluid. Give students an idea of the amniotic sac by showing them the water-filled balloon with the marble in it. (For more drama you may wish to fill the balloon and add the marble with the class watching.) Pass the balloon around, instructing students to handle it carefully. Through touching and gentle shaking the balloon, they will be able to experience how the fluid protects the object from shock—just as the amniotic fluid protects the fetus from outside movements.

2. **Activity.** Divide the students into groups of two or three and assign each group a month of fetal development to research and report on. Groups can find information and copy or draw pictures describing what takes place during their assigned month. If desired, assign additional groups to study the phenomenon of twins, the importance of prenatal care and good nutrition, or some causes of birth defects.

   Give groups the opportunity to make presentations on their findings to the whole class. Display the student illustrations of the chronological development of a baby on the bulletin board.

### Second session

3. Show the teacher visual of the stages of labor. Explain that by the time the baby is to be born it usually has settled into a head-down position in the mother's uterus (feet-down is called a breech position). Labor is the name for the physical effort of the mother during childbirth. Labor and delivery commonly last 6–12 hours.

   During labor the muscles of the uterus contract and push the baby's head against the cervix. The contractions become stronger as labor progresses. The pressure of the baby's head against the cervix causes the cervix to stretch and thin out. (This has been compared to the ribbing of a turtleneck sweater stretching and thinning before the neck opening begins to expand.)

When the cervix is completely open (fully dilated), the baby passes through the birth canal (vagina). The doctor or midwife examines the baby, and then often lays it on the mother so that she may see and touch it.

The doctor places a clamp on the umbilical cord and cuts it (the cord is 20 inches or longer). This does not hurt because the cord has no nerves. Over the next week(s) the baby's stump of cord will dry up and fall off. The place where it was attached is the navel or belly button.

Shortly after the baby is delivered, the placenta (afterbirth) also passes out of the mother.

During pregnancy the mother's breasts prepare to produce milk to feed the baby. If the mother chooses to breast-feed her baby, she will begin to nurse the baby shortly after birth.

In some cases it may be difficult for a woman to give birth to her baby in the usual way. In these cases the doctor will perform a surgery known as a C-section or cesarean delivery. In a C-section the doctor makes an incision in the woman's abdomen and through the wall of the uterus, and then lifts the baby out. Then the doctor stitches the incision shut.

4. Conclude these sessions by reading Psalm 139. Our loving God has known us from the very beginning of our lives. God cares for and watches over us every day of our lives.

● ● ● ● ● ● ● ● ● ● ● ● ● ● ● ● ● ● ● ● ● ● ● ● ● ● ● ● ● ● ● ● ● ● ● ● ● ● ● ● ● ● ● ● ● ● ● ● ● ● ● ●

## Related Activity (Optional)

- Health notebook: Ask students to write about what they think is the most awesome thing about the creation of a baby and the process of development and birth.

# LESSON 5: RISKY BUSINESS

## Preparation/Materials
- Student books
- Calculators, one per student group

## Objectives
- Students will review sexually transmitted diseases, with a focus on HIV/AIDS.
- Students will discover that abstinence/celibacy or a mutually faithful and monogamous marriage relationship are the only means of truly "safe sex."

## Background
Sexually transmitted diseases (STDs), formerly called venereal diseases, are on the rise worldwide, and some of these diseases are among the world's most serious. Here are basic facts about some of these diseases.

- Gonorrhea is caused by bacteria that attacks the urethra of both male and female and the female's cervix. The infection can lead to scar tissue and sterility. Once bacteria get into the bloodstream, they can cause liver and joint damage—and eventually death.
- Syphilis, also a bacterial infection, causes sores to form on the male/female genitals. Other symptoms are fever, sore throat, rash, swollen glands, and aching joints. Although the symptoms may disappear—even for years—the infection is still present. If untreated, the disease will destroy body tissues and organs. Antibiotics can cure syphilis and prevent damage to the body.
- Chlamydia bacteria infect the male's urethra and female's fallopian tubes. There are often no clear symptoms of this infection until it is at a serious stage. Symptoms are a discharge from the vagina or penis. Chlamydia can create scar tissue and lead to sterility. Antibiotic medication can treat this infection.

- Herpes is a virus causing painful sores on the genitals. During birth a baby can pick up the virus as it passes through the birth canal. Although medication is available for treating symptoms, there is no cure for herpes.
- Hepatitis B, a viral liver infection, is often spread by sexual contact. Symptoms are persistent chills, fever, nausea, and a generalized feeling of sickness. Hepatitis B usually clears up on its own. A vaccine may soon become available to prevent Hepatitis B.
- AIDS stands for Acquired Immune Deficiency Syndrome. The acronym tells much about the disease: (1) it's an acquired disease—not genetic or hereditary; (2) it's a disease that attacks the body's immune system; (3) it weakens the immune system, making the body deficient in white blood cells to fight the disease; (4) it's not a specific disease, but a condition that leads to various opportunistic diseases.

The human immunodeficiency virus (HIV) causing AIDS is passed through an infected person's blood, semen, or vaginal secretions. Although the virus has been found in tears and saliva, there is no known case of anyone being infected in this way. HIV can remain silent in the body for 10 years or longer with the person looking and feeling perfectly healthy—and passing the virus to others.

Scientists still do not know what exactly triggers the onset of AIDS, but finally the person experiences symptoms such as fever, fatigue, night sweats, and weight loss, swollen lymph glands, and chronic diarrhea. Later on the person may develop rare cancers or a serious respiratory infection called *pneumocystis carinii* pneumonia.

Although there is no cure for AIDS, one drug, called AZT, has helped to prolong the lives of people who have HIV/AIDS and to slow the progress of those with early symptoms. AZT can produce some serious side effects. Other drugs are available to treat conditions caused by HIV infection and HIV/AIDS. The scientific community is testing a variety of experimental vaccines, but developing a vaccine for HIV is tricky because this clever virus mutates. Be sure to obtain updated information from community medical organizations or HIV/AIDS hotlines before teaching this lesson.

Teaching about HIV/AIDS is a challenge for teachers. Why should children learn about HIV/AIDS? First of all, to keep themselves from getting HIV/AIDS. Their lives may literally depend on having correct information and motivation. But also, so that they will be able to respond in an informed and compassionate way to people who have been affected by HIV/AIDS. The gospel mandate calls us to respond in love and to reach out to those suffering because of HIV/AIDS.

• • • • • • • • • • • • • • • • • • • • • • • • • • • • • • • • • • • • • • • • • • • • • • •

## Lesson

1.  Begin by reviewing two main concepts covered in earlier lessons: sexual intimacy is good and pleasurable in a marriage relationship and one possible outcome of intercourse is pregnancy. Tell the students that there are various methods of birth control. Explain the meaning of *birth control* (a way to attempt to prevent pregnancy). (The depth of your presentation on this topic may be governed by school policy.)

    Stress that the only completely effective way of avoiding pregnancy is to not have sex. Dispel any myths or misconceptions students may have (for example, that a woman can't get pregnant the first time she has intercourse or during menstruation).

2.  Review the meaning of the term *STD*—sexually transmitted disease. Define an STD as an infection that is passed from one person's body to another's during sexual contact. Elicit the names of some kinds of STDs (students learned about STDs in grade 5). Some STDs are chlamydia, herpes, gonorrhea, and syphilis. Some STDs affect only males, some affect only females, and some affect both sexes. Most of these diseases are curable if they are treated early enough; however, some are not curable. Use background information as appropriate during this discussion of STDs.

    Note that one STD that has received a lot of news coverage is AIDS. The full name of this disease is Acquired Immune Deficiency Syndrome, and it is caused by the Human Immunodeficiency Virus (HIV).

3.  **Student book.** Read and discuss "Questions and Answers About AIDS." Then answer the "Think It Over" questions as a class.

    1.  *Answers will vary but should reflect that it is unreasonable to be afraid of getting HIV/AIDS through casual contact.*
    2.  *People with HIV can be infected with the virus and look and feel healthy. The virus does not produce symptoms right away, and, in fact, may not produce symptoms for years. Make sure that students understand the implications of this for infecting others. You may also wish to explain that even though a blood test can show the presence of HIV, if a person has been infected within the past six months, the test may be negative.*

3. *Student answers should show awareness of their responsibility to make decisions to obey God's law by abstaining from sex before marriage and avoiding drug abuse.*

4. *God commands us to love our neighbor; God shows us—through no merit of our own—love and mercy. We are called to reflect God's mercy in our relationships with others.*

5. *Student answers may include learning more about HIV and AIDS, praying for those with AIDS, visiting them, helping with household and shopping chores, and showing compassion and love.*

In the discussion talk about the relationship of the spread of AIDS to homosexuality. You may wish to simply state that the sexual contact that spreads HIV can be between men and women or between those of the same sex. Students may know the names of some celebrities who were homosexuals and died from AIDS.

During the discussion also explain the term "safe sex," a value-free term used in the media and one many students are most likely familiar with. Explain that when TV ads and other materials warn about HIV/AIDS, they often urge people to practice "safe sex." By this they mean using a condom, which is a thin, tight-fitting rubber sheath, over the penis during intercourse. The idea is to prevent direct contact and to prevent the exchange of body fluids that can pass HIV. (Actually the use of spermicide with condoms is the best way to cut risk, but this fact is not usually given.) Using condoms reduces the possibility of HIV infection, but condoms are not totally safe (they may slip or break during intercourse). Tell students that the term "safe sex" is misleading. Have students define what the only "safe sex" is: waiting until marriage for sex and having sex only with one's husband or wife.

4. Consider doing this activity to show how fast HIV can spread. Provide a calculator for each group of students, and draw two stick figures on the board, one boy and one girl. Tell students to suppose that one of these people is unknowingly carrying HIV. The two of them have injected drugs and have shared needles. Have students put a 2 in the calculator to represent two people who have/or have been exposed to HIV.

On the next day draw two more stick figures on the board. Tell students that the original two people have each infected someone else. Have them put "times 2 equals" in the calculator. Continue in this manner. having student groups keep track of the day and the number that could possibly be infected. By about the 27th day the numbers will run off the calculator.

(We are indebted to Judy Willis of the State of Iowa Public School System for this activity.)

• • • • • • • • • • • • • • • • • • • • • • • • • • • • • • • • • • • • • • • • • • • • • • • • • • • • •

## Related Activity

• Assign group research projects on various STDs or on various topics related to HIV/AIDS.

# LESSON 6: GROWING UP AND REACHING OUT

## Preparation/Materials

- Prepare cards for group discussion, one per student group. On each card write an example of a situation or relationship that causes a dilemma. Examples: A popular girl invites you to a party, but your best friend isn't invited. A boyfriend pressures his girlfriend to do things she doesn't want to do (sexual contact, disobey parental rules).
- Student books

## Objectives

- Students will discuss the qualities of friendship that relate to friendship of both the same sex and the opposite sex.
- Students will learn to analyze different perspectives on the use of sexuality according to God's guidelines.
- Students will discuss and develop healthy, Christian standards for marriage and dating.

## Background

Students will approach this lesson with varying opinions and levels of interest. The development and level of sexual interest varies with every individual. It is important not to make students who are not yet interested in members of the opposite sex feel uncomfortable. It is critical, however, to promote the development of ideas and values regarding healthy, Christian relationships. Society offers a view of sexuality and sexual relationships that differs radically from the Christian ideal. Students need a Christian perspective in order to critically analyze our society's flood of sexually explicit material.

## Lesson (2 sessions)

1. Develop with the students a list of desirable qualities of friendship that relate to both same-sex and opposite-sex relationships. Include qualities such as honesty, integrity, loyalty, kindness, helpful and caring attitude, similar interests, ability to keep confidences.

   Review God's law of love: Love God with all your heart, and treat others in the same way that you would like to be treated. This is a good guideline for all relationships (from acquaintances to good friends to dates to marriage partners).

   Review God's guidelines for sexual relationships: Sexual intimacy is to be reserved for and used only within marriage. You may wish to briefly talk about the relationship of friendship to marriage. God created man and women to be helpers to each other. When a marriage relationship is based on friendship, commitment, and trust, partners can find great support and pleasure in one another.

2. **Activity.** Ask the class to critique examples of relationships or situations according to the standards that they developed in Step 1.

   Have the class break up into groups of four or five. Give each group a card describing a dilemma in a relationship. Each group should discuss the implications of the situation described on their card and then decide what they think may be positive or negative about the situation. Then each group should pass its situation cards to the next group. Make sure each group discusses at least two situations. (If time permits and interest is high, allow student groups to discuss each situation.) Finally, open the discussion to the whole class.

3.  Next, assign one of the relationship ideals (both for friendship and marriage) to each group. Ask each group to come up with an example from culture or from their personal experience that shows the effects of either keeping or breaking the ideal.

    Have students share the results of their assignment. Conclude that what is portrayed in the media is not always what is good or acceptable according to God's guidelines. In our own lives we also sometimes fail to do what is best because of the influence of sin. Talk about the importance of making choices based on God's will but also the importance of asking forgiveness for wrong choices. Stress that with God's help we can make new beginnings.

4.  **Student book.** Assign students to read "Boys and Girls." Have students answer the "Think It Over" questions in pairs or groups.

    1.  *Answers will vary.*
    2.  *Student answers should reflect an awareness of the influence of society of ideas about sexuality.*

    Discuss the selection as a class.

5.  Focus on the messages from the media about relationships between sexes. What are the lyrics of songs that students currently listen to? What do the articles in the magazines they read tell them? What are the messages from TV programs they watch?

    Assign students to keep track of messages they hear or see about male/female relationships for 3–5 days. Then have a class discussion based on the results of their findings.

• • • • • • • • • • • • • • • • • • • • • • • • • • • • • • • • • • • • • • • • • • • • • • • • •

## Related Activity

*   Health notebooks: Have the students think about the role of friendships in their own lives. Ask them to write in their journal about how important friends are to them right now or about another lesson-related topic.

# LESSON 7: WHERE DO YOU COME FROM? (FAMILY—NUCLEAR AND EXTENDED)

## Preparation/Materials
- Student workbook activities 1 and 2
- Make a transparency of workbook activities 1 and 2 to use with the overhead (see Teacher Resources).
- Be prepared with personal information to use to fill out a sample of each activity worksheet (Steps 1 and 2).

## Objectives
- Students will understand that they belong to a nuclear family, an extended family, and the family of God.
- Students will explore their family history.
- Students will develop an appreciation for the family in which God has placed them.

## Lesson

1. **Student workbook activity 1.** Explain that in this lesson students will be gathering information about their family. Place a copy of Student Activity 1, the family group chart, on the overhead. Explain that this sheet organizes information about the nuclear family. Define the term *nuclear family*. Then model how to fill out the family group sheet, using information about your own parents and siblings.

   Under the "Sources of Information" heading at the bottom of the worksheet, list any documents that are available to verify the information contained on the upper part of the form (for example, birth certificates, marriage certificates, etc.).

   Finally, write in date and location of profession of faith and the date and location of baptism as available. Discuss how this marks a person's inclusion in yet another family, the family of God.

   (*Note:* In order to avoid misunderstanding, it is better to write the dates on the worksheets with the day first, the month (written out) second, and then the full year—15 May 1942.)

2. **Student workbook activity 2.** Define *extended family*. Place a copy of Student Activity 2 on the overhead. Demonstrate how to complete the family tree chart. Again, use personal information to fill in the chart.

3. Have students take home the worksheet containing the two student activities for this lesson. (If you wish students to have completed samples of the worksheets for reference, provide copies of those completed in Steps 1 and 2.) They may begin to fill out the activities in class, but most of the information will have to be gathered as homework. You may wish to suggest that they begin by writing information in pencil and use ink only when the chart is finished. To get access to family information, students can ask parents' permission to photocopy birth, baptism, or marriage certificates.

4. In addition, assign a family history project. The information gathered in the previous activity may serve as a springboard for this project. Offer a variety of ideas to the class, but encourage the students to be creative.

   Some project suggestions include making a family time line or a family coat of arms, writing a play about family traditions, using a box or crate to make a mini-museum in which to display family mementos. Another option is to design a chart that includes more extended family members than the Student Activity 2 chart (for example, including siblings and cousins).

   Be sensitive to students whose family units may not fit a traditional pattern. If the past is painful, for example, to a child in a foster-care situation, point out that the students will probably be someone's ancestor in the future. In this case, the student might choose to assemble a personal history project that would tell a future descendent about what important events and accomplishments have happened in his or her life.

● ● ● ● ● ● ● ● ● ● ● ● ● ● ● ● ● ● ● ● ● ● ● ● ● ● ● ● ● ● ● ● ● ● ● ● ● ● ● ● ● ● ● ● ● ● ● ● ● ● ● ● ● ● ● ●

## Related Activities

1. Make student resources available.
   Some suggestuions and activities are on
   the resources list.

2. Integrate with social studies, and research
   family structures in other cultures.

# LESSON 8: THE CHRISTIAN FAMILY— WITHIN AND WITHOUT

## Preparation/Materials

- Bible
- Materials and resources for Step 4 as desired
- Optional: transparency/overhead or large sheets of chart paper (see Step 2)

## Objectives

- Students will understand that the Christian family is built on God's Word and is supported by love for each other and love of God.
- Students will consider how love can be practiced by the family both within the home and within the community.
- Students will consider the effect of societal influences on the family.

## Background

The *Horizons Health* curriculum for grade 4 introduces the Word of God as the basis for the Christian family. Students at that grade level are asked to draw the simple outline of a house, whose walls stand for "Love of God" and "Love for Each Other." The fourth graders then write a few specific examples of love from their own experience to mount inside the house.

In this lesson we suggest you use the same visual aid. However, sixth grade students should be able to expand their thinking beyond their own experience. Their list of loving qualities should include ideals that may be difficult to achieve but are worth striving for. Your students can also begin to see beyond the walls of their own home to examine the positive effect of a Christian family that shares its love with the members of the wider community.

If in your school this lesson is being presented simultaneously with the fourth grade lesson, consider having your class show their projects in a presentation or hallway display for the younger students.

• • • • • • • • • • • • • • • • • • • • • • • • • • • • • • • • • • • • • • • • • • • • • • • • • • • •

## Lesson

1. Review the fourth grade lesson by drawing on the board a simple outline of a house. Label the floor or foundation, "Word of God." Title the walls, "Love of God" and "Love for Each Other." Cap the roof with the words "Christian Family."

   Discuss the meaning of the drawing and its labels. Read excerpts from Genesis 2. Review that God's plan is not for us to live in isolation, but to live in loving families. God's Word is the foundation of a Christian home. Explain that love for God and for each other are the strongest supporting structures in that home.

2. Work with your class to develop a conceptual web, representing their understanding of a Christian family. (You may wish to work on the board, an overhead, or a large sheet of paper.) The model should incorporate the basics as reviewed above, but should include more specific characteristics or examples as well.

For example, the interactions between family members could be defined as shared memories, kindness, compassion, honor, cooperation, forgiveness, mutual dependence, trust, and loyalty—with examples included of each. Specific duties of parents to nurture their children and of children to obey their parents can also be included. Another idea to incorporate is the importance of the Christian family connecting to the community through service, hospitality, and church involvement.

3. Focus on societal influences on the family. Brainstorm with your class the attitudes, practices, and influences of modern society on the family. Discuss how these conflict or mesh with a Christian view.

   Develop a list of issues that a Christian family must confront. Depending on the size of the web you have constructed, you may prefer to add the societal influences to the web, showing them with arrows pointing back to the center of the web.

4. Assign one of the following activities related to the lesson discussion, or have students—working on their own or in groups or pairs—choose one of the activities/suggestions to develop a project. (You may want to have students working on projects first develop a proposal to submit for your approval.)

   Suggestions for student activities/projects:
   - A letter to present or future family members in which the student describes how he or she would like family members to be able to treat each other.
   - A short story (fiction or nonfiction) that explores one of the issues discussed in this lesson.
   - Look up passages in the Bible related to hospitality and service to others and translate these passages into the student's own words.
   - Build a model of a house out of cardboard/make a poster that shows the model of a Christian family and visually illustrates some examples.
   - Research a family-related topic. Then develop a way to present the information to the rest of the class. Possible topics include problems of children whose parents are divorced, the pitfalls and perks of stepfamilies, the effect of TV viewing on children, latchkey kids, the need for community support in a marriage, prayer in family life, how families cope with serious illness.
   - Compose and perform a song about Christian love in the family.
   - Write and perform a skit about family life.

## Related Activities

1. Focus on the relationship of family and friends. Make a worksheet on the theme "A friend respects my feelings, my family, my faith." Write the three categories as column headings.

   First, lead a general discussion of how friendship relates to family. Give some examples that you might include if you were to fill out the worksheet. Also give some positive examples of ways that you could communicate these needs to a friend.

   Next, ask students to complete the worksheet, writing in each column ways in which they hope their own friends will show respect for their feelings, family, and faith.

2. Discuss conflicts that sometimes arise between family and friends. Consider choosing a class panel to discuss conflicts such as the following: when parents approve/disapprove of friends, what I get from my friends that I can't get from my family.

3. Have students chart how much time during each day they are with family, with peers (outside of school time), and alone (outside of time spent sleeping).

   What do the results show? Are they surprised?

# LESSON 9: FOR THEY SHALL BE COMFORTED

## Preparation/Materials

- Bible
- Unit evaluation in student workbook
- Prepare and duplicate (one copy per student) a list of local resources for helping those who are grieving (hospice; support groups related to terminal illnesses, death, divorce, Christian family counselors, pastors).
- Optional: Duplicate and distribute "Some Sources of Help" from the Teacher Resources section.
- Optional: Obtain a copy of *Hey World, Here I Am!* by Jean Little (Kids Can Press, 1986).

## Objectives

- Students will review and develop their understanding of the stages and symptoms of grief.
- Students will identify sources of help available to people who are dying and grieving.
- Students will discover some simple ways in which they can help and comfort others.
- Students will be reassured by the Christian belief that Christ has destroyed the power of death and that one day believers will be resurrected.

## Background

Your students have already experienced grief. It may have been a small loss, such as misplacing a favorite toy or perhaps the death of a pet. Others will have already experienced the death of a significant person in their lives. But what exactly is grief?

In her book, *Where Has Grandpa Gone?* (Zondervan, 1983), Ruth Kopp attempts to define grief. She writes, "Grief is the sum total of the feelings we have when we suffer a loss. What we learn about grief through observing others is the behavior that expresses the feelings."

Because some of these behaviors and feelings may be confusing for children, it is helpful for them to learn that there are names for these reactions and that their responses are normal. Children should also know that although there are many typical expressions of grief, there is no standard. Everyone's way of grieving is as unique as a fingerprint.

Theresa Huntley in her book *Helping Children Grieve* (Augsburg, 1991) writes a helpful chapter on the common behaviors of grieving children. In fourth grade (Unit 2, Lesson 11) children studied some of these behaviors. They discussed denial, anger, guilt, bodily distress and shortened attention span. These behaviors differ from the typically defined stages of grief, which usually include denial, anger, bargaining, depression, and acceptance. This lesson reviews the fourth grade material, but it also introduces bargaining, depression, and acceptance as part of the grieving process.

C.S. Lewis, writing about his feelings after his wife's death, begins with the words "No one ever told me...." Perhaps it is impossible to completely explain grief—to fully understand grief, one must feel it. But it is important to begin to talk about grief with our students. As Kopp writes:

> Losses, and the grief we experience because of them, strip us and cleanse us. They can leave us stronger and more ready to go on to new experiences, new responsibilities, new joys, and new loves. They can leave us freer than we were, less restricted in our choices and the possibilities for our lives. The way in which we handle the grief process and accomplish the painful task of mourning determines whether this will be the outcome of our grief. (p. 50)

As Christian educators we can prepare our students for grief by talking about death honestly and openly with sensitivity and faith. For we know that we need not fear death. In dying, Christ has destroyed the power of death. Through Christ we too will have victory.

• • • • • • • • • • • • • • • • • • • • • • • • • • • • • • • • • • • • • • • • • • • • • • • •

## Lesson (1–2 sessions)

1. Read Matthew 5:4 and Romans 12:16. Tell the class that it is a Christian's privilege and responsibility to identify with others in both their joys and their sorrows.

2. Recall that grief is felt on the occasion of some great loss—for example, a death, divorce, or difficult move. Remind the class that it is hard to feel what others are feeling, but we usually find clues in what people say or how they act. Then lead the class through the following reactions to grief.

   • Denial:

   "No, it's not true. I don't believe she died."

   "He went away, but he didn't die. He'll come back. I know he will!"

   Denial is the mind's way of pushing the grief away for a while. It's a way of taking a break from dealing with the loss. Denial is a common first reaction to death. It's not healthy to stay in this stage for a long time.

   • Anger:

   "Why did she leave me?"

   "He knows I need him. Why did he go away?"

   "God could have saved my friend!"

   Feeling angry is okay. It is normal. Anger should be freely expressed, but in appropriate ways such as punching a pillow or taking a run.

   • Bargaining:

   "I'll do anything she asks me—if only she gets better!"

   "I'll read and pray every day if you'll only make him better" (bargaining with God).

   In bargaining, a person often promises a change in behavior to keep or bring back a loved one. Bargaining is another way the mind pushes away the reality of death that is so hard to accept.

   • Guilt:

   "If only I had (or hadn't) …"

   "It's all my fault. I did something bad."

   Death of a loved one is not a punishment for something you did.

   • Bodily distress:

   "I feel so tired. It's even hard for me to get up and get dressed."

   "My stomach doesn't feel good. I don't want to eat."

   It's normal to feel this way. It may be the body's way of handling confusion or fear or sadness. In time the grieving person will feel better.

   • Shortened attention span:

   "I can't concentrate on anything."

   "I feel like I'm in a different world."

Of course. The death of someone close is painful. Both grownups and children feel this way. These feelings will go away with time, too.

- Depression:

"I don't want to go fishing" (or some other activity always enjoyed with the person who has died).

"There's no point in going to school/work."

Depression causes life to seem hopeless or meaningless. The person is beginning to look to the future, but grief keeps him or her from seeing the positive things it will hold.

- Acceptance:

"Things are going to be all right."

"I'm ready to go on with my life."

Some people think that accepting a death means that they don't love or miss the person who has died. That's not true. Acceptance means recognizing the finality of death (at least on this earth) and being ready to "get on with life."

The Christian hope is the reason that Christians can accept death and have peace about the future.

3. Give students the list you have prepared of local resources. Explain that these are sources of help available to assist the students and their friends and families. Go over the list briefly. Give students the opportunity to add information they may have about support groups or other resources.

If you have not prepared such a list in advance, distribute the handout from the Teacher Resource section entitled "Some Sources of Help." Ask students if they know of any resources of this kind and compile a list of their responses.

4. Next help the class identify some things Christian friends can do for people who are grieving.

If you have a copy of Jean Little's book *Hey World, Here I Am!* read the selection entitled "When Someone I Love Is Hurt." Use the reading to stimulate student thinking about empathy. Ask: "How does the writer feel when someone she loves is hurt? (The writer hurts, too; she doesn't feel like doing any of her normal activities.) Have you ever felt like the writer in this situation? (It is normal to feel this way.) Would it help to have some ideas of what to do when someone you love is hurting?" (Yes.)

Ask class members what they think they would want others to do for them if they were grieving. Have individual students write down their ideas. Then have volunteers share their lists. Some important suggestions to include are these:

—prayer

—recognizing that everyone feels grief differently

—being available to listen

—encouraging the grieving person to express his or her feelings

—maintaining a normal life and routine as much as possible
—including the grieving person in ways you normally would
—celebrating good memories
—helping out with the concrete details of life

5. Read about the death of Lazarus in John 11. Point out that Jesus grieved with his friends Mary and Martha. This is evidence that Jesus shares the grief that we feel. He knows grief, and he understands the pain of grief.

   Close by reading some verses from 1 Corinthians 15 about the Christian hope.

6. **Unit evaluation.** Use the worksheets to review and evaluate.

   *Matching:*
   *1. e;  2. h;  3. g;  4. f;  5. b;  6. a;  7. i;  8. c;  9. d*

   *Short answers:*
   1. *Answers may include growth spurt, change in facial features, voice changes, skin changes, increased perspiration, appearance of pubic/body hair, development of reproductive organs.*
   2. *Through sexual contact; through blood-to-blood contact, injecting drugs with shared needles; from infected mother to baby; through blood transfusions.*
   3. *It cannot be passed through ordinary, casual contact.*
   4. *When an individual begins puberty, his or her timetable is partly determined by heredity.*
   5. *Possible answers include various support groups, counselors, pastors.*
   6. *Denial, anger, bargaining, guilt, bodily distress, shortened attention span, depression, and acceptance.*

   *Short essay:*
   1. *Answers will vary, but should reflect awareness of the stages of each lifetime.*
   2. *Answers will vary, but should reflect an understanding that God's law is given for the good of human life, to make community possible.*
   3. *Answers will vary, but should reflect the class discussion in Lesson 8.*
   4. *Answers may include prayer, being available to listen, encouraging the grieving person to express feelings, including your friend in ways you normally would, helping out with the concrete details of life.*

## Related Activities

1. Point out that while acceptance is a healthy resolution of grief, it does not mean that death is good. Death is an intrusion in creation. Paul writes of death as an enemy of Christ and of Christians. Read 1 Corinthians 15:26.

2. Invite a counselor or pastor to talk to the class about how he or she helps those who are grieving.

3. Health notebook: Have students research various funeral/burial practices in North America and other countries.

4.  Create a "Talking to Parents" worksheet about death for students to use to initiate a discussion on the lesson topic with parents. Some possible questions/topics for the worksheet include the following: "What was your first experience with death? Did you feel angry about the death? What other reactions did you have? How did your Christian faith help you?"

5.  Make books available to the class that deal with death and grief. Some suggested titles: *I Heard the Owl Call My Name* by Margaret Craven, *Ordinary People* by Judith Guest, *The Empty Chair* by Bess Kaplan, and *The Golden Bird* by Hans Stolp

# Unit 6

# Choosing a Healthy Lifestyle

Lesson 1:  Why Bother?

Lesson 2:  Be a Picky Eater—Choose Wisely!

Lesson 3:  Nutrients for Health (2 Sessions)

Lesson 4:  Checking Up on Fats, Sugars, and Salt

Lesson 5:  Nutrients and Your Cells (Optional)

Lesson 6:  The Dieting Obsession

Lesson 7:  Your Physical Best (2 Sessions)

Lesson 8:  Exercise and Body Composition (2 Sessions)

Lesson 9:  Skills Fitness

Lesson 10:  Shiny Bright and Smelling Right

Lesson 11:  Skinformation

Lesson 12:  Time Out

Lesson 13:  How Are You Doing?

## Goals

- Students will develop an understanding of some basic components of a healthy lifestyle.
- Students will decide to make choices that contribute to a healthy lifestyle.

## Background

"Children *by nature* gravitate toward healthy activities and habits. At the most fundamental levels they genuinely *want* to have strong and sound bodies and minds," writes Kenneth Cooper in *Kid Fitness* (Bantam, 1991). Helping children form healthy living patterns is particularly important in view of numerous studies which show that millions of North American children—most of them from middle- and upper-middle-class homes—are on a fast track to becoming unhealthy adults. The way we live has a tremendous affect on our health, both now and in the future. Taking even small steps toward a healthy lifestyle can have a surprisingly beneficial effect.

Although *Horizons Health* seeks throughout the curriculum to motivate students to make choices that contribute to a healthy lifestyle, this unit focuses on making healthy choices in the areas of nutrition, physical fitness, and personal health care. Consider adding lessons on lifestyle issues that appear to be a particular problem for your class or in your community.

## Vocabulary

Plan to integrate the following vocabulary

| | | | | |
|---|---|---|---|---|
| carbohydrates | minerals | proteins | vitamins | saturated fats |
| pulp | unsaturated fats | starches | complex carbohydrates | |
| fiber | sodium | osmosis | diffusion | dentin |
| filtration | anorexia | bulimia | calorie | net weight |
| calipers | acne | plaque | cardiorespiratory fitness | |
| enamel | calculus | body composition | | |

cell parts:

| | | |
|---|---|---|
| membrane | nucleus | cytoplasm |

## Unit Resources (Search online for similar resources if these are no longer available.)

Resources section of the MyPlate website.
https://www.choosemyplate.gov/resources/videos.
Contains many overview videos and videos suitable for kids.

"Physical Activity Facts." Centers for Disease Control and Prevention.
https://www.cdc.gov/healthyschools/physicalactivity/facts.htm.
Information and downloadable PDFs focused around youth.

Brand, P., and P. Yancey. *Fearfully and Wonderfully Made*. Grand Rapids, Michigan: Zondervan, 1980.

"Children's Mental Health." Centers for Disease Control and Prevention, 2020.
https://www.cdc.gov/childrensmentalhealth/index.html.

*Super You*. Rosemont, Ill.: National Dairy Council, 1988.
> A children's guide to fitness and nutrition, this resource offers a wide variety of exercises and activities. Contact National Dairy Council, 6300 N. River Road, Rosemont, Illinois 60018; phone 708-696-1020.

## Lesson Resources (Search online for similar resources if these are no longer available.)

### Lessons 2–5

"Read the Label Youth Outreach Materials." U.S. Food & Drug Administration.
> fda.gov.
> Printable infographics, activities, and information for students.

"Healthy Eating Toolkit." Action for Healthy Kids.
> https://www.actionforhealthykids.org/nutrition-toolkit/.
> This page contains blog posts, ideas, and activities for kids.

"7 Nutrition Activities for Elementary and Middle School Students." Houghton Mifflin Harcourt.
> https://www.hmhco.com/blog/nutrition-activities-elementary-middle-school-students.
> List of activities that includes links.

"Diet and Dental Health." Mouth Healthy by the American Dental Association.
> https://www.mouthhealthy.org/.

*Schools v Cancer Nutrition Guide, Middle School*. American Cancer Society, Inc., 2018.
> cancer.org/schools.
> PDF about the importance of nutrition, written for the parent or teacher (but students will understand the material as well).

"Food & Fitness." The Nemours Foundation, 2020.
> https://teenshealth.org/.
> This page links to sections about health/nutrition topics, suitable for middle school.

"Exercise Tips for Kids and Teens." NASM.
> https://blog.nasm.org/fitness/kids-and-exercise.
> Resource containing information about benefits, exercise frequency, movements, and risks.

"Read the Label Youth Outreach Materials." U.S. Food & Drug Administration.
> fda.gov.
> Printable infographics, activities, and information for students.

### Lesson 6

"About Eating Disorders." The Healthy Teen Project, 2020.
> https://healthyteenproject.com/about-eating-disorders/.
> This page provides an overview of different disorders and disproves common myths.

*Educator Toolkit*. NEDA.
> https://www.nationaleatingdisorders.org/.
> PDF that provides information and resources for educators.

"Free curricula for grades K–12 on eating disorders." Bulimia Guide and health body image."
> https://bulimiaguide.org/.
> Links to educational material and resources.

**Lessons 7–9**

"Physical Activity in Young People." Physiopedia.
    physio-pedia.com.

"Promoting Youth Fitness." Nationwide Children's Hospital, 2020.
    www.nationwidechildren.org.

Robinson, Sharon. *Promises to Keep: How Jackie Robinson Changed America*. Scholastic, 2004.

Ignotofsky, Rachel. *Women in Sports: 50 Fearless Athletes Who Played to Win*. Ten Speed Press, 2017.
    Book for Grades 5-12.

Tebow, Tim. *Shaken: Young Reader's Edition: Fighting to Stay Strong No Matter What Comes Your Way*.
    WaterBrook, 2020.

*SHAPE America: Society of Health and Phhysical Educators*. SHAPE America.
    https://www.shapeamerica.org/.
    Provides lessons and resources.

Scioscia, Mary. *Bicycle Rider*. New York: HarperTrophy, 1983.
    This biography of world-famous bicyclist Marshall Taylor tells how Taylor got into bicycle racing.
    The owner of a bike shop gives Marshall a job and enters him in the annual bicycle race after
    he watches Taylor doing great tricks on his bicycle. For grades 2–6.

**Lessons 10–12**

"Smile Smarts Dental Health Curriculum." Mouth Healthy, American Dental Association.
    https://www.mouthhealthy.org/en/resources/lesson-plans/smile-smarts.
    Printable PDFs separated by different grade levels.

"10 Ways to Teach Preteen Hygiene." Scholastic Inc., 2020.
    https://www.scholastic.com/parents.

*Teacher's Guide: Germs (Grades 6 to 8)*. The Nemours Foundation/KidsHealth, 2015.
    Lesson, article links questions, and activities about hygiene and germs.

"Parent Resources: Nicotine Vaping Prevention."
    CATCH.org.
    Free parent resources from the CATCH My Breath Program.
    The videos and information are also suitable for kids.

"For Kids & Teens": Tobacco Education Resources.
    healthychildren.org from the American Academy of Pediatrics.
    A list of tobacco use resources with links, suitable for kids and teens.

# LESSON 1: WHY BOTHER?

## Preparation/Materials
- Bibles, one per student
- Art materials for making a bulletin board display (*See* Step 4)

## Objectives
- Students will identify biblical norms for making lifestyle choices.
- Students will recognize their responsibility for making lifestyle choices.

## Background
One of the major emphases of *Horizons Health* is the Christian's responsibility to live a healthy lifestyle. Students are encouraged to view their body as God's creation and as the temple of the Holy Spirit. They are encouraged to honor God with their body and present it as a living sacrifice to God. But whether or not they take up the challenge is a personal decision. No one can force students to make healthy choices. This lesson presents students with the challenge to seriously consider the importance of living a healthy lifestyle.

• • • • • • • • • • • • • • • • • • • • • • • • • • • • • • • • • • • • • • • • • • • • • • • • • • •

## Lesson

1. Begin this introductory unit lesson by having students brainstorm components of a healthy lifestyle. What does a healthy lifestyle involve? (Physical fitness, food of the right kinds and amounts, dental care, taking precautions to prevent disease—vaccinations, personal hygiene, careful handling of food, getting enough rest, controlling stress, emotional health, social health.) List student suggestions on the board.

2. Ask students why we should bother with all the effort that goes into looking after our nutritional needs, getting fit, practicing daily hygiene habits, and so on. Is it worth all the effort?

   As students suggest reasons, record their answers. Be sure to include the most important reason: "God tells us to."

   Discuss the relationship of this last reason to the others on the list. If obeying God is the basic reason for living in a healthy way, what role do the other reasons on the list have? Or discuss the difference between living in a healthy way in order to obey and serve God with doing so for purely selfish reasons.

3. Have students read the following Bible passages. What do they say about how God wants us to live?

   - Genesis 1:28. God has given humans the task of taking care of creation, and this task includes taking care of our bodies.
   - 1 Corinthians 6:12-20. The following note on the passage from the NIV Study Bible (Zondervan, 1985) provides a helpful framework for discussion:

"Food for the stomach and the stomach for food." Paul quotes some Corinthians again who were claiming that as the physical acts of eating and digesting have no bearing on one's inner spiritual life, so the physical act of promiscuous sexual activity does not affect one's spiritual life. "The body is not meant for sexual immorality, but for the Lord." Paul here declares the dignity of the human body: It is intended for the Lord. Although granting that food and the stomach are transitory, Paul denies that what one does with the body is unimportant. This is particularly true of the use of sex, which the Lord has ordained in wedlock for the good of mankind.

Ask: "Does God force us like robots (or like puppets manipulated by strings) to do his will?" The point is that when we love God, we want to do God's will.

4. Create a bulletin board centered on the lesson theme. Students can cut out letters to form words that express one of the main ideas of the lesson. They can also find pictures of people doing things that relate to the theme (for example, exercising, eating healthy foods, and so on). Two suggested bulletin board themes: "Honor God With Your Body" and "Choosing a Healthy Lifestyle."

5. Assign students to write down everything they eat during the next 24 hours. Tell them to write down all snacks as well as regular meals. They will need this information for the next lesson's activity.

● ● ● ● ● ● ● ● ● ● ● ● ● ● ● ● ● ● ● ● ● ● ● ● ● ● ● ● ● ● ● ● ● ● ● ● ● ● ● ● ● ● ● ● ● ● ● ● ● ●

## Related Activities

1. Health notebook: Ask students to write a paragraph on a lesson-related topic such as "Why bother to aim for a healthy lifestyle?"

2. Spend some time discussing why God created us with the ability to choose. Read and talk about Genesis 2:16. You may also wish to look at how specific choices affected the lives of biblical characters the class is currently studying.

# LESSON 2: BE A PICKY EATER— CHOOSE WISELY!

## Preparation/Materials

- Student workbook activity
- Student books
- Optional: examples of standard measures to help students determine amounts of serving sizes (for example, a tablespoon, one cup, ½ cup, sample of 2–3 ounces/grams of a food)

## Objectives

- Students will evaluate their daily diet.
- Students will review the basic food groups.
- Students will review the connection between eating a variety of foods from all food groups and a healthy diet.

## Background

"The U.S. government's 1990 guidelines urge an ambitiously varied meal plan: three to five servings daily of vegetables, two to four of fruit, as well as six to eleven of breads, rice, pasta, and grains and two to three of meat, eggs, poultry, and dried beans. As far as America is concerned, most people don't even come close. A mere 9% of adults manage to consume five servings of fruits and vegetables each day, according to the National Center for Health Statistics. By and large, Americans simply don't like vegetables.... Nonetheless, failing to match daily dietary guidelines is no reason to go running for the vitamin bottle. 'What you do one day or one week isn't the whole story,' stresses Jeanne Goldberg, assistant professor of nutrition at Tufts. 'It's what your general eating patterns are.' Blitzing on junk food for a day or two is no problem if over the long haul, a diet regularly contains fruits and veggies." (*Time*, April 6, 1992)

*Note:* In 2010 the USDA created MyPlate, a new symbol and interactive food guidance system. The new food guidance system utilizes interactive technology found on **MyPlate.gov**. MyPlate contains interactive activities that make it easy for individuals to key in their age, gender, and physical activity level so that they can get a more personalized recommendation on their daily calorie level. Teachers may wish to refer to this website to create a sample menu for sixth-grade students.

This lesson helps students to become aware of their eating patterns.

Puberty is a time of active growth and often of strenuous activity. A balanced diet is needed at this time more than ever. Foods must be rich in protein to make new muscles and body tissue. They must contain plenty of minerals for the growth of bones, plenty of vitamins for general health, and foods rich in carbohydrates to provide necessary energy.

## Lesson

1. **Student workbook activity.** If students have lists of what they ate in the last 24 hours, have them use the lists to fill in the chart. Otherwise give students some time to remember and jot down what they've eaten (including all snacks). (Students may need some help in figuring out where combination foods belong. Recall that a combination food is the sum of its parts: Macaroni and cheese, for example, contains both pasta and cheese.)

When individual students have completed question 3, they can look at MyPlate in the student books (in the section "Choosing a Healthy Lifestyle" under "Getting Your Nutrients") to check on how many servings of each are recommended daily. [*Note:* The serving suggestions were calculated using the MyPlate.gov website and are for an 11-year-old boy who is active for 60 minutes or more a day.] How did the amounts they ate stack up against MyPlate guidelines? To help evaluate their daily diet, students should complete the remaining questions on the worksheet.

Allow about 15–20 minutes for the activity.

2. **Discussion.** Consider using questions such as the following to discuss the activity.
   "What food group did you have the most of? The least?"
   "Did you have enough (name groups by turn)?" (Note students should eat at least the lowest recommended amount; if they are very active, they may need more. Each individual's needs vary.)
   "What about Fats, Oils, and Sweets? Those are the kind of foods many of us eat too much of? What are some ways to cut down?" (Point out that this is not a food group. People get plenty of fats and sweets through eating from the five food groups. Note that everyone enjoys eating these foods once in a while.)
   "Did you eat different foods because of this assignment? If you did, how did you change what you ate? That might show you something about how you could change your daily diet."
   "How can we be sure to eat a balanced diet? (Eat from all food groups in recommended amounts.)

3. **Closure:** "Have you ever heard of this common sense way to be sure to eat enough healthy foods? Eat something brown, green, red, yellow, and white at each meal. Eating foods of different colors can help you make sure you're eating a variety of different kinds of foods."

## Related Activities

1. Explore the influence of family lifestyle and ethnic background on eating habits. For example, have students record information such as what meals the family eats together, time the family eats dinner, who does the cooking, and so on. Then have students find out how these things were done when their parents were children living at home. What are the most common differences? What effects do students think these differences have?

2. Health notebooks: Ask students find articles on nutrition. What claims do the articles make? Students can write a paragraph highlighting one of their article's main ideas. Find ways for class members to share what they found. Discuss the content of some of the articles—particularly those that tie in with the lessons on nutrition.

3. Work with students to create a food-group game. Make 10 to 15 questions for each of the five food groups. The questions could be about certain foods, number of servings, or a food group's contribution to health. Have students write each question on a card. Also make a puzzle of MyPlate shape on paper, and cut the puzzle into five pieces (one piece for each category).

To play the game, student teams should take turns selecting a card and answering the question. A correct answer earns one serving of a food group. When a team earns enough "servings" to match the minimum number of servings for the food group, it wins a block of the plate. By winning all five blocks (or the most blocks) the team wins the game. (This game is taken from *Instructor* magazine's "Eat Right America poster [February, 1993]. The poster was created by the Dietetic Association and its Foundation [1992].)

4. Enjoy poems about food. One resource is Arnold Adoff's *Eats: Poems,* which contains poems that delightfully express feelings about food.

# LESSON 3: NUTRIENTS FOR HEALTH

## Preparation/Materials

- Student books
- Student workbook activity
- Optional: magazines with food pictures, class supply
- Optional: student resources on nutrition

## Objectives

- Students will review the functions of the six classes of nutrients: proteins, carbohydrates, minerals, vitamins, fats, and water.
- Students will identify the major sources of these nutrients.

## Background

In this lesson students review the six main groups of nutrients.

Each group of nutrients provides something essential for body processes.

| FOOD GROUP | NUTRIENTS |
| --- | --- |
| 1. Grains | Mainly vitamins (especially of the B group) and carbohydrates. Some minerals. Provides fiber. |
| 2. Fruits | Mainly carbohydrates and proteins. Some minerals and vitamins. |
| 3. Vegetables | Mainly carbohydrates and proteins. Some minerals and vitamins. |
| 4. Dairy | Mainly fats and proteins. Some minerals and vitamins (D and B) and carbohydrates. |
| 5. Proteins | Mainly protein. Some fats, minerals, and vitamins. |

Note that some foods are said to be *complete proteins,* proteins that contain all eight of the essential amino acids that we must get from foods. Eggs, milk, and meat are in this category. Many vegetables, particularly those that come from the seeds of plants, contain protein, but some of the essential amino acids are present in quite small amounts. So to get complete protein on a vegetarian diet, it is important to eat complementary plant foods. Beans and grains, for example, eaten together provide complete protein.

Vitamins and minerals, although vitally important, are required in relatively small quantities. Each is needed to perform specific functions in the body. Vitamins are not a source of energy, but they are important in the conversion of food to energy. There are about 13 or 14 vitamins the body needs and can obtain from food sources; however, the daily nutrition requirements are known for only 10 of these. Vitamins are usually classified into two groups: the fat-soluble vitamins A, D, E, and K, and the water-soluble ones, vitamin C and the B-vitamin group.

"The fat-soluble vitamins are absorbed with the fats in foods. If not used, they can be stored in moderate quantities. Although a daily supply of these fat-soluble vitamins is not essential, it is preferable to choose foods containing them each day to ensure that reasonable amounts are always available. In contrast, the water soluble vitamins are not stored in appreciable amounts; excess quantities are excreted in the urine. Thus, adequate supplies must be provided on a continuing basis for optimum good health.

"When vitamins were first discovered less than 60 years ago, their chemical composition was not known. As each vitamin was isolated it was labeled with a letter of the alphabet.

Not until their composition was determined were they identified by specific chemical names. Some (Vitamins A, D, E, and K) are still commonly known by their alphabetical names.

"Research revealed that 'vitamin B' was actually a group of several vitamins, almost all of which are now known by their chemical names. The B-vitamin group includes thiamin, riboflavin, niacin (nicotinic acid), vitamin B6 (pyridoxine),

vitamin B12 (cyanocobalamin), folic acid, pantothenic acid, and biotin. Choline and inositol are sometimes included in this group." (*Handy Nutrition* [Dairy Bureau of Canada, 1984])

*Note:* In grade 5 students studied the six basic groups of nutrients. Using comparison cards, they also compared the amounts of specific nutrients in various foods.

## Lesson (2 sessions)

1. Recall the previous lesson's activities in which students analyzed their food choices and reviewed food groups. Ask: "Why do you need a variety of foods from the different food groups to stay healthy and look your best? Why does your body care what you eat? (Different foods contain different nutrients. Each nutrient has its own particular function in the body.) What is a nutrient?" (A substance in food that your body needs to do its work—for example, to replace tissue or to grow.)

2. Review the main groups of nutrients with the class.

   Consider using the following activity for the review. Explain that students will each choose a slip of paper on which is written the name of a nutrient. They will each look up the information about their nutrient in the student book ("Getting Your Nutrients") and then prepare to describe the nutrient for the rest of the class, telling what it does for health and what foods are good sources. Their presentations will be very short—not longer than 1–1½ minutes. Since there are six basic nutrients, some nutrients will have more than one presenter. (Another option is to provide additional resources and to assign some students to report on other vitamins and minerals—for example, riboflavin, vitamin B6, vitamin B12, folic acid, vitamin D, phosphorous, iodine, magnesium, and zinc.)

   **Student workbook activity.** Have students turn to the student workbook activity to organize the information about their nutrient. Besides filling out the worksheet, students should create a poster, poem, or narrative about the nutrient. Some students may wish to cut out magazine pictures of foods or to take several actual foods from home that are good sources of the nutrient. Other students may enjoy dressing up as their nutrient or as a food that supplies the nutrient.

   Give students the rest of the session to complete the worksheets and to plan and prepare for their presentations. Collect and review the completed worksheets. (This activity is adapted from Michigan Model, Grade 7, Module 1.)

## Session 2

3. Listen to the student descriptions of nutrients. To keep the activity moving along and to give all an opportunity to present, choose one student to be timekeeper.

4. **Closure.** End the lesson by answering the three "Think It Over" questions at the end of "Getting Your Nutrients" in the student book.

> 1. *You need nutrients to grow, for energy, and to repair and maintain your body cells.*
> 2. *Foods that are alike and that do the same things for your body are put into one group. The basic food groups contain all the nutrients needed for healthy eating.*

*Note:* In 2010 the USDA introduced MyPlate, a new symbol and interactive food guidance system. The new food guidance system utilizes interactive technology found on **MyPlate.gov**. MyPlate contains interactive activities that make it easy for individuals to key in their age, gender, and physical activity level so that they can get a more personalized recommendation on their daily calorie level. Teachers may wish to refer to this website to create a sample menu for sixth-grade students.

● ● ● ● ● ● ● ● ● ● ● ● ● ● ● ● ● ● ● ● ● ● ● ● ● ● ● ● ● ● ● ● ● ● ● ● ● ● ● ● ● ● ● ● ● ● ● ● ● ● ●

## Related Activities

1. Have students create a crossword puzzle, acrostic, or word search about the food groups and/or six main nutrients.

2. Make a worksheet based on the Basic Nutrient Chart in the student book. Provide some of the information on the chart, but leave some blanks under each of the three headings for students to fill in.

3. Have students make up a poem or chant about the main nutrients.

   Example:
   Proteins, minerals, vitamins, fat
   And carbohydrates are where it's at!
   And when the N team is in the lead,
   These and water is all you need.

   (Adapted from M.R. CHEP, Michigan State University/Michigan Department of Public Health, 1984.)

4. If the classroom is equipped with computers, obtain computer software that allows students to analyze a meal in terms of nutrients.

# LESSON 4: CHECKING UP ON FATS, SUGARS, AND SALT

## Preparation/Materials

- Student books
- Samples of labels to demonstrate how to check for fat, sugar, and salt content
- Labels from various products—for example cereal, peanut butter, canned soups, tomato products, and crackers. (Request students to bring labels from home. Try to have labels from different manufacturers for the same type of product for comparison.)

## Objective

- Students will become aware of healthy choices connected with fats, carbohydrates, and salt.
- Students will be able to discover the amounts of fats, sugars, and sodium in processed foods by deciphering food labels.

## Lesson

1. **Student book.** Read and discuss "Close-up: Fats," "Close-up: Carbohydrates," and "Be a Sodium Sleuth." The first two sections have suggestions for ways to make wise choices about fats and carbohydrates. The last section raises awareness of the large amounts of salt in processed food and offers some ways to avoid using too much salt.

   During the discussion of fats, look at MyPlate with the class. Ask students to identify which food groups have the most fat and which have the least. Stress that although we need some fat in our diet, we can get what we need if we eat the right amounts from the different food groups. Note, however, that eating too much from groups that contain the most fat isn't healthy either. Recall how a build-up of fatty substances in the blood vessels leads to heart disease. Answer the "Think It Over" questions with the class.

   ### Close-up: Fats / Close-up: Carbohydrates
   1. *Saturated fats most often are of animal origin; they are solid or semisolid at room temperature. Unsaturated fats are of vegetable origin; they are liquid at room temperature.*
   2. *Choose proteins—chicken, turkey, fish, lean meats, and beans—that are lower in fat; cut away visible fat; limit foods that are high in fat; use little or no fat in cooking; check fat content on food labels.*
   3. *Complex carbohydrates contain more nutrients with fewer calories.*

   ### Sodium Sleuth
   1. *Hot dogs, processed cheese, canned soups, canned meats and fish, bacon, condiments such as soy sauce and garlic salt, olives, catsup, any kind of salted snack chip.*
   2. *Answers will vary.*

2. Give students the opportunity to read labels of processed foods to compare kinds and amounts of fat. Also check labels for the amount of sugar and sodium. Review some basic facts about reading food labels: (a) ingredients are listed in order by weight; (b) the term *net weight* refers to the weight of the food, without the packaging.

   To help students spot sugar on the labels, you may wish to make a list on the board of names for student reference (dextrose, glucose, sucrose, fructose, lactose, corn syrup or corn sweetener, molasses). In addition, fatty acids and cholesterol are names for fat products that students may not be familiar with.

3. Have students working in groups compare the same type of product made by different manufacturers (for example, have one group compare two or three kinds of rice cereals). Each group should list the differences it finds. Does one have much more sugar or sodium than another? Students can share their results with the class.

4. **Health notebook.** Ask students to keep a record for three days of the fats they eat. Have them identify whether the fats are saturated or unsaturated. Which type of fat did they eat the most of?

5. **Closure.** Summarize the main lesson ideas about controlling the amounts of animal/saturated fats, sugars, and sodium that we eat. Elicit from students what the label activity showed about how to be good consumers and about the importance of knowing what we're eating.

• • • • • • • • • • • • • • • • • • • • • • • • • • • • • • • • • • • • • • • • • • • • • • • • • •

## Related Activities

1. Ask volunteers to list grocery items that have low-salt substitutes and to make the list available to the class.

2. Make bar graphs to show the amounts of sugar or sodium in three or four different foods.

3. Make posters featuring the suggestions in the student book for limiting fats, sugars, and salt. Encourage them to make up catchy jingles that others will remember. Display the posters in the school hallways.

4. Develop ads for a food low in fat, sugar, or sodium. Steps for developing ads include choosing an audience for the food/ad, deciding the main advertising message, picking key words or thoughts (cover who, what, when, where, and why), and creating the ad.

# LESSON 5: NUTRIENTS AND YOUR CELLS

## Preparation/Materials
- For diffusion demonstration:
  one glass of water
  some ink or other colored liquid
- For filtration demonstration:
  one glass
  ground coffee, a few tablespoons
  hot water
  one paper coffee filter
  one rubber band
- For osmosis demonstration:
  one egg
  small glass tumbler, just large enough to
      hold egg upright
  vinegar, enough to cover half of the egg
  tack and hammer to make a hole in the top
      of the egg

## Objective
- Students will identify diffusion, filtration, and osmosis as the processes by which all cells receive nutrients and oxygen.

## Background
One of the main functions of food is to provide the body with energy. Before food reaches the cells of the body, it must be broken down by the digestive system into substances (nutrients) that the body can use. Then these nutrients pass from the small intestine into the bloodstream. From there the nutrients along with oxygen are delivered to the body's cells. The cell lets in food substances and oxygen, and lets out carbon dioxide and waste products through the cell membrane. This is done through the processes of *diffusion, filtration,* and *osmosis.*

Diffusion allows the passage of a substance by dissolving and diffusing it through the permeable membrane. "Diffusion, in chemistry, is the mixing of the atoms or molecules of one substance with those of another. It is caused by the natural movements of atoms and molecules. It differs from the mixing caused by stirring or shaking or the blowing of the wind" *(World Book Encyclopedia).*

Filtration forces the substance through the membrane.

"Osmosis is the movement of liquid from one solution into another through a membrane that separates them. The process is essential for the survival of living things" *(World Book Encyclopedia).* During osmosis, a liquid passes through a semipermeable membrane. A semipermeable membrane allows only some solutions to pass through, and keeps others out.

Much of this lesson has been adapted from Michigan Model, Grade 6, Phase III.

## Lesson
1. Begin by telling students that this lesson is about how the nutrients in the foods they eat actually arrive inside their body cells. Elicit from students the role of the digestive system in breaking down food and changing it into substances/nutrients the cells can use.
2. Review basic cell facts. Remind students that a human body has millions and millions of cells. *World Book Encyclopedia* says that a human being has more than 10 trillion cells (10,000,000,000,000).

Almost all cells have the same basic parts. Draw a cell on the board, and label its three parts: the membrane (the outer covering that holds the cell parts together), nucleus (the small, round part of the cell near its center that controls the cell's activities), and cytoplasm (the gelatin-like substance that is inside the cell membrane and around the nucleus). Recall that the nucleus also contains the DNA which controls heredity.

Also recall some structures found in the cytoplasm—empty places for storing water, nutrients, and waste, a power station or mitochondria, and lysosomes—chemicals that break down fats and do other important jobs.

Elicit from students basic information they have previously learned about the cell:
- Cells are as different in form and structure as a giraffe and a mouse.
- Cells come in all sizes and shapes. Some are so small that a million could be comfortable on the head of a pin. Others are very large. Cells may be shaped like discs, rods, spheres.
- Review the structure of the body. A cell is the basic unit of the body. Groups of the same kinds of cells group together to make tissues which have a special function. A group of tissues that have a special function are called an organ. Several organs and body parts make up a system. The systems combined make up the body.

Stress that, however, the cell is where the processes take place that keep our bodies working. If we are to be healthy, our cells need to be healthy. They need to receive nutrients to do the job.

3. Write the words *diffusion, filtration,* and *osmosis* on the board. Tell students that these are three processes by which the cells get the nutrients and oxygen they need to stay alive. Explain that although the processes are complicated, these simple demonstrations will give them some idea of how cells absorb nutrients and oxygen from the blood.

- Diffusion. In this process one substance mixes with another by natural movements. To demonstrate diffusion, add ink to a glass of water. The ink moves randomly and gradually into the water. Once the ink is completely mixed with the water, the color of the water becomes the color of the ink. "Each molecule of ink has its own constant and random motion. The motion of the ink molecules causes them to spread through the water. The water molecules also move about and become mixed with the ink molecules." *(World Book Encyclopedia).*

- Filtration. Through this process substances are forced through the cell membrane. To demonstrate filtration, make some coffee using a filter. Place a paper coffee filter over the top of an eight-ounce glass. Push in the center of the filter slightly and then fasten the filter to the outside of the glass with a rubber band. Put ground coffee into the center of the filter, and pour hot water through it. The water is heavier than the air in the glass, so it goes through the paper, together with oils from the coffee. The coffee grounds stay behind. The coffee has been made by filtration. The water was forced through the membrane/filter paper, and because of the contact with the coffee grounds, it looks and tastes different.

- Osmosis. There are materials which will allow some solutions to pass through but keep others out. These are called semipermeable membranes. The process by which some substances pass through such semipermeable membranes is called osmosis. The skin or cell membrane that lines the shell of an egg is an example of a semipermeable membrane.

  Take a short glass tumbler, just large enough to hold an egg upright. Pour in enough vinegar so that half of the egg will be covered. Place the egg in the glass, and let it stand for 24 hours. Then pour out the vinegar and gently lift out the egg, touching only the top part. The bottom of the egg will show some thin parts. Gently rub the bottom of the egg with your finger. The action of vinegar has partly dissolved the shell and made it crumbly. It will easily rub off. Expose some of the skin or cell membrane of the egg. Put the egg back into an empty glass (skin side down), and add enough water to cover the area of exposed skin. Make a puncture or small hole in the top of the egg (using a tack and a gentle tap from a hammer and making sure the skin has been punctured through). After a short time, the white of the egg will ooze out of the top hole. Water has entered the egg from below through the skin, which is a semipermeable membrane. The skin will not let the white of the egg (which is protein) pass through. The water in the bottom of the glass is still clear. Because water has entered the egg, and the white of the egg cannot pass through the skin, it has to go some place, so it seeps out of the hole in the top of the egg.

4. **Closure.** Point out that when we eat nutrients, we are providing our body with what it needs to stay alive. Tell students that the healthier the food we eat, the healthier the body is. The basic unit of the body needs to constantly be supplied with the nutrients and oxygen it needs. Elicit from students the names of the three processes that help to deliver nutrients to the cells (diffusion, filtration, and osmosis).

## Related Activities

1. Study the mitochondria and the process of oxidation in the cells. How does the body maintain its internal temperature?

2. Volunteers may enjoy demonstrating osmosis with an experiment using a sugar solution and water, which is described and illustrated in the *World Book Encyclopedia*.

# LESSON 6: THE DIETING OBSESSION

## Preparation/Materials
- Optional: Magazine pictures of skinny models (if possible, both men and women)
- Some examples of advertisements for over-the-counter weight-loss products
- Student books

## Objectives
- Students will recognize the dangers of strict dieting during growing years.
- Students will identify two eating disorders—anorexia and bulimia.
- Students will grow in self-acceptance and in acceptance of others.

## Background
Two very serious eating disorders are anorexia nervosa and bulimia nervosa. These disorders are related to the fear of obesity and are potentially life threatening, requiring intensive treatment.

Anorexia is a disorder involving self-starvation and extreme obsession with weight. It is characterized by prolonged and severe refusals to eat. The overwhelming fear of becoming obese does not diminish even with radical and obvious weight loss. A person with anorexia sees their body as too fat (even if it is skeleton-like). The condition can lead to irreversible bodily damage and death.

Bulimia is characterized by intense, recurring episodes of binge eating followed by drastic efforts to avoid weight gain, usually including vomiting or using laxatives. Bulimia leads to serious physical problems such as hair loss, erosion of tooth enamel, tooth loss, and irritation or diseases of the digestive system.

*Note:* It is important to adjust this lesson to fit your classroom situation. Be particularly aware of the feelings of students who have weight problems. Handled sensitively, however, this lesson can be helpful in leading class members to accept physical differences.

## Lesson

1. Begin the session by showing pictures of skinny models. Ask students to describe how the models look. Also ask them if this is the way most people look. Is it the way we all should look? What message do the media give about the "right" way to be? *Note:* You may want to leave out pictures and just discuss how media and advertisements generally portray 'attractive' people.

   Talk about how our weight-conscious society wants everyone—especially women—to fit an unrealistic ideal. This pressure causes a lot of hurt. And it leads young people to start trying very early to control their weight. In fact, it often leads to strict dieting that is unhealthy for young people. Some young people have an unhealthy fear of getting fat—even though they aren't overweight at all.

2. **Student book.** Read and discuss "Eating Disorders."

   Look at the diagram of three basic body types, and identify the characteristics of each. Point out that at this time of their lives, students are growing and changing so much that probably they can't even figure out what body type they are. But also point out that not everyone can look like the North American ideal because not everyone has that kind of body shape. An endomorph, who has a rounder shape, is not going to become an ectomorph—no matter how much he or she tries to lose weight. The only way to know if you're at the weight that is best for you is to check with a doctor.

Also make the point that during these years of physical development, class members are going to be different sizes and shapes depending on their different timetables. During puberty young people may suddenly go through a growth spurt—and gain weight. Students can help each other by being kind and by not calling attention to differences.

Stress that this time of the students' life is not the time to diet. List reasons why dieting is not a good idea during growing years (except under doctor's supervision):

- Dieting can stunt your growth. During puberty/adolescence young people need plenty of basic nutrients such as minerals and vitamins for their bones to be strong. Cutting back too far on calories can stunt growth.
- Dieting can interfere with your physical development. A severe lack of nutrients can delay the beginning of puberty. Studies show that strict dieting has this effect. Besides, recall that everyone needs a certain amount of body fat.
- Dieting can lead to eating disorders. Being caught in a harmful cycle of dieting and overeating may lead to the disorders described in the student book.

(These three points are adapted from *Growing and Changing: A Handbook for Preteens* by Kathy McCoy and Charles Wibbelsman, M.D. [Perigee, 1986].)

3. **Health notebook.** Give students a few minutes to write down their responses to the lesson. Be sure to respect student privacy and not press anyone to share responses.

4. Review main ideas of the student reading with the "Think It Over" questions. You may wish to have students write their answers to these two questions.

    1. *Answers should include the importance of eating plenty of food to get nutrients they need at an age when they are developing and changing rapidly. They may also include the possibility of getting caught up in an unhealthy cycle of bingeing and dieting. Stress that even if young people really are overweight, a strict diet at their age should only be undertaken with medical supervision.*

    2. *Anorexia nervosa—limiting food to the point of starvation—and bulimia—bingeing followed by purging; being unreasonably afraid of getting fat, not accepting one's physical self. Keep in mind that anorexia and bulimia may have deep psychological causes, so be careful not to oversimplify the causes.*

5. **Closure.** Stress that although there is nothing wrong with wanting to look our best, constant dieting and unhealthy behaviors around food will not help you in the long run and will cause harm. The way to look our best is to eat a variety of healthy foods and to get enough exercise. You may wish to tie in with the lesson introduction, pointing out that overemphasizing looks and making having a beautiful body all-important is a form of self-worship.

● ● ● ● ● ● ● ● ● ● ● ● ● ● ● ● ● ● ● ● ● ● ● ● ● ● ● ● ● ● ● ● ● ● ● ● ● ● ● ● ● ● ● ● ● ● ● ● ● ● ●

## Related Activities

1. Explore the reasons why people eat. Brainstorm a list of reasons or do a clustering activity. Some reasons to include: being part of a group, relieving boredom, following a habit (for example, always having a snack after school or always eating while watching TV), cheering ourselves up when we're down, rewarding ourselves, doing what's expected of us (social situation). Have students identify which of these reasons have to do with our emotional or mental life and which are part of our social life.

2. Center class devotions or a Bible study on the theme of inward beauty or integrity. Discuss 1 Samuel 16:1-13 (the story of Samuel anointing David), Luke 16:15, and John 2:25.

# LESSON 7: YOUR PHYSICAL BEST

## Preparation/Materials
- For Step 2 activity:
  music to accompany exercising
- Student books
- Student activities 1 and 2

## Objectives
- Students will identify the main parts of health fitness.
- Students will understand the role of each part of health fitness.
- Students will develop a one-week fitness schedule.

## Background
Physical fitness consists of health fitness and skills fitness. Health fitness has four basic components: cardiorespiratory endurance, muscle strength, muscle endurance, and flexibility. "Cardiorespiratory endurance is the increasing capacity of the blood vessels, heart, and lungs to receive blood, to deliver nutrients and oxygen, and to remove waste from working muscles. The ability of muscles to develop tightness and move objects is muscular strength. Flexibility involves the ability to move a limb or body segment through a full range of movement. If over a period of time the muscles' ability to keep pushing an object is improving, then muscular endurance is improving" (M.R. CHEP [Michigan Department of Health, 1984]).

The benefits of physical fitness are tremendous. When we are physically fit, every body part improves in structure and function. The heart and lungs work more efficiently; the heart moves more blood through the body and the lungs hold more air. The body makes better use of nutrients; bones and muscles become stronger.

Other benefits of fitness include more energy for daily activities, better posture, reduced stress levels, and a more positive mental outlook. Overall physical appearance improves, too, which in turn contributes to a healthy self-image. Social health improves as well.

Another important consideration is this: Fit children usually become fit adults (the opposite is probably true as well). The ages 9 to 11 are a crucial period during which children are beginning to grow rapidly and form attitudes and habits towards fitness that they will keep as adults.

Most schools have physical education programs that introduce students to the components of physical fitness. However, students (and families) should be aware that physical education programs at school can only provide a beginning of fitness. Students must begin to take responsibility for their own fitness and plan ways to be active and to exercise. They should also become aware that too much time spent watching television or playing computer games is not healthy.

If your school has a physical education teacher, consult with him or her as you plan these lessons on fitness. However, if your school's physical education program is very limited, you may wish to consider taking more responsibility for physical fitness and to plan to incorporate exercise routines or other fitness activities into the class's daily schedule.

The reference charts at the end of the lesson are adapted from Michigan Model, Grade 7, Module 1, Lesson 6.

• • • • • • • • • • • • • • • • • • • • • • • • • • • • • • • • • • • • • • • • • • • • • • • • • •

## Lesson (2 sessions)

1. Introduce these lessons on physical fitness by asking students about the kinds of exercise they enjoy and how they feel during exercise or active games. Note that the next several lessons will be about physical fitness, particularly about exercise. Ask students to define *physical fitness.* Accept all responses, using them to lead into the student book selection.

2. **Student book.** Begin by reading and discussing "What Is Physical Fitness?" Use the "Think It Over" questions to stimulate discussion about the Christian view of physical fitness. Stress that physical fitness, in particular health fitness, is for everyone—for people of all ages and abilities.

    1. *People being in their individual, physical best condition.*
    2. *Lead a discussion of the Christian view of the body and fitness. As stewards of God's creation, which includes being stewards of our bodies and physical health, we have the responsibility to take care of our bodies. Also, when we are physically fit, we are better able to fulfill our responsibilities to serve God and others. Note, however, that many people in our society use fitness for self-glorification and spend an inordinate amount of time on it.*

3. Introduce the first four parts of health fitness: muscular strength, muscular endurance, flexibility, and cardiorespiratory fitness. Lead the class in an overview of each of these parts of health fitness by having students briefly practice them. Spend about 20 minutes on this activity, using most of the time on an activity promoting cardiorespiratory fitness (aerobic exercise).

    Organize the classroom so that there is room for standing and moving, or move the class to a larger, more suitable space (gym, lunch room, playground, stage of the auditorium). Then lead students through examples of each type of exercise. If possible, play music to go with each type of exercise. The music will make the activity more fun and will help students to focus on the activity.

    Stress that before students do a strenuous exercise routine, it is important to warm up the body first to get muscles and joints ready for action. Warm-up exercises serve to raise the body's temperature, make the muscles more limber, and prevent injury. Review why cool down after exercise is necessary (prevents soreness, helps gradually lower heart rate back to normal).

    • Flexibility. Use a flowing, gentle musical selection with about 80-90 beats a minute. Do some basic reaching and stretching exercises: waist side-bends, toe-touches, arm-reaches, standing stretch, hamstring stretch. Instruct students to relax and breathe comfortably. Don't bounce or jerk. Hold each position for about 10 seconds. (As flexibility improves, students can hold each stretch for 30 seconds.) If it hurts, ease up a little.

- Muscular strength. Use music with a strong, but quite slow beat (such as a march, about 110 to 120 beats a minute). Have the class do exercises such as push-ups or curl-ups. Stress controlled movements to strengthen and tone muscles.

- Muscular endurance. Use music similar to or slightly faster than that used in the previous category. Activities using muscles for longer periods of time than normal build endurance, so repetition is the key here. Keep up the exercise long enough for students get the feel of endurance.

- Cardiorespiratory fitness. Use music that is lively and will keep students moving quickly. Have students warm up, and then lead the class in some aerobic activities such as running in place or jumping rope. Note that to be effective aerobic exercise must be kept up for at least 20 minutes.

### Session 2

4. **Student book.** Read and discuss the material describing the four parts of health fitness introduced in the previous session ("Exercise Improves Your Muscles" and "Exercise and Cardiorespiratory Fitness"). Use the "Think It Over" questions for discussion.

    1. *Exercise that makes the heart and lungs work hard and is kept up for an extended period of time. You may wish to explain that aerobic means "with air." Aerobic exercise is exercise that uses a lot of oxygen. Students should realize that aerobic exercise must be done regularly.*
    2. *Makes the heart muscle stronger. As a result, the heart is able to pump more blood with each heartbeat and can rest longer between beats. Blood vessels are less likely to develop atherosclerosis, or fatty deposits. Chest muscles that work with the lungs become stronger, so lung capacity improves and lungs work efficiently.*

During discussion of the need for cardiorespiratory fitness recall concepts about heart health/heart disease covered in Unit 4. You may wish to have students review this information.

5. **Student workbook activity 1.** Tell students that they will be setting up a one-week fitness/exercise program for themselves. In order to do that, they have to know how to do aerobic exercises correctly. Briefly review the previous session's aerobic practice for physical fitness. Using the teacher reference information "Aerobics, Exercise, and Heart Rate," help students determine their resting heart rate.

Walk the class through the steps of taking their target heart rate. Check to make sure that each student understands how to determine his or her heart rate before (the resting rate) and after exercising.

6. **Student workbook activity 2.** Assign students to use the chart in the workbook activity to make an exercise plan to follow for one week. They should include exercises/activities for building each of the four components discussed/practiced in this lesson.

Urge students to set up a program that encourages fun as well as fitness-building. Consider having students try to include family members in some of their activities. Have students hand in their plans for you (or the physical education director) to review before they get started.

At the end of the week have students assess their fitness plan. Have them write answers to questions such as the following in their health notebooks:

"Did you stick with your fitness activity plan from the beginning to the end of the week? What helped you? What hindered you?"

"Did friends or family members encourage you or discourage you from exercising?"

"Did your resting heart rate change? Explain."

"How do you feel about exercising now?"

"Are there ways you could revise your exercise plan to make it better?"

"What was the most important thing you learned from this activity?"

(This activity is adapted from Michigan Model, Grade 7, Module 1.)

7. **Closure.** Elicit from students the definition of physical fitness and the four parts of health fitness covered in this lesson. Tell students that in the next lesson they'll be learning about body composition and health fitness.

• • • • • • • • • • • • • • • • • • • • • • • • • • • • • • • • • • • • • • • • • • • • • • • • •

## Related Activities

1. Ask students to prepare questions/answers on the lesson materials. The questions can be used for a class quiz or for a partner quiz. Groups of interested students may wish to develop games using their questions.

2. Discuss the physical, mental, and social benefits of exercise. Have students work in groups to discuss and list their ideas. Then meet in full-class session for discussion.

   Some benefits to include for mental health are relieving stress (working off anger, worries, tension), feeling good about self, having a feeling of accomplishment. Social benefits of exercise include opportunities to interact with others in group sports, learning communication in group sports, making new friends. Physical benefits include having better posture, being ability to take part in activities without tiring, preventing diseases (such as heart disease), preventing injury.

3. Have students illustrate the benefits of exercise by making posters or giving skits. Or have them make posters that urge people to exercise and be physically fit.

4. Ask students to write a description of someone who is physically fit. Review the definition of physical fitness—each person being at his or her own physical best.

## How Exercise Can Help Improve Your Heart, Blood, and Blood Vessels

Exercise can

1. Increase the number and size of your blood vessels (better and more efficient circulation).
2. Increase the elasticity of blood vessels (less likelihood of breaking under pressure).
3. Increase the efficiency of exercising muscles and blood circulation (muscles and blood better able to pick up, carry, and use oxygen).
4. Increase the efficiency of the heart (able to pump more blood with fewer beats—better able to meet emergencies).
5. Increase tolerance to stress and promote greater sense of personal control and well-being (this means you will be less likely to be caught in stress-pressure syndrome).
6. Decrease triglyceride and cholesterol levels (less likelihood of fats being deposited on the lining of the arteries).
7. Decrease clot formation (less chance of a blood clot forming and blocking blood flow to the heart muscle).
8. Decrease blood sugar (reduced chance of blood sugar being changed to triglycerides).
9. Decrease obesity and high blood pressure (people who are obese and have high blood pressure are more prone to heart disease).
10. Decrease hormone production (too much adrenaline can cause problems for the arteries).

## Aerobic Exercise and Heart Rate

*Why aerobics?*
Although there are many benefits from aerobic activity, one of the main purposes is to exercise the heart muscle. This is accomplished by raising the working level of the heart with dynamic exercise and maintaining this working level for a period of time. The heart pumps oxygen-rich blood to the muscles as they demand it. During aerobic activity the muscles demand up to 12 times more oxygen than during ordinary activity. Thus, the heart is exercised at a rate determined by muscle movement. This can be measured by ascertaining the heart rate.

*What is a heart rate?*
Simply put, your heart rate is the number of times per minute that your heart pumps fresh blood to the rest of the body.

During aerobic activity the heart rate should be monitored periodically in order to maintain the proper working level, a figure often called "target heart rate."

*What is a target heart rate?*

Target heart rate is the term we give to the working level or training range of the heart during aerobic activity. This figure is usually around 70-85% of the maximum heart rate for your age group. This allows normal metabolic functions of liver, spleen, etc., about 15-30% of the available oxygen supply to continue operations. Target heart rate varies with each individual and should be computed in advance of aerobic activity. This target heart rate should remain the goal during aerobic exercise.

*What is my personal target heart rate?* (See student worksheet "My Target Heart Rate")

*What if I am not working within my target heart rate zone?*

Most experts agree that aerobic activity must be performed for a minimum of 20 minutes during a state in which the oxygen transport system is *challenged*. (The heart is the muscle which pumps the oxygen rich blood through the body as the lungs supply the fresh oxygen.) Normally this is about 70-85% of capacity, however, under certain conditions 60% will often provide the challenge to the body. Recent illness, medication, loss of sleep, de-conditioning, high blood cholesterol, or pregnancy are a few good reasons why your body might feel challenged at a 60% rate. Theoretically, the body will burn more fat at a 60% rate as opposed to an 85% rate because the body can continue to metabolize fat and can work for a longer period of time.

Going over the target heart rate to 90-95% can cause oxygen debt. The hard work of the muscles requires more oxygen than the system can supply. Breathlessness and fatigue set in and cause the muscles to demand so much of the oxygen supply that there is little left for regular body metabolism. The body stops burning fat (a metabolic process) and the oxygen supply must go to the muscles. Once the state of oxygen debt is reached, the body is unable to continue dynamic activity.

*How can I maintain my target heart rate during aerobic activity?*

Monitoring the heart rate regularly is the key to personalizing an aerobic workout and maintaining your target heart rate. This can be achieved with a watch or clock with second intervals. This is the most useful tool in exercising the heart. Make the most of it. Always take your heart rate during the intervals provided during an aerobics class. Make a conscious effort to maintain your personal target heart rate. Any heart rate count which is below your target range can be corrected by increasing speed and size of body movements. Likewise, any heart rate count which is above your target range can be corrected by reducing body movements and slowing down a bit. *Avoid stops and starts* in activity which might cause ups and downs in your rate. Working within your target heart rate range will allow maximum benefits and minimal body stress.

**REMEMBER: AEROBIC EXERCISE MUST BE MAINTAINED FOR AT LEAST 20 MINUTES TO BE EFFECTIVE.**

# LESSON 8: EXERCISE AND BODY COMPOSITION

## Preparation/Materials
- Student books
- Student workbook activity

## Objectives
- Students will define *calorie.*
- Students will recognize the connection between food/calorie intake, level of activity, and body fatness.

## Background
Weight loss diets, which can stunt normal growth and development and possibly lead to serious eating disorders, are harmful to children. Instead, increasing regular physical activity is the way to improve muscle tone and to reduce the chance of developing a weight problem. Activity "burns up" part of the body fat when it has used up the calories provided. More vigorous activities require more energy (and calories) than less vigorous ones. A balance between calories in and calories out helps to keep us at our proper weight.

The calorie used in nutrition to indicate the unit that measures heat production in the body is actually a kilocalorie, or large calorie. It is "the amount of heat needed to raise the temperature of one kilogram of water one degree celsius" (*Foodworks,* 1986). (Note: in technical writing this calorie is spelled *Calorie.* A *Calorie* is 1000 times greater than a calorie (lower case c).)

## Lesson (2 sessions)
1. **Student book.**
   - In the section "Exercise and Body Composition" read and discuss "Good Body Composition Means…"

   - Have students identify the different reasons why the body needs some fat.

   - Write the word *calorie* on the board. Explain that a calorie is a unit of measure. Elicit from students different kinds of measure (a mile/kilometer measures distance, a pound/kilogram measures weight, a gallon/litre measures volume). What does a calorie measure? (The energy or heat that a food produces as well as the amount of energy the body uses during an activity.)

   - Have students identify different types of fuel and how we use them. For example, water and heat make steam—which is energy. What are some things students have seen steam do? (Lift off a radiator cap or a pan lid.) Elicit other examples of fuels that create energy.

   - Read and discuss "Calories In and Calories Out." Ask students to describe in their own words what happens when we take in more calories than we use and how we can balance calories in (food intake) and calories out (activity level).

   Point out that young people around their age need between two and three thousand calories every day. A person who is very active needs more than a person who is less active. In addition, individual needs also vary. Briefly recall the importance of obtaining the necessary calories by eating foods high in a variety of nutrients and not so high in calories.

- Examine the calorie-use chart with the students. Possible discussion questions: "Which activities will use the most calories? Which will use the least? Are you surprised by any of the numbers?"

  Also check the sidebar information on burning off the calories in a candy bar. If students eat three chocolate bars a week, how many minutes will it take to work off the calories? Pose a few other quick math questions that highlight the fact that a candy bar is a high-calorie food.

2. **Student workbook activity.** Divide the class into groups, and assign each group one of the situations on the worksheet to read and discuss. Group members should answer the questions together, with individual students making notes on their own worksheets. Allow about 15 minutes for this activity.

   Lead a class discussion that summarizes the lesson and checks on student understanding of the concept of calories and energy balance. Recall the class discussions about strict dieting being unhealthy for young people in the growing stage of life (Lesson 6). Emphasize the fact that weight is not always a good indicator of body composition. Also, reassure students that gaining weight during these growing and changing years is common. Besides, in most cases it is temporary. As they move through adolescence and become taller, their weight will be redistributed.

   (This group activity is adapted from Michigan Model, Grade 7, Module 1.)

3. Assign students to pick three sports or activities listed on the "Calorie Use Chart" in the student book and to calculate how many calories they would use by doing each activity three times a week—each time for 30 minutes.

4. Use the "Think It Over" questions to review of main lesson concepts. You may wish to make this a written quiz or a quick oral review.

   1. *A person with good body composition has the right amount of fat in comparison to lean body mass, which includes muscles, bones, tissues, and organs.*
   2. *Body fat does important things in the body: helps keep body warm in cold weather, protects internal body organs, stores specific vitamins, and stores energy.*
   3. *Calories in is the amount of calories, or units of energy, in the food we eat; calories out is the amount of calories our bodies use.*
   4. *Regular exercise can help control the amount of body fat by increasing the amount of calories the body uses.*
   5. *This question relates to the chart. People with larger bodies burn more because they need more energy then smaller people to do the same activity.*

## Related Activity

- Health notebook: Have students compare life in North America today with life 50–60 years ago to determine how the daily activity level has changed. Students could compare transportation, methods of doing household chores, and other things. What conclusions can they draw?

# LESSON 9: SKILLS FITNESS

## Preparation/Materials

- Student books
- Decide which activity to use in Step 2. If you wish to do activities demonstrating the six parts of skills fitness, plan what you will do and obtain materials as desired.

## Objectives

- Students will recognize the six parts of skills fitness.
- Students will understand the relation of innate abilities to skills fitness.
- Students will develop in their acceptance of individual differences in physical skills.

## Background

Agility, coordination, balance, speed, power, and fast reaction time are specific skills that are necessary to excel in various sports and jobs. Individual abilities in these skills vary widely.

Some of these differences have to do with body build and with inherited abilities. Nonetheless, determination and effort can help those with limited natural abilities in some areas to develop and improve those areas.

How much effort individual students are willing to invest in developing skills fitness depends on their interests in sports or other activities that require these specific skills. As you teach this lesson, encourage students to judge their personal physical potential and to try to fulfill it. However, make a clear distinction between health fitness and skills fitness. Although skills fitness is part of all-around physical fitness, it is not directly related to health fitness. Individual skills fitness goals may vary from person to person depending on individual needs or interests, but health fitness is necessary for all students.

• • • • • • • • • • • • • • • • • • • • • • • • • • • • • • • • • • • • • • • • • • • • • • • • • • •

## Lesson

1. **Student book.** Read and discuss "Skills Fitness." Go over each skill with the class. Look at the illustrations of the skills, and have students read the captions. Answer the "Think It Over" questions.

    1. *Agility, coordination, balance, speed, power, fast reaction time.*
    2. *Several may be helpful to each job, but these are primary. Brain surgeon/eye-hand coordination; construction worker/agility and balance; computer operator/eye-hand coordination; professional soccer player would need all to be a good player.*

    Discussion. Note that students are still developing and exploring their abilities. Perhaps even though some of these skills may be difficult for them now, as their bodies change the skills may become easier. In addition, make the point that extra effort in a weak area can make a big difference.

    Consider also highlighting the fact that although many of these skills are necessary for various sports, many are also necessary for certain jobs.

2. Do one or more of the following activities:

    - Give the class the opportunity to do some activities that demonstrate the six parts of skills fitness. (Note: The idea is not to measure student abilities in this lesson.)

You may wish to have students rotate through a series of stations. Partners can help each other with measuring and timing. Depending on your classroom situation and your choice of activities, you may be able to do these activities in the classroom.

*Agility*

Line jump. Materials: masking tape. Make a line on the floor with masking tape. Balance right foot on the line. Jump, landing to the right of the line on left foot. Jump, landing to the left of the line on right foot. Jump again, this time landing on the line on left foot. Try doing this sequence two-three times.

Shuttle run (measures running agility). Materials: two blocks of wood (2 inches by 2 inches by 4 inches), stopwatch. Mark two parallel lines on the ground about 30 ft. apart. Place the wood blocks behind one of these lines. Start at a parallel stance behind the start line (opposite the blocks). Lean weight on one foot prior to pushing off. At the signal "go," run from the starting line to the blocks. Pick up one of the blocks, run back to the starting line, and place (not throw) the block behind the starting line. Then make one more run to get the second block and carry it back across the starting line. The time stops as the runner crosses the starting line with the second block. Record time to the nearest tenth of a second. Do this twice.

*Balance*

Hopping. Close eyes and try a hopping activity. For example, stand on one foot and hop backward (at least five times). At the end of the last hop, keep standing on the same foot, balancing for at least two seconds. Repeat the exercise, this time with the other foot.

*Coordination*

Juggling. Materials: two rubber balls. Try juggling two balls. (Students who are good at this might want to try three.)

Wall kick (eye-foot coordination). Stand behind a line 5m from a wall, kick the ball to the wall and then kick it again on the rebound. Trap the ball with feet and kick from behind the line. Place an extra ball 5 m behind the line to count the number of times the ball hits the wall in 30 seconds. Do this twice; record the best attempt.

*Speed*

Running in place. Materials: stopwatch. Stand with legs slightly apart. At a signal run in place for 10 seconds. A partner can be the timekeeper; the jogger can count the number of steps (one count for each time a foot touches the floor). Record the best of two attempts.

45-M dash. Stand in a parallel stance behind the start line. Lean weight on one foot prior to pushing off. At the signal, run as fast as possible to the finish line. Record the number of seconds (to the nearest tenth of a second) it takes to complete the dash.

*Reaction time*

Flip and react. Materials: cardboard or paper tube. Place the tube on a table so that almost half of it extends beyond the table surface. Hit the end of the tube to flip it off the table. The idea is to catch the tube in the air. Do this five times and record number of catches.

*Power*

Wall jump. Stand sideways to a wall and extend arm (usually side with dominant hand) up a high as possible. Mentally, or with a piece of chalk, mark the spot on the wall. Then drop arm, bend knees, and jump as high as possible. If you wish, have students also mark the wall with chalk at the peak of their jump. Then measure the distance between the reach mark and the jump mark (to the nearest half inch). Allow time to practice before measuring.

Standing broad jump. Make a mark on the floor with masking tape. Lie down and place heels up to the line. Then place a mark on the floor at the top the head. Standing at one line, try to jump beyond the second line. Stand with toes against the line, bend knees, and swing arms forcefully backward. Then swing arms forward and outward while jumping.

- **Health notebook.** Ask students to write about an activity they now enjoy or would like to learn. Which of the skills discussed in this lesson would they like to develop or which would they need? What kind of practice would help them to achieve their goal?

- Have students design a fitness course that includes activities that use the various elements of physical fitness. Give them the opportunity to lay out the course in the gymnasium or playground and to enjoy using the course. You may wish to keep track of how often students use the course, number of repetitions at each station, and so on. Perhaps establish a point system. Designing a fitness course makes a good culminating activity for the lessons on physical fitness. If students have done this in fourth or fifth grade, point out that now they should be able to make a more sophisticated design—one that takes into account what they have learned about health fitness and skills fitness.

3. **Closure.** Elicit from students the six parts of skills fitness. Make the point that our interests will help us determine which parts of skills fitness we want to work on and develop. Stress that, in contrast, health fitness is something for everyone to develop.

●  ●  ●  ●  ●  ●  ●  ●  ●  ●  ●  ●  ●  ●  ●  ●  ●  ●  ●  ●  ●  ●  ●  ●  ●  ●  ●  ●  ●  ●  ●  ●  ●  ●  ●  ●  ●  ●  ●  ●  ●  ●  ●  ●  ●

## Related Activity

- Ask volunteers to research the training programs of athletes in different sports. What kinds of training programs do they have? Sports magazines are good sources of this kind of information.

# LESSON 10: SHINY BRIGHT AND SMELLING RIGHT

## Preparation/Materials
- Student books
- Magazines that contain advertisements for personal care products, several for each student group

## Objectives
- Students will recognize the relationship between good hygiene and appearance.
- Students will identify key considerations in selecting body, hair, and dental care products.

## Background
Much of the material for Lesson Steps 2 and 3 have been adapted from Michigan Model, Grade 7, Module 1.

• • • • • • • • • • • • • • • • • • • • • • • • • • • • • • • • • • • • • • • • • • • • • • • •

## Lesson (2 sessions)

1. Ask students what shiny, clean hair, fresh breath, clean teeth, and smelling good have to do with living a healthy lifestyle. (They are all part of personal daily health care.) Note that personal daily health care not only contributes to good health, but also to appearance. "Looking good" and good personal health habits are closely connected.

   Highlight the fact that as students grow up, their changing body means they need to pay closer attention to personal health care. Sweat glands are becoming more active, and underarm perspiration may be noticeable. Skin is becoming oily. Teeth need special attention because at this age young people are likely to get cavities. Consider describing some old tactics that won't work anymore.

   > *Fake baths.* Splashing water on your hands or face or feet (or wherever else your parents are likely to check or notice) and pretending that you took a bath or shower.
   > *Underwear marathons.* Seeing how long you can wear one pair of underwear before your mother notices.
   > *Toothbrush Tease.* Wetting your toothbrush to make people think you brushed your teeth—when you really didn't.
   > *The After-Gym Sprint.* Dashing out of gym class ahead of everyone else to avoid taking a shower.

   (Taken from *Growing and Changing: A Handbook for Preteens* by Kathy McCoy and Charles Wibbelsman, M.D. [Perigee, 1986].)

2. **Student book.**
   - Divide the class into three groups. Provide several magazines with personal product ads to use to trigger student awareness of advertising approaches and relevant

hygiene facts. Have students read the following articles in the student book: "Healthy Hair," "Keep Smiling," and "Smelling Good." Then assign one of the topics—Hair Care, Oral/Dental Hygiene, and Body Odor Control—to each group. Using personal experience, the magazines, and the articles, each group should make a list of at least four things to consider when buying or using a body care product. (Allow about 10 minutes for this activity.)

| Body Odor Control | Hair Care | Oral/Dental Hygiene |
|---|---|---|
| Means of application? (spray, roll-on, stick, etc.) | Designation according to hair type or texture? (e.g., dry, oily, etc.) | Type of tooth brush? Waxed or unwaxed floss? Toothpaste or gel? Mouthwash? |
| Ingredients? | Ingredients? | Ingredients? Fluoride? Whitener? Tartar Control? |
| Effectiveness?<br>• Will it keep me dry? (antiperspirant)<br>• Will it control odor? (deodorant) | Effectiveness? Detangling or conditioning properties? | Effectiveness? Plaque removal? Fresh breath? |
| Scented-Unscented? | Dandruff control? | Flavor? |
| Recommended by? | Recommended by? | Recommended by? |
| Packaging? | Packaging? | Packaging? |
| Cost? | Cost? | Cost? |

Examples of some considerations:

• Have student groups make up a name for a new deodorant, shampoo, or toothpaste and develop a slogan to promote it (based on items identified in the previous step). They can decide how to present their product to the class (advertisement drawn on the board or a poster, group skit, and so on). They should also have a spokesperson prepare to tell the important considerations that the group identified.

• Have groups (or an individual representative from each group) present their product, slogan, and key considerations. Before each group presents, give the rest of the class copies of the appropriate Student Activity handout for reference and for making notes. (Allow about half an hour for this second part of the activity.)

3. Discussion questions:
   - "What techniques do advertisers commonly use to make you buy their body care products?" (Exaggeration, "perfect" models, statistics, doctor recommendation, celebrity endorsement, "sex appeal," economy, effectiveness, and so on.)
   - "Which techniques actually have influenced you to buy one product instead of another?"
   - "Which techniques 'turn you off'?"
   - "How knowledgeable do you think the average consumer is about the health effects or the hygiene facts that underlie smart choices of one body care product over another?"

4. **Student book.** Assign students to read "Dental Health Facts" to review the problems of tooth decay, gum disease, and proper brushing techniques. Have them answer the "Think It Over" questions.

   1. *By removing the sources of infection: plaque, sugar, and bits of food. Bacteria in plaque use sugar in foods to form acids that destroy enamel, penetrate the tooth, and lead to cavities.*
   2. *Calculus is hardened plaque; once calculus builds up under the gum line it can cause gums to separate from teeth and allow bacteria to attack the bone supporting teeth; a dentist must remove calculus using a special instrument.*
   3. *Answers will vary. Students should include diet, frequency of snacking, and poor brushing and flossing habits.*

5. Review proper care of eyes and ears. Cleaning eyes should be gentle (soap and other chemicals can cause irritation). Any infection which causes the eye to become red, painful, swelled, or teary, or the vision to be blurry requires medical attention. Ears (in, around, and behind) should be cleaned with a washcloth each day. Avoid putting anything in the ears other than a washcloth, because anything smaller might get lodged inside the ear and damage it. If earwax builds up, it should be cleaned away carefully. If it gets packed down, it can cause earache, loss of hearing, or ringing in the ears. Never scrape in or around the ears or poke sharp objects in them. This can damage or infect the eardrum. A buildup of wax should be syringed out by a doctor.

6. Summarize the main ideas of the lesson: During teen years when hormonal changes are occurring and people commonly have problems with perspiration, oily hair, or dental disease, it is good to know that with a little careful label reading and knowledge of hygiene facts, we can be shiny bright and smelling right!

• • • • • • • • • • • • • • • • • • • • • • • • • • • • • • • • • • • • • • • • • • • • • • • • •

## Related Activity

- Review the relationship of good hygiene practices to the prevention of infectious diseases. Particularly emphasize the importance of not sharing personal hygiene items with others and washing hands before handling food and after using the toilet.

# LESSON 11: SKINFORMATION

## Preparation/Materials
* Write a scrambled word on the board (see Step 1)
* Box labeled Rumor Box (shoe box size is fine)
* Student books
* Bell and buzzer or horn

## Objectives
* Students will review basic facts about the nature and functions of the skin.
* Students will differentiate between facts and myths about common adolescent skin problems, including acne, cold sores, athlete's foot, and warts.
* Students will consider the impact of tanning on the skin, including the long-term risk of skin cancer from too much sun during their youth.

## Background
The skin is the body's first line of defense. Because it protects against injuries and infections, it is important to look after the skin. Proper care for skin will keep it supple and strong. However, the changing body of an adolescent requires special skin care. Because sweat glands become more active and the skin becomes more oily at this stage, daily baths or showers are important. It is necessary to wash away sweat and oil so that the pores of the skin do not clog with dirt and oil.

Athlete's foot is a fungal infection that causes itching and burning spots on the feet and often blisters between the toes. This infection occurs when a person's feet are constantly hot, sweaty, and moist. It is important to avoid wearing the same shoes every day, especially if they are non-ventilated running shoes. Wearing cotton socks or applying baby powder to keep feet dry will aid in avoiding infection.

In adolescence, hormone levels increase, which in turn causes the many oil glands in the skin to become more active. When excess oil blocks the pores of the skin, blackheads and pimples are created—often resulting in acne. To deal with this problem, young people should wash the face twice a day to remove oil and bacteria from the skin and to keep the pores open. Hair should be washed frequently also to remove excess oil from the scalp and face area. In washing the affected areas, be careful not to dry out the skin. Skin needs some oil to stay soft and healthy. Very dry skin may crack, which allows bacteria to enter and cause infection. If acne does not respond to proper skin care, a dermatologist may need to prescribe special treatment.

Long time exposure to the sun's ultraviolet rays makes you more likely to suffer from skin cancer and have lined, prematurely aged skin. Special precautions are necessary, particularly with the reduction of the ozone layer. It is important to stay out of the sun when the rays are most direct, between 10:00 A.M. and 2:00 P.M. A sunscreen provides a barrier to prevent the sun's harmful rays from penetrating the skin. A high SPF level of sunscreen is particularly important for fair-skinned individuals.

Warts are a common viral infection of the skin, which are found on the hands, knees, and soles of feet. A doctor can remove them or give advice about over-the-counter products.

Cold sores or fever blisters are also caused by a virus. They usually occur with a fever or cold, or can follow exposure to the sun and wind. Although they usually clear up within one week, recurrent cold sores may be more serious and should be examined by a doctor.

It is important to always consult a doctor if anything unusual happens to your skin. Good skin care can keep skin looking wonderful and healthy for years.

## Lesson

1. Write the following scrambled words on the chalk board before class:

   | | |
   |---|---|
   | XPCOLOIENM | (Complexion) |
   | ECAN | (Acne) |
   | SARWT | (Warts) |
   | HSEELATT TOFO | (Athlete's Foot) |
   | RUSNUBN | (Sunburn) |
   | LOCD OSERS | (Cold sores) |

   Start the class by giving students two minutes to figure out the scrambled words. Tell students you'll give them a hint: all have to do with their skin, or XPCOLOIENM (point to the first word on the board). Ask if anyone can guess what the word is. If no one can quickly decipher the word, provide the answer *complexion.* Then give students time to figure out each of the others. Provide clues as necessary to speed up this warm-up activity.

2. Note that each of skin problems written on the board are of special concern to young people and that in this lesson the class will learn more about these problems. First of all, the class is going to think about various things they have heard about the cause, cure, or prevention of these problems.

   - Ask students to take out a piece of paper, tear it into three pieces, and on each piece write a complete sentence that states something they have heard about these skin problems.

     Examples:
     cause—Chocolate causes acne.
     cure—You can cure warts by rubbing a quarter over them three times a day.
     prevention—To avoid warts, don't touch mushrooms.

   - Collect the slips of paper and place them in a TRUE/FALSE or RUMOR box.

3. **Student book.** Assign students to read the following articles in the student book: "Basic Skin Facts," "Acne Facts," "Sun and Skin Facts," and "Other Common Skin Problems." Tell students that in a few minutes they'll do a rumor exercise, but in preparation they should read over the articles. Provide time for students to do the reading.

4. Choose a panel of students to discuss the statements about skin. Consider selecting four students for the panel and one student to be the moderator. Have the panel sit at the front of the class. The moderator should take one statement and read it aloud to the class. Then the panel should decide whether the statement is true or false, or whether they don't know.

Have both a bell and a buzzer (or toy horn) of some sort to signal correct and incorrect panel responses. Ring the bell if the panel response is correct, and sound the buzzer or horn if the response is wrong or questionable. Use this as an opportunity to step in and clarify misconceptions or raise questions if there is not enough information to determine the correct answer.

Be prepared for a wide variety of ideas about causes, cures, and prevention of the skin problems. If some very unusual statements surface, ask for a volunteer to research the question and share the findings with the class tomorrow. This activity should be fun, lively, and encourage critical thinking.

Close the activity by noting that our ideas about health care may be based on unreliable information—on rumors, made-up cures, and so on. Stress that reliable information is available from nurses or doctors or from resources in the library, etc. Also point out that complexion problems are normal for adolescents. As they have learned, acne can begin around age 11 and disappear around age 20. Some people never have it, but some people do. Students can control acne with good skin care practices.

4.  **Health notebook.** Assign students to list as many good skin care practices as they can—based on the class discussion and handouts.

• • • • • • • • • • • • • • • • • • • • • • • • • • • • • • • • • • • • • • • • • • • • • • • •
## Related Activities

1.  Have students create a how-to manual for adolescent skin care. The manual can include basic information about skin care, an advice column, and cartoons or jokes.

2.  Review ways to take care of other sense organs, such as eyes and ears.

# LESSON 12: TIME OUT

## Preparation/Materials
- Choose activity for Step 6
- Art materials for activity in Step 6, as desired

## Objective
- Students will develop their understanding of the role of sleep and recreation in a healthy lifestyle.

• • • • • • • • • • • • • • • • • • • • • • • • • • • • • • • • • • • • • • • • • • • • • • • • • • • • •

## Lesson

1. Ask students to recall the last time they got less sleep than usual. How did they feel? Accept all responses.

2. Have students draw cartoons or comic strips showing how people feel and act when they don't get enough sleep.

3. Give students an opportunity to share their cartoon ideas. On the board write the words *physical, mental/emotional,* and *social.* Do their cartoons show physical, emotional, or social results of lack of rest? (Physical results: tiredness, sleepiness, difficulty keeping eyes open, headache; mental/emotional results: crying or getting angry easily, feeling irritable, having a hard time thinking and concentrating; social results: being uncooperative, needing extra help/support, affecting others in a negative way.) What might be the spiritual results if someone consistently ignores sleep needs?

4. Briefly review some of the important things that happen during sleep. Use the following information as basis for discussion questions.
   - Heart rate, breathing rate, and some other body processes slow down.
   - With these processes slowed down, the body has more energy to build and repair body cells.
   - Muscles and other body parts get a rest from activity.
   - About an hour of dreaming takes place during a night's sleep. According to experiments, people dream about four or five times a night. Each period of dreaming lasts anywhere from a few minutes to about a half hour. Much about dreaming is still a mystery, but scientists do know that dreaming is very important to health. Experiments show that when people are awakened and not allowed to dream, they become very tired and irritable.
   - We cannot make up for lost sleep. Sleeping late on Saturday morning does not make up for other short nights. The healthiest sleeping schedule is sleeping about the same amount time each day.
   - People need varying amounts of sleep. Most sixth graders need about nine to ten hours a night.

5.  Use the following questions to stimulate thinking about the need for relaxation in order to reduce fatigue:
    *   "What about time out during the day? When might we need time out from daily schedules to relax in order to reduce fatigue?" (Define *fatigue* as a feeling of weariness or extreme tiredness.)
    *   "What might cause you to feel mentally tired? Why do we have breaks in the school schedule?"
    *   "What other things might cause a person to feel tired?" (Emotional upsets, worry, anxiety, stress.)
    *   "What message does fatigue give us?" (That we need a change.)
    *   "How can planning help reduce these kinds of tiredness?" (Talk about how lack of planning creates stress.)

6.  Do one or more of the following activities.
    *   Make individual plans, or schedules, for the next day. Have students make sure they allow time not only for everything they must do but also for relaxation. Have students follow the plan the next day. Discuss results. How does good planning help to reduce stress/emotional fatigue?
    *   Write paragraphs describing activities students enjoy doing for relaxation. Or have students write about an experience that caused them to feel very fatigued. What kind of fatigue did the experience cause? What would be a good way to get over the fatigue?
    *   Make time-out mobiles. Students can work in groups to make the mobiles. Encourage them to use their creativity to show the importance of rest for a healthy lifestyle. Make magazines available in case groups wish to use magazine pictures.

7.  **Closure.** Summarize lesson concepts. Stress that consistently not getting enough rest damages health. Encourage students to take responsibility for getting the rest they need to enjoy each day's activities.

●　●　●　●　●　●　●　●　●　●　●　●　●　●　●　●　●　●　●　●　●　●　●　●　●　●　●　●　●　●　●　●　●　●　●　●　●　●　●　●　●　●

## Related Activities

1.  Have students chart their sleeping times. Do they notice a difference in the amount of sleep they need depending on the weather, day of the week, amount of stress?

2.  Ask students to research and report on some of the following topics connected with sleep: why babies need so much sleep, why people yawn, diseases connected with sleep (for example, narcolepsy), the different stages of sleep.

3.  Construct sleep-related math problems. For example, compute the number of hours spent sleeping in a week, a month, or a year. Compute how many days of a year are spent sleeping.

# LESSON 13: HOW ARE YOU DOING?

## Preparation/Materials
- Student workbook activity
- Unit evaluation in student workbook

## Objectives
- Students will take inventory of basic aspects of a healthy lifestyle.
- Students will develop goals to improve their health practices.
- Students will review unit concepts.

• • • • • • • • • • • • • • • • • • • • • • • • • • • • • • • • • • • • • • • • • • • • • • • • •

## Lesson

1. **Student workbook activity.** Have students complete the health survey. Explain that this survey will help them to evaluate how they are doing in the basic health practices covered in this unit. Tell students that these surveys will not be graded or seen by others. Students can figure their scores by adding up the total number of checks in each section.

   Discuss how to interpret the scores. Explain that the scores give them an idea about how they are doing presently in maintaining and promoting their own health.

   Encourage students to bring the surveys home to discuss with their parents. Students who have very low scores in one area may need help from parents to make changes.

2. **Unit evaluation.** Use the worksheets to review and evaluate.

   *Fill in the blanks:*
   1. large intestine; 2. salt; 3. physically fit; 4. carbohydrates; 5. cardiorespiratory; 6. Flexibility; 7. Saturated; 8. Proteins; 9. minerals; iron; 10. The six skills are agility, coordination, balance, speed, power, and fast reaction time.

   *Short Answer:*
   1. Complex carbohydrates contain more nutrients with fewer calories; they also contain fiber. Simple carbohydrates are generally high in calories, but contain few or no nutrients.
   2. Muscular strength, muscular endurance, cardiorespiratory fitness, flexibility, and good body composition.
   3. Saturated fats, which come from animal sources, are high in cholesterol. Eating too much saturated fat appears to increase the amount of cholesterol in the blood, which, in turn, may lead to the buildup of plaque on the walls of the body's blood vessels.
   4. By doing aerobic exercises at least three times a week for 20–30 minutes each time.
   5. Eating from all the food groups is necessary to obtain all the nutrients the body needs to function at its best.

6. *Possible student answers include the following: Add little or no salt at the table or during cooking; flavor foods by using a variety of herbs; limit intake of salty foods such as potato chips; check on salt content of processed foods by reading food labels; use low-salt products.*

7. *Exercise helps control the amount of body fat by increasing the amount of calories the body uses.*

8. *Possible answers include the importance of eating plenty of food in order to get the nutrients needed during this time of physical growth and development. In addition, a cycle of drastic dieting and then bingeing may lead to more serious eating disorders.*

9. *Possible answers include regular brushing, flossing, eating teeth-healthy foods and limiting sweets, regular dental visits.*

10. *Sleep gives your body a chance to build and repair body cells; it gives your muscles and other body parts a rest from activity; it also gives you the dreaming time you need to stay healthy.*

11. *Changes of puberty bring more active sweat glands, stronger body odors, underarm perspiration, oily skin, and oily hair. Frequent showers and shampoos and use of antiperspirants become more important.*

*Short essay:*

1. *Answers will vary. Student answers should reflect awareness of the responsibility we have to care for the body God has given us and to use our bodies to honor God.*

## Related Activities

1. Health notebook: Students may wish to chart their progress or ways they are working to improve their lifestyle with a graph, timetable, or health log. This will encourage them by providing a visual reminder of their goals and accomplishments.

2. Create acrostics based on a word such as *fitness.* Use each letter to begin a sentence about a health practice. Make a list of key unit words students should incorporate into the sentences *(nutrients, food groups, fats, salt, sugar, cardiorespiratory fitness, flexibility, strength, endurance, body composition, exercise, personal health care, plaque, calculus, sleep, fatigue.)*

# Unit 7

# Drugs and Your Health

# Goals

- Students will develop an understanding of the harmful effects of substance abuse.
- Students will develop an understanding of the way substance abuse affects others.
- Students will choose not to misuse or abuse drugs.

# Background

According to current statistics, 26 percent of children now starting kindergarten will use alcohol before they have finished grade 4. By grade 6, one in six will have used marijuana. Children are using drugs at a much younger age than in previous generations. And they are getting addicted faster because the drugs are so powerful.

One important factor is that drugs are so readily available now. At one time children would have had difficulty knowing where to find drugs. These days children are a targeted market.

Another factor is that the media fosters a substance-dependent mindset. TV and other media bombard children with commercials that encourage reaching for pill bottles to ease discomfort. Commercials and advertisements promote the use of alcohol to relax and have a good time.

Teachers have a vital role in helping children develop the right attitudes toward substances. Use this unit to arm students with convincing reasons for not abusing substances and to introduce them to ways of saying no.

# Vocabulary

Plan to integrate the following vocabulary:

| | | | |
|---|---|---|---|
| internal balance | neurotransmitter | synapse | chemical reaction |
| neuron | dendrite | tolerance | withdrawal |
| dependence | medicine | depressant | over-the-counter |
| stimulant | hallucinogen | inhalant | prescription medicine |
| steroid | cannabis | narcotic | alcoholism |

# Unit Resources (Search online for similar resources if these are no longer available.)

"Lessons and Activities for Teaching Kids About Drugs." Best Drug Rehabilitation, 2015.
  http://bestdrugrehabilitation.com/.
  This drug and alcohol rehab facility links resources and materials, lesson plans, and activities that cover a variety of drugs; suitable for grades 5–12.

The Children & Teens section of drugabuse.gov provides a variety of videos and informative sections.

"Substance Use." American Academy of Pediatrics.
  healthychildren.org.
  Articles written for teens, but this substance use section would be suitable for most ages.

"Videos on Drugs and Addition." Scholastic.
  http://headsup.scholastic.com/students/video-collection.
  A variety of short videos about drug abuse.

# Lesson Resources (Search online for similar resources if these are no longer available.)

### Lessons 1–2

"Inhalant Prevention: Lesson Plans for 4th Grade and Above." Utah Poison Control Center.
> https://poisoncontrol.utah.edu/.

"Drug Facts." National Institute on Drug Abuse.
> https://teens.drugabuse.gov/teens/drug-facts.
> This page provides information and answers frequently asked questions for commonly abused drugs, written for middle school to high school students.

"Activities, Games, and More Games: Drug Use and Effects." National Institute on Drug Abuse.
> https://teens.drugabuse.gov/teens/games.
> Review games about the dangers of drug use and abuse.

### Lessons 3–5

"Resources: Alcohol and its effects (physical and social)." Alcohol Education Trust.
> https://alcoholeducationtrust.org/.
> Includes teacher notes, lesson plans, printable activities.

*Teacher's Guide: Alcohol (Grades 6 to 8)*. The Nemours Foundation/KidsHealth, 2016.
> classroom.kidshealth.org.
> This PDF links articles, lists questions, and includes worksheets.

### Lesson 6

*Teacher's Guide: Peer Pressure (Grades 6 to 8)*. The Nemours Foundation/KidsHealth, 2016.
> classroom.kidshealth.org.
> Lesson plan, articles, activities, and questions related to peer pressure with alcohol and drugs.

"Facts on Drugs: Teen Guide to Making Smart Decisions." Scholastic, 2008.
> http://headsup.scholastic.com/.
> This page has links about peer pressure and making decisions.

"15 Ways a Teen Can Say No to Alcohol and Drugs." American Addiction Centers Resources, 2010.
> https://www.treatmentsolutions.com/.

"Saying No! A Drug Prevention Lesson." Education World, 2011.
> https://www.educationworld.com/.

# LESSON 1: KEEPING YOUR BALANCE

## Preparation/Materials

- Student books
- Nerve Cell Teacher Visual. Enlarge the visual of the nerve cell or make a transparency to use on the overhead.
- Student workbook activity
- Samples of labels of several over-the-counter medications that contain warnings of side effects.
- Optional: a completed copy of Unit 4, Lesson 2, workbook activity 8 of nervous system diagram to use as a visual

## Objectives

- Students will understand how the body works to maintain internal balance.
- Students will develop an understanding of the role of the nervous system in maintaining internal body balance.
- Students will recognize that medicines and other drugs affect that balance.

## Background

The body is constantly making adjustments to maintain internal balance. The nervous system has the primary role in this delicate balancing act. This lesson helps students to understand the importance of internal balance and the effects of interfering with it.

• • • • • • • • • • • • • • • • • • • • • • • • • • • • • • • • • • • • • • • • • • • • • • • •

## Lesson (2 sessions)

1. **Student book.** Ask students to turn to the section entitled "Drugs and Your Health." Read and discuss "Keeping Your Balance."

   You may need to spend some time explaining the idea of internal balance. Describe or elicit from the class some activities in which balance is important (for example, performing on a balance beam or tightrope walking). Or have students try standing on one leg with their eyes closed to experience trying to keep in balance. Make a comparison to what goes on inside the body.

2. **Student workbook activity.** Give a mini-lecture about the nervous system's role in maintaining internal body balance. Illustrate with an overhead or an enlarged copy of the nerve cell made from the visual in the Teacher Resources section. Have students complete the worksheet as you identify and explain each part of the nerve cell.

   Use the following teaching strategies and information as appropriate for your class.

   Review the main parts of the nervous system: brain, spinal cord, and nerves. Explain that the nervous system helps keep the body in balance by sending messages between different parts of the body. It also processes the information coming into the body.

   To help students understand how the nervous system works, compare it to a telephone network. The brain is the central computer or switchboard of the system. The nerves are the telephone wires, running from the brain to the individual telephones (or parts of the body) and back to the brain. They carry information from the mouth, ears, eyes, and skin telling the brain what's going on outside the body. Then they carry instructions from the brain to muscle cells telling them what to do (voluntary movements). But many of the messages in this system control what goes on inside your body—without your being aware of it. What are some of these internal processes that the brain controls? (Heart rate, feelings of hunger and thirst, breathing, thinking and feeling, growth rate, sexual development, amount of fluid in the body, and internal balance.)

Each nerve consists of long, thin cells called neurons. Each neuron (like other cells) has a main part, a cell body with a nucleus. From the cell body several dendrites and one long feeler, called an axon, branch out. (Some neurons—for example, those in the brain—have short axons; other neurons—for example, those running from the spinal cord down the leg may be over three feet/one meter long.) The dendrites receive messages from other cells. The axon links each nerve cell/neuron to other nerve cells and to muscle cells. It carries the message away from the cell body to the dendrites of other neurons (or to muscles or glands).

Messages travel along the nerves in a way similar to the way messages are sent along telephone wires—by electrical signals. When the signal reaches the end of an axon, it must jump across a gap, or synapse, to reach the dendrite of the next nerve cell (neurons do not directly touch each other). To do this the electrical signal is changed into a chemical message. The chemicals pass the message across the gap, or synapse, to the next nerve cell. The chemicals that form the message are called neurotransmitters. This chemical message is received by the end of the dendrite of another neuron. The message is changed back into an electrical signal by the dendrite. The time it takes for the message to jump the gap between nerve cells takes about 1/10,000 of a second.

Stress that the nervous system is of enormous importance in maintaining the body's balance. It is constantly sending messages to and from the body systems to make small or large adjustments—mostly without our conscious control—to keep the body in balance. Lead students to understand that any interference in this system will upset the internal balance of the body.

Provide a few examples of how the body responds to try to restore body balance. (A cut activates white blood cells, platelets, etc. to converge and try to stop the bleeding and prevent infection. Blood vessels are automatically closed by the process of clotting. The body also reacts to changes in temperature to keep internal body balance. When the body starts getting too cold, blood vessels near the skin constrict to keep blood away from body's surface and conserve heat. When the body gets too warm, the vessels widen to get more blood to the surface. Perspiration also helps cool the body.)

At this point you may wish to have students complete the Student Activity worksheet by describing in their own words how the message is carried from one nerve cell to another.

*Note:* Consider ending the first session at this point and doing Steps 3–7 in a second session.

3. **Student book.** Read and discuss "Medicines and the Body's Balance." Tie in the discussion to material covered in the previous session on internal balance with questions such as the following.

    • "What are some ways that medicines work to help the body maintain or restore balance?" (Help—with vaccines—to form antibodies that kill germ invaders, help fight infections, and help various body parts/systems to function within normal range—for example, if blood pressure is too high, medicines can help bring it back to normal range, etc.)

    • "What is the effect on the body of taking medicines you don't need?" (Would most likely upset body balance. A healthy body is already in balance. Use example of medication for high blood pressure.)

4. Use the "Think It Over" questions to review the class's understanding of medicines and their proper use. Consider assigning pairs to answer the questions before going over the material with the class.

    1. *A drug causing changes in your body; medicines are meant to help the body restore internal balance.*
    2. *Each individual's body chemistry is unique.*
    3. *Over-the-counter medicines, or OTCS, can be bought without a prescription; prescription medicines are stronger medicines that can be obtained only with a prescription. Ask students to provide examples of each type of medicine.*
    4. *By not following directions on drug container labels—both prescription and OTCS, by self-diagnosing and using others' medications, by taking OTCs when you don't need them. Stress that medications contain chemicals that change the body's chemical balance. Also stress first trying other ways of dealing with minor upsets—such as eating, rest, and/or exercise.*
    5. *Guidelines to include: Not taking medicine without the permission of a responsible adult; reading medicine labels and following directions; being aware of possible side effects; discontinuing the use of medicines that have surprising side effects and checking with an adult and a doctor; not taking others' prescription medications; keeping labels on containers and medicines in correct containers; keeping medicines out of reach of small children.*

5. Allow students to examine the warning labels of some OTCs to reinforce the idea that over-the-counter medications can affect the body's internal balance.

6. Have students (possibly working in groups) identify ways to deal with minor problems without taking medicine. For example, what could they do for muscle aches and pains,

upset stomach, or a garden-variety headache? After group discussions, have spokespersons report to the class. (Or have students demonstrate one or more solutions with a skit.) Student suggestions might include eating and/or drinking something, resting or sleeping, relaxing in some enjoyable way, getting exercise, changing routine in some way. Discuss whether these are things that students actually do or whether they are more likely to reach for painkillers or other medications. Note, however, that students should report any persistent problems—even though they may appear minor—to an adult. It is important to seek reliable medical care for persistent problems.

7. **Closure.** Summarize (elicit from students) basic ideas about body balance covered in the lesson.

● ● ● ● ● ● ● ● ● ● ● ● ● ● ● ● ● ● ● ● ● ● ● ● ● ● ● ● ● ● ● ● ● ● ● ● ● ● ● ● ● ● ● ● ● ● ● ● ● ●

## Related Activities

1. Create posters to highlight ways to treat mild physical discomfort without taking medicine. Some posters could use the theme of maintaining internal balance. Place the posters in the hallway to raise consciousness about dependence on OTCs.

2. Health notebooks: Explore the affect of advertisement on the use of medicine. Ask students to find an advertisement of an OTC for their notebooks and to write a paragraph telling what the product is supposed to do and how the advertiser tries to catch their attention.

3. Have interested students research and report on acupuncture and/or "natural" medicines. Why are these types of treatments becoming popular? Is this a good trend or not?

# LESSON 2: DRUG ABUSE AND THE BODY'S BALANCE

## Preparation/Materials
- Student books
- Teacher Visual. Enlarge the visual or make a transparency of it for use with an overhead.
- Optional: Obtain additional student resources on various types of drugs.

## Objectives
- Students will identify basic groups of illegal drugs and the characteristics of each group.
- Students will recognize the harmful effects of these drugs on a person who abuses them.

• • • • • • • • • • • • • • • • • • • • • • • • • • • • • • • • • • • • • • • • • • • • • • • • •

## Lesson (2 sessions)

1. **Student book.** Read and discuss the opening paragraphs of "Drug Abuse and the Body's Balance." Review the meaning of the terms *tolerance, dependence,* and *withdrawal.*

   Talk about how the drugs get into the body's bloodstream. Alcohol enters the bloodstream very quickly through cells in the stomach and small intestine. Inhaled drugs can enter the bloodstream right through cells in the nose. Ask: "How would drugs that are in smoke (marijuana, tobacco) enter the bloodstream? (Through the lungs.) What about drugs that are injected?" (They are usually injected right into blood vessels.) You may wish to have students turn in the student books to the drawing of the circulatory system (Unit 4) to have them notice how the bloodstream carries the drugs throughout the body.

   Tie in to the previous lesson with these questions:
   - "What do you think is the effect of nonmedicinal drugs (usually what people mean when they use the term *drugs*) on the body?" (They upset the body's balance. Stress that some drugs interfere with the body's nervous system by affecting how the brain works. The drugs actually change the chemical reactions in the brain. That's why these drugs are called mind-altering drugs. Cocaine, LSD, marijuana, and alcohol are all examples mind-altering drugs.)
   - "Do you think that the body is able to restore balance if a person keeps abusing drugs?" (Continued abuse can break down parts of the body, and the body may lose the battle.)

2. Divide the class into seven groups, and assign each group a drug category discussed in the student book (depressants, stimulants, hallucinogens, narcotics, cannabis, inhalants, and steroids). Explain that each group is responsible for teaching the rest of the class about its assigned topic. Student groups should create a teaching plan and also a quiz (with answers). Provide a transparency or an enlarge copy of the Teacher Visual for groups to use to point out what parts of the body are affected by the drugs.

Give one session for preparation. Circulate around the classroom, giving help as necessary. You may wish to check student questions/answers for accuracy.

Have student groups give their presentations. The class can take the quizzes right after each presentation or in a separate session. Student groups can give the answers or grade the papers.

Alternative option: Make this a written research report. Student groups would not only be expected to study the student book information but also do some independent research. (This is an opportunity to teach research skills and to give students practice in using library reference materials.) After completing their research, they should write a report about their type of drug.

3. **Health notebook.** Ask students to find articles about drug abuse in current magazines or newspapers for their notebooks. Use the articles to discuss current problems/issues in drug abuse. These articles can also be used for a language arts assignment. Allow students several days or a week to collect the articles.

4. **Closure.** Answer the two "Think It Over" questions in the student book. Tell students that in a subsequent lesson they'll be learning about the drug most misused and abused in North America.

   1. *Answers will vary. Call attention to the dangers of alcohol—one drug that may be readily available.*
   2. *Answers will vary, possible answers include increased crime, increased illness of various kinds, breakdown of society's social health/families, increased cost of health care.*

● ● ● ● ● ● ● ● ● ● ● ● ● ● ● ● ● ● ● ● ● ● ● ● ● ● ● ● ● ● ● ● ● ● ● ● ● ● ● ● ● ● ● ● ● ● ● ● ● ● ● ● ●

## Related Activities

1. Invite a representative of a local drug abuse prevention organization to give a presentation in the class. Many organizations (including the local police department) have drug abuse education programs for students.

2. Have student groups develop a written report on their assigned topic. Then have them incorporate the written report in a display that becomes the basis for a class oral report.

   Directions for making the display:
   Use a box (one for each group of students) at least large enough to mount their reports on one side. Cut out the top, bottom, and one side of the box. Then tape the two open sides together to make a three-sided display. Attach the report on one side of the box.
   Use the other two sides for drawings (for example, of plant sources of the drug) or for additional information gleaned during research.
   Each group should explain its display in an oral report. Student groups should work out ways for everyone in the group to take part in the oral presentations (in groups of three, each student could explain one side of the display).

# LESSON 3: UNDERSTANDING THE EFFECTS OF ALCOHOL

## Preparation/Materials
- Student workbook activity
- Student book

## Objectives
- Students will recognize the pressures to drink alcohol in our society.
- Students will recognize the short-term effect of alcohol on the body.

## Background

Alcohol is North America's most used and most abused drug. The National Institute on Alcohol Abuse and Alcoholism (NIAA) in the United States estimates that one in ten Americans who drink is an alcoholic. Alcohol use is a factor in a large percentage of violent deaths: 50 percent of traffic deaths, 70 percent of drownings, 55 percent of suicides. Of course, not everyone who uses alcohol abuses it. Many people drink moderately and know and respect careful limits.

Some people choose not drink alcohol at all. Among them are Christians who believe that alcohol is off limits for them because the potential for harm is so great. But others believe that they can use alcohol in good conscience if they use it moderately. Some of these people are Christians also. They point to the time when Jesus made gallons and gallons of wine at the wedding feast at Cana and to the Lord's promise that his people will drink wine with him at the messianic banquet. Both groups of Christians believe that *abusing* alcohol is wrong. The Bible makes clear statements about alcohol abuse (see Ephesians 5:18, for example).

Of course, for those below the legal age, using alcohol is against the law. Not only is using alcohol illegal, it is also very harmful for young, growing bodies. So, the basic message to students is "just say no." Because students are surrounded in our culture by images of people drinking and having a good time and may hear little about the negative side of using alcohol, use this lesson to inform students about the hazards of alcohol use. The idea is not to use scare tactics but to give them accurate information and help them form proper attitudes.

*Note:* Subsequent lessons deal with alcohol advertisement, alcoholism, and refusal skills.

• • • • • • • • • • • • • • • • • • • • • • • • • • • • • • • • • • • • • • • • • • • • • • • •

## Lesson

1. Ask: "What are two common drugs that we didn't discuss in the previous lesson? (Alcohol and nicotine.) How are these drugs different from those we discussed in the last lesson? (They are legal for adults to use.) How are these drugs similar to those discussed in the last lesson?" (They are also drugs that upset the body's internal balance. Nicotine is a stimulant, and alcohol is a depressant—although it may affect different people in different ways.)

   Tell students that in the next few lessons they'll learn about the effects of alcohol on the body and about some pressures in our society to use alcohol.

2. Work with the class to identify some of the subtle and not-so-subtle pressures in our society to use alcohol. Ask students for suggestions, and write them on the board.

Include the following pressures on the list: ads for alcohol, having alcohol readily available, having older siblings and family members who drink, seeing people use alcohol in movies and on TV, and the direct pressure of being offered a drink.

Discuss each of the pressures listed on the board. How does each make us think that alcohol use is natural?

Have students decide which of the pressures listed is the strongest. Consider having them number the pressures according to the level of pressure they exert.

3. **Student book.** Ask students to describe how people who have drunk too much act or feel. Have students read "Short-Term Effects of Alcohol" in the student book to help them understand how alcohol does this to the body.

   Spend some time discussing the three main things that will influence the amount of alcohol in the blood: how much a person drinks, how fast a person drinks, and the size of a person.

   Also mention possible long-term effects of continual alcohol abuse: liver disease, loss of brain cells, and cancer.

4. **Student workbook activity.** The crossword puzzle answers include terms from "Short-Term Effects of Alcohol" in the student book. Have student pairs work together to complete the puzzle. You may have to work with the class to solve some of the more difficult clues.

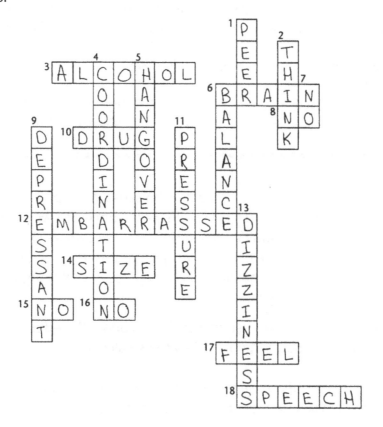

5. **Closure.** Briefly review the lesson's main ideas:

"What are three things that determine the effect of alcohol?" (The effect of alcohol depends on how much you drink, how fast you drink and how large/small you are.)

"How does alcohol affect the body?" (Affects how a person thinks and feels, affects body coordination, and can make a person sick.)

"What might happen to someone who abused alcohol over a long period of time?" (Liver disease, cancer, loss of brain cells.)

● ● ● ● ● ● ● ● ● ● ● ● ● ● ● ● ● ● ● ● ● ● ● ● ● ● ● ● ● ● ● ● ● ● ● ● ● ● ● ● ● ● ● ● ● ● ● ● ● ● ● ●

## Related Activity

•   Show students a film about alcohol abuse.
    See Lesson Resources for suggestions.

# LESSON 4: WHAT'S THE HIDDEN MESSAGE?

## Preparation/Materials

- Obtain three to five samples of advertisements for alcohol. Ads should show a variety of messages (for example, appealing to the desire to have fun and friends or to be popular, powerful, wealthy, or attractive).
- Optional: Make enlargements or transparencies of the advertisement samples to use in class discussion.
- Supply magazines with alcohol advertisements for class use, or request students to bring two alcohol advertisements to class.
- Student workbook activity

## Objectives

- Students will identify common appeals used in alcohol advertisements.
- Students will recognize the purpose of the appeals.
- Students will consider how to resist such appeals.

## Lesson

1. Introduce the topic of advertising and alcohol with questions such as the following:
   - "Have you ever bought something because of an ad? Did the product do what the ad said it would?" (Give students time to discuss any experiences they have had.)
   - "Why do companies make ads?" (To sell products.)
   - "What do most ads leave out or ignore?" (Any problems with products or any bad effects of using the product. Use the example of cigarettes, and note that now the government makes the tobacco companies warn about the bad effects of smoking.)
   - "What do most alcohol advertisements show?" (Beautiful people having fun, etc.)
   - "What do alcohol ads leave out?" (The effects of alcohol abuse.)
   - "Why don't alcohol companies put warnings in their ads?" (Afraid that people won't buy their product.)

2. Discuss various examples of ads. If possible, put the ads on the overhead. Note that people trying to sell alcohol appeal to the needs and desires of their potential customers. Talk about each ad, asking questions such as the following:
   - "What does the ad try to show about their kind of alcohol?" (For example that healthy, beautiful people drink the wine or that handsome, wealthy men use whiskey).
   - "What is the message that the advertiser wants you to get from the ad?" (That you too will be beautiful, healthy, handsome, or wealthy.)
   - "Does the ad give a true picture or not?" (Lead students to recognize the strategy each ad employs.)

- "Is the ad aimed at people of a certain age level?"
- "If a person were to misuse alcohol in the situation pictured, what might happen?" (Lose coordination and fall off the horse, say things he or she would be embarrassed about later, and so on.)
- "How do you think you can keep from being tricked by ads?" (Answers will vary. Make the point that knowing what ads are trying to do and thinking critically about the ads are good ways to fight back.)

3. **Student workbook activity.** Have students study two alcohol advertisements (if necessary, first finding advertisements in magazines), and then answer the questions on the worksheet.

   Give students the opportunity to share their ideas, particularly about resisting ads.

# LESSON 5: COPING WITH ALCOHOLISM

## Preparation/Materials
- Student book
- Invite a representative from Alateen to talk with the class, or obtain a film showing how family members cope with alcoholism.

## Objectives
- Students will identify two warning signals for alcoholics.
- Students will identify two strategies for coping with an alcoholic.
- Students will identify at least one community agency that helps alcoholics and their families.

## Background
Alcoholism and other forms of substance abuse harm the person who does the abusing, but they also harm the person's family members and friends. Articles appearing in Christian magazines make it clear that Christian homes are not immune to abuse-related problems.

In an article in *Christian Educators Journal* (October-November 1988) Jeane L. Grys describes how the substance abuse of a family member has affected her life:

> Not only does [substance abuse] cause harm to the substance abuser himself, but it also causes ill effects on close family members. Often these family members are unaware of the cause of the emotional stress and distorted thinking they are experiencing.

My own life is an example of not recognizing the effects of living with substance abuse. For 27 years I've struggled with who I am. I grew up thinking it was wrong to express my feelings, and I never really trusted anyone. I was the quiet, shy kid who sat in the front of the room. I would never admit there was something wrong. What would have happened if a teacher at my school would have been able to detect the cause of my difficulties? Would I have been open to speak about what was happening in my life or how I was feeling? ...

I wonder how many of the youth in our classrooms are influenced by substance abusers. Observing the behavioral extremes of such young people can be frightening to a teacher, especially one who cares enough to link a problem with its cause. Some victims withdraw; they don't talk, trust, or feel. Others are outspoken. They misbehave until teachers find themselves drawing away from them—when what the students actually need is our willingness to understand and reach them. Yet, the ill effects may be more subtle. They may show up in the areas of academic achievement, social skills, emotional maturity, or spiritual growth.

Much of this lesson is adapted from Michigan Model, Grade 6, Phase VI.

• • • • • • • • • • • • • • • • • • • • • • • • • • • • • • • • • • • • • • • • • • • • •

## Lesson
1. Tell students that today they are going to be learning about a form of alcohol misuse called alcoholism. Tell them that alcoholics are people who are *unable to control their drinking*. Alcoholics come from various backgrounds and family situations, are male or female, young or old. When people are alcoholics, their drinking behavior affects others—family, friends, co-workers.

2. If possible, show a video or interview about a family coping with alcoholism in the family. Or, invite an expert to speak with the class.

3. **Student book.** Assign students to read the article entitled "Coping with Alcoholism." Go over the material with the students.

   Use the "Think it Over" questions to stimulate further discussion.

   1. *Answers will vary. Sometimes family members get the idea from the alcoholic who blames them. Family members can also feel that in some way they have failed the person who has alcoholism.*
   2. *Answers will vary. Suggested responses would include the idea that it's easier to cope with problems when you have a trusted friend or adult to talk to. Sometimes people who have been through the same thing may know of and can share information about helpful resources.*
   3. *Answers will vary. Many times the alcoholic doesn't want others to know how much he/she is drinking.*

4. **Closure.** Point out that there are both Christians and non-Christians who are alcoholics. Both need professional help. Explain that God uses professional help to support alcoholics and their families in trying to recover. But also tell students that many recovering alcoholics have testified how the power of God gave them the strength to resist their powerful craving to drink. And God's power can also help family members cope with alcoholism.

• • • • • • • • • • • • • • • • • • • • • • • • • • • • • • • • • • • • • • • • • • •

## Related Activity
• Have volunteers find out about local resources available to help those with alcohol and other drug abuse problems.

# LESSON 6: SAYING NO

## Preparation/Materials

- For the Cookie Experiment:
  box of cookies (the more irresistible the better!)
  prepare an instruction card for each of six students as follows:
  - on three cards write, "Take one cookie, eat it slowly, and try to pressure everyone else at the table to eat a cookie. Give them a lot of pressure (talk them into it)."
  - on two cards write, "Resist the pressure for about three minutes. Then finally give in and take a cookie."
  - on one card write, "Do not take a cookie, no matter what!"
  name tags—Jane, Mary, John, Gene/Jean, Don/Dawn, Louis/Louise
- Unit evaluation in student workbook

## Objectives

- Students will identify strategies for refusing drugs.
- Students will examine reasons for alcohol and drug abuse.
- Students will identify ways—other than drug abuse—to meet needs and solve problems.

## Background

Educating about what drugs and alcohol do to the body is one way to help prevent chemical abuse. Another way is to prepare students to cope with pressure from others to use drugs. As students learn specific strategies for refusing drugs, they develop self-confidence for dealing with situations that are almost certain to arise.

## Lesson

1. To simulate a situation in which some students are pressured, do the Cookie Experiment.

   Explain the following ground rules before beginning the role play:
   No put-downs.
   Stay in the role (explain what this means).
   Don't use people's real names.
   Try to make the role play as real as you can. Remind students in the class as well as students in the role play to be aware of feelings throughout the role play.

   Ask for six volunteers, and have them sit around a table or desk on which is placed a box of cookies. Give each student a name tag and a prepared instruction card (before passing out the cards, ask them not to show the card to anyone else).

   Be clear about beginning and ending each role play segment (for example, say, "Begin role play" or "Cut role play"). Remind students to speak loudly enough so that everyone can hear them.

   Then have the students interact with each other, according to the instructions on their cards. Allow the activity to go on for about four or five minutes.

At the end of the role play, ask questions such as the following:
- "John and Mary, how did you feel when the others were pressuring you? How did you feel when you finally gave in and took a cookie?"
- "How did the rest of you feel when Jane wouldn't take a cookie? How did you feel when John and Mary finally gave in?"
- "Jane, how did the pressure feel? How did it feel not to give in? How did you feel about yourself? How did you feel about the others?"
- "How did you feel when Jane wouldn't give in? What do you think a person who gives in to pressure is afraid of?"

If interest is high, you may wish to repeat the activity at another time with other participants.

(This activity is adapted from *Sound Off* by Lindenberger, Ebrecht, and Baldes [Marquette, Michigan] and the M. R. CHEP Program of the Michigan Department of Health.)

2. Follow up on the activity by asking student pairs or groups to develop some practical strategies for refusing drugs.

   Begin by posing one or more concrete examples. Example: During half-time or a slow spell during an evening sports event, two students step outside the gym. They run into other classmates—or older students—who offer them drugs. Try to develop a situation that is realistic for your school and community.

   Give students a few minutes to discuss and to decide on how to refuse the drugs.

   Share their responses. Perhaps vote on what students think is the best way to deal with the situation.

3. Go over the following strategies for saying no. After each is discussed, have two volunteers role play a situation using the strategy.
   - The simplest way to resist pressure is to say, "No, thank you." Note that saying this plainly shows that you've made up your mind and you really mean it.
   - Suggest another activity. ("No, thanks. I'm going to play catch. Want to join me?" or "No, I don't want any. I'm going to go get a hamburger.")
   - Say why not. If students use this strategy, they must phrase the answer so that it doesn't seem like a lame excuse. Excuses often lead to more pressure.
   - Give an objective fact, such as "Smoking smells up my clothes." But caution that it is better to avoid lecturing. ("Don't you know that smoking destroys your taste buds?")
   - State your opinion. ("I don't like the taste of beer.")
   - Go away. Simply leave. If those pressuring you won't take no for an answer, this may be the best course.
   - Make sure your body language matches your verbal message. If you send mixed signals, those who are pressuring you will take your body language as the real message.

Note that looking directly at the person and maintaining eye contact sends a message of calmness and self-confidence. Body posture and tone of voice are also important. Demonstrate (or have student volunteers demonstrate) ways to say no assertively, but not too aggressively.

4. **Health notebook.** Ask students to write their reflections on the Cookie Experiment. Or, if you prefer, have them write a paragraph on one of these questions:
   - "Do you think it's possible to say no without hurting others' feelings? Explain."
   - "Do you think it's all right to walk away if the other person won't accept no as an answer? Explain."
   - "Do you think that what you've learned today will help you to refuse drugs? Give reasons for your answer."
   - "Which of the different strategies do you think will work the best? Explain."

5. **Unit evaluation.** Use the worksheets to review and evaluate.

   *Matching:*
   *1. c; 2. b; 3. j; 4. a; 5. g; 6. h; 7. d; 8. e; 9. i; 10. f*

   *Short Answers:*
   1. *Possible answers include nail polish remover, glue, paint thinner, gasoline, cleaning fluids, lighter fluid. Follow the instructions on the container for safe use. Proper ventilation when using these substances is important.*
   2. *Some people use steroids as a shortcut to body building; they can cause stunted growth, acne, mental health problems, severe liver and kidney damage, and appearance of characteristics of the opposite sex.*
   3. *Because the user needs more of a drug to have the same effect, the user tends to use more and more of a drug.*
   4. *The drug user thinks that he or she can't do without the drug. For example, a person who becomes mentally dependent on marijuana may think that he or she needs the drug in order to do well on a test.*
   5. *How much a person drinks, how fast a person drinks, and the size of the person.*
   6. *Because ability to think is changed, the person's judgment, inhibitions, and emotions are affected. Because ability to move is changed, the person's coordination and balance are affected. Heavy drinking may also cause physical reactions such as vomiting and hangovers.*
   7. *Possible answers include the following: has trouble remembering what occurred during drinking session; has trouble stopping drinking; difficult to get along with after drinking; becomes angry when questioned about drinking; sneaks alcohol; frequently drinks alone; finds excuses to drink; breaks promises to quit drinking.*

*Short essay:*

1. *Advertisers try to convince people that using alcohol will bring fun, happiness, beauty, wealth, power, friends, sex appeal; thinking critically about ads helps people to resist their sales pitch.*

2. *Answers will vary, but should reflect the awareness of the dangers of drug abuse and the Christian calling to honor God with our bodies.*

● ● ● ● ● ● ● ● ● ● ● ● ● ● ● ● ● ● ● ● ● ● ● ● ● ● ● ● ● ● ● ● ● ● ● ● ● ● ● ● ● ● ● ● ● ● ● ● ● ● ● ●

## Related Activities

1. Have students brainstorm a list of reasons why people use drugs (looking for fun, adventure, excitement; escape from stress/a way to relax; a way to cope or escape from problems). Then ask student groups to identify other ways to meet those needs. Have groups share their ideas with the rest of the class.

2. Show students a film about refusal skills. See Lesson Resources for suggestions.

3. Ask pairs of students to work together to practice saying no in various ways. Have them try aggressive, passive, and assertive responses.

# Unit 8

# Focus on Safety

## Goals

- Students will choose to take responsibility for their safety and the safety of others.
- Students will be aware of safety precautions for preventing injury and harm.
- Students will become familiar with emergency and first aid procedures.

## Background

"A child's judgment develops slowly. Young children can't judge traffic speed and distance, and their peripheral vision may be limited. This is why they often run into the street while playing—and why nearly half of the children killed in traffic accidents are pedestrians. Or consider teenagers. They have a hard time seeing the consequences of their actions, they tend to have a feeling of invulnerability ('It can't happen to me'), and they are susceptible to peer pressure. This developmental stage lends itself to reckless driving and accounts for many early deaths as well as numerous and permanent brain and spinal cord injuries" (from *Facts About the 1990 Health Objectives: Injury Prevention*).

Students in your classroom are at various stages of development, but by sixth grade many may be beginning to adopt the teenage attitude described in the previous paragraph. That attitude may be due in part to the way North American media often glorify taking physical risks. In the Christian view, however, human beings have a God-given task to care for creation—and that includes being caretakers of ourselves and others. Help students to see that acting in a safe and responsible manner is one way to honor God by confessing that we are not our own.

A note on unit teaching strategies: Many community organizations have valuable resources for teaching safety topics. Audiovisuals, speakers, and brochures (for students and parents) are typically available—often at little or no cost.

## Vocabulary

| | | | | |
|---|---|---|---|---|
| appropriate | inappropriate | sexual abuse | personal safety | offender |
| victim | incest | assertive | nonassertive | aggressive |
| frostbite | hypothermia | wind chill | heat exhaustion | heatstroke |
| ultraviolet rays | natural disaster | hurricane | typhoon | cyclone |
| tornado | earthquake | blizzard | tsunami | |

## Unit Resources (Search online for similar resources if these are no longer available.)

"Unit 7: Injury Prevention and Safety Promotion." U.S. Centers of Disease Control and Prevention, 2020.
> https://www.cdc.gov/healthyschools/bam/injury.htm.
> This page includes lessons and PDFs about all areas of safety.

"Information on Safety in the Home & Community for Parents with Children (Ages 4-11)."
> Centers for Disease Control and Prevention.
> https://www.cdc.gov/parents/children/safety.html/.
> Contains a lengthy list of topics with information on each area of safety.

# Lesson Resources (Search online for similar resources if these are no longer available.)

### Lessons 1–2

"Helmet Safety." Centers for Disease Control and Prevention, 2018.
 https://www.cdc.gov/healthyschools/.

"Pre-Teens." Safe Kids Worldwide.
 https://www.safekids.org/safetytips/field_age/pre-teens-10-14.
 This page links to safety topics such as bike safety, fire prevention, and pedestrian safety.

*Before the Fire: Prevention Works!* Prevention 1st.
 http://prevention1st.org/.
 This PDF has lesson plans and links (including videos), separated by grade level.

### Lesson 3

"Resources for Kids." Childhelp.
 https://www.childhelp.org/resources-kids/.
 The page of the website provides a list of things kids should know and a suggested book list.

"Prevent Child Sexual Abuse: Facts about sexual abuse and how to prevent it." Stop It Now!, 2020.
 This PDF provides details information and resources. More information (printable and topic-specific) can be found on stopitnow.org.

"Child Abuse and Neglect Prevention." Centers for Disease Control and Prevention.
 https://www.cdc.gov/violenceprevention/childabuseandneglect/index.html.
 This web page provides a short video, links to more detailed information, and a downloadable PDF.

### Lessons 4–5

"Reasons First Aid Training Should be done in School." American Academy of CPR and First AID, Inc., 2019.
 https://www.onlinecprcertification.net/.

"CPR Facts & Stats." American Heart Association.
 https://cpr.heart.org/en/resources/cpr-facts-and-stats.

"First Aid Steps." American Red Cross.
 https://www.redcross.org/.

Mannequins for practicing artificial respiration are available from a variety of sources.
 Contact local paramedic agencies or the Red Cross.

### Lessons 6–7

*Do1Thing: Emergency Preparedness.* Do1Thing, 2020.
 http://do1thing.com/.
 A non-profit for emergency preparedness.

*Ready.* Ready, 2020.
 https://www.ready.gov/.
 Website about emergency prepardness that includes a section for kids.

"Emergency Preparedness In School." Community for Accredited Online Schools, 2020.
 https://www.accreditedschoolsonline.org/resources/emergency-preparedness-in-school/.

# LESSON 1: BEING SAFETY CONSCIOUS

## Preparation/Materials
- Student workbook activity
- Newspapers with articles about accidents, class supply. You may wish to have students bring several old newspapers from home.

## Objectives
- Students will become aware of the importance of using seat belts.
- Students will develop safety awareness.

- Students will be able to articulate the Christian perspective on safety.

## Background
Most of the unit lessons address the specific topic of safety by reviewing safety rules or providing information about potential safety hazards. However, knowing safety rules and following them are two different things. This lesson aims to help students understand and articulate the "why" of safety.

● ● ● ● ● ● ● ● ● ● ● ● ● ● ● ● ● ● ● ● ● ● ● ● ● ● ● ● ● ● ● ● ● ● ● ● ● ● ● ● ● ● ● ● ● ● ● ● ● ● ● ● ● ● ●

## Lesson

1. **Student workbook activity.** Introduce the unit with an activity about the use of seat belts. Have the students complete the survey forms. Encourage them to be as honest as possible. Make this an anonymous survey—no names on papers.

   Tabulate the results on the board or on a chart. Then discuss the results, and draw conclusions about students' current use of and knowledge about safety belts. During the discussion include the following seatbelt safety facts.
   - Wearing a seat belt in the back seat is important because it gives added protection to the wearer in case of an accident and it prevents the back seat passenger from being thrown forward into a front seat passenger and causing injury.
   - Most accidents happen within 25 miles of home. No matter how short the trip, wear a belt.
   - In many provinces and states, babies and very young children are required by law to be restrained in car seats. The safest place for a child is in the back seat, secured by a seat belt or a properly installed car seat.
   - Pregnant women should also wear seat belts. If seat belts are worn properly, they protect mother and unborn child.

2. Use the survey as a springboard for discussing attitudes toward safety. Ask students why they think most accidents happen. Note that most people are aware that safety belts do cut down traffic injuries and death; nonetheless, many people still do not bother with seat belts. Lead a discussion on the attitude toward safety that most likely lies behind this behavior. This is a good opportunity to bring in a Christian perspective on safety. Discuss questions such as the following.
   "Do you think most accidents can be prevented? Why or why not?"
   "What are some basic causes of accidents?" (Being in a hurry, being careless or distracted—sometimes because of anger or excitement, not thinking about consequences.)

"Why should Christians use sensible safety precautions?"
"Why do we not have to constantly worry about our safety?"
"Do we have a responsibility for the safety of others? Why or why not?"
"What are specific examples of how our attitudes toward safety affect others?"

3. **Health notebook.** Ask students to look through newspapers to find an article telling about an accident. Have them tape the article to a sheet of notebook paper and then write a brief explanation of what caused the accident, if/how the accident could have been prevented, and the accident's result.

Have students share their accident articles and comments. You may wish to use the assignment to create a bulletin board display.

Another option is to have students write one or more paragraphs based on the class discussion in Step 2. The article activity can be an assignment to be completed outside of class.

• • • • • • • • • • • • • • • • • • • • • • • • • • • • • • • • • • • • • • • • • • • • • • • • •

## Related Activities

1. Distribute additional copies of the Student Activity, and have students survey others— neighbors, family members, friends. Tabulate and compare the results to those of the class survey. Are there significant differences or similarities? Integrate with math and use the information to make graphs.

2. Make available in the classroom a variety of materials on safety. *See* Lesson Resources for suggestions. You may wish to have students contact local organizations for free pamphlets and other educational materials.

3. Research your province's or state's law on seatbelt use. Consider holding a debate based on the findings.

   Two debate topics:
   Is the law an infringement on individual rights?
   Does having a law make people more likely to use seat belts?

4. Have students working in groups develop lists of daily activities and the accidents most likely to occur during each. Then have them identify specific ways to cut the risk of accident during each activity.

# LESSON 2: REVIEWING BASIC SAFETY RULES

## Preparation/Materials
- Brush up on basic safety rules.
- Materials for making student posters
- Student workbook activity

## Objective
- Students will review safety rules covered at earlier levels.

• • • • • • • • • • • • • • • • • • • • • • • • • • • • • • • • • • • • • • • • • • • • • • • • • • • • • • •

## Lesson

1. Review basic safety rules.
   - Write on the board names of categories of accidents (for example, falls, burns, poisonings, traffic accidents) or of broad safety categories (for example, fire safety, pedestrian safety, bike safety, swimming safety, boating safety, preventing electric shocks, food safety).
   - Divide the class into groups, and have each group develop a list of safety rules for one category. The rules should be short—if possible, no more than 4 or 5 words.
   - Go over the lists with the full class. Add any important rules that were omitted.
   - Have each group make one or more posters illustrating rules of its assigned category. Students might wish to create a safety character (like Smokey the Bear) for the poster. Another suggestion is making mobiles with different rules written on parts of the mobile.
   - Display the posters in the school hallway.

2. Have students create safety acrostics to further help them review safety rules. They can base the acrostic on their name (first or last) or on a safety word or words.

   Example using bicycle safety rules:
   
   **D**on't forget to use hand signals.
   **A** bike should be kept in safe condition.
   **W**atch for drivers making right-hand turns.
   **N**ever ride out into the street without checking for cars and trucks.

   Example using fire safety rules:
   
   **S**top, drop, and roll to put out a clothing fire.
   **A**void overloading electrical outlets.
   **R**eplace damaged wiring.
   **A**rrange an escape route.
   **H**andle matches carefully.

   **B**e careful around campfires.
   **E**veryone should store flammable substances properly.
   **C**rawl low in smoke.
   **K**eep matches away from young children.

3. **Student workbook activity.** Discuss the items on the home hazard safety checklist. Have students complete the checklist at home with their parents.

● ● ● ● ● ● ● ● ● ● ● ● ● ● ● ● ● ● ● ● ● ● ● ● ● ● ● ● ● ● ● ● ● ● ● ● ● ● ● ● ● ● ● ● ● ● ● ● ● ●

## Related Activities

1. Have groups of students develop the lists of rules into charts or posters to hang around the room.

2. As a class, make up a poem or chant about safety. Or have individual students make up safety jingles.

3. Health notebook: Assign students to groups. Have each group look for articles about accidents in one category covered in the lesson. Groups can discuss the articles and identify the safety rules that apply to the situations described.

# LESSON 3: SEXUAL ABUSE PREVENTION

## Preparation/Materials
- Obtain and study teacher resources on prevention of sexual abuse.
- Make student resources available.

## Objectives
- Students will define sexual abuse.
- Students will differentiate between appropriate and inappropriate touch.
- Students will practice self-protection skills.
- Students will identify sources of help.
- Students will enlarge their vocabulary/ knowledge about dealing with sexual abuse.

## Background
Some may question the need for child abuse education in Christian schools, but reliable research has shown that abuse does occur in Christian families and communities. And the rate of abuse is comparable to or only a little lower than that of the population as a whole. So although we may wish to believe that the problem does not exist in Christian communities, the facts do not support that view. Christian communities need to face the reality of abuse and help students develop skills for dealing with it.

Each level of *Horizons Health* addresses the problem of sexual abuse. Since this is a sensitive subject, it is important for the school to contact parents/caregivers in advance and inform them of lesson content. You may wish to do this by letter or by meeting with parents (or your school administrator may prefer to hold a meeting to which parents of all grades are invited). Good communication with the home will give parents the opportunity to work with the school and to reinforce safety concepts.

The central focus of this lesson is safety, not sex education. In this unit students have been learning about safety—traffic safety, fire safety, home safety, bicycle safety. Now they are learning about one more type of safety—safety from sexual assault. (There are communities that do not have sex education programs, but that *do* teach prevention of sexual abuse.) Students who are aware of the danger of sexual abuse and know how to protect themselves are less likely to become victims of sexual abuse.

To be effective, sexual abuse prevention education needs to cover the following basic areas in age-appropriate ways: (1) recognizing sexual abuse/differentiating between appropriate and inappropriate touch, (2) learning self-protection skills and techniques, and (3) identifying resources for help. We want to emphasize that presenting information on the subject of sexual abuse is not sufficient. Students also need to develop skills—decision-making skills and self-assertive protection skills. They must not only understand what inappropriate touch is, but must clearly understand what they can do about inappropriate touch.

It's also vital to present the material in a nonthreatening way. Introduce the topic of touch in a way that makes you and the class feel comfortable. Although having the classroom teacher present the material is preferable, if you are unable to teach the lesson comfortably, consider asking another qualified person to teach it, perhaps another teacher on the school staff. This is an important safety lesson, and it should be presented in a supportive environment.

As you teach the lesson, be clear and direct; use correct names when referring to body parts. If a child should begin to report abuse during class (an unlikely event), offer to talk with him or her later, and follow the protocol established by your school for reporting child abuse.

Since *Horizons Health* includes material on sexual abuse at each level, in grade 6 students should be familiar with basic concepts about appropriate/inappropriate touch and skills for self-protection. At this level, however, students do learn some new vocabulary and learn a definition of incest. The lesson, for the most part a review, is in a question and answer format in order to give teachers the opportunity to identify and correct student misconceptions or weak areas.

●●●●●●●●●●●●●●●●●●●●●●●●●●●●●●●●●●●●●●●●●●●●●●●●●●●●●●●●●

## Lesson

1.  Deal with students' embarrassment by stating that the topic of this lesson, personal safety, can be an uncomfortable topic to talk about, but it is an important safety topic. Ask: "What is personal safety?" (It deals with learning about ways to protect our "person," our bodies, from harm.) In personal safety we learn to recognize situations that may be disturbing or become harmful and think about ways to prevent harm.

    Create a climate conducive to open communication. Make clear that students will be expected to respect questions and comments of other class members during discussion. Also encourage class members to actively participate as you teach the lesson.

2.  Begin by discussing some situations that give students the opportunity to practice decision making (avoid using names of class members). Ask: "What do you think you would do in this situation?"

    Cindy is at a movie with friends. The man sitting next to her is very friendly and asks questions such as "What's your name?" "What school do you go to?" "Where do you live?" (Say, "I'm not allowed to tell you that." If he persists, move, and report incident to theater attendants and parents.)

    Jim is riding home from a friend's house on his bike. When he's still several blocks from home, his bike chain breaks. He's trying to figure out what to do when a friendly young man, about 20–25 years old stops and offers to give him and his bike a lift home. (Include the following: say no politely, stay away from the young man's car; if he persists, make noise, run towards people or nearby house; report to adults.)

    When Susie answers the telephone one night, the person calling doesn't say who he is, but says some things having to do with the private parts of the body. (If necessary, review what the private parts of the body are. Define as area covered by bathing suit or underwear or name parts of the body using correct anatomical terms: breast, vulva, vagina, penis, scrotum, anus, buttocks. Students should hang up right away and not talk to the person. They should tell parents. If parents aren't home and the calls continue, they should call the police and/or telephone company.)

    Sally's house is right next to a big park. The family has the following rule about playing at the park: Sally may only play there if one of her older siblings or parents are at home and she tells them when she is going to the park. The weather is beautiful today, and Sally decides she'll ignore the family rule and take a quick bike ride through the park on her way home from school. She'll be home soon and nobody will even know that she broke the rule. So off Sally goes. But as she's riding through the park an older teenager on a motorcycle starts following her. (Go towards people; go to emergency contact in neighborhood and not to own house; report the problem to an adult.)

Children in Terry's neighborhood like to play in a deserted lot. After school Terry is going to meet friends there to play catch. Terry is the first one to arrive. A man comes from behind some bushes and exposes his penis (private parts). (Run away and report to adult/police.)

During Nikki's piano lesson her teacher, Mr. Kole, has been touching her a lot—putting his arm around her, rubbing her arm, etc. His touch makes her uncomfortable. (Move away from him, take his hand away, tell him she doesn't like to be touched like that, tell parent, and find a new piano teacher.)

Sloan and his boys' club leader are on an outing (fishing, seeing a ball game or movie) together. On the way home the leader touches Sloan's private parts and tells him to keep it a secret or he'll get even with Sloan. (Say no, get away or move away, report incident to parent or other trusted adult.)

3. Use the following list of questions as a basis for further discussion:
   • "Some of the situations we've just talked about involve touching. Sometimes touches can be confusing. Sometimes we're not sure if a touch is all right or not. How can we tell?" (Feelings and touches are closely related. Touches that are disturbing or make us feel unhappy, frightened, guilty, or perhaps angry are not good. Some may be wrong. We should act on "no" or "uh-oh" feelings and tell an adult.)
   • "What is sexual abuse?" (Comment that although all the situations in Step 2 involve personal safety, the last one about Sloan involves direct sexual abuse. Sexual abuse is a forced sexual touch. The adult forces or tricks the child into touching the adult's private parts or into letting the adult touch the child's private parts.)
   • "Is sexual abuse against the law?" (Yes. It's a crime. The law does not allow adults—who are stronger and may have power over a young person—to use their position to force or trick children into a sexual touch.)
   • Consider teaching the following new vocabulary:
        *offender:* the person doing the abuse
        *victim:* the person being abused or taken advantage of—in this case the children
        *incest:* sexual abuse by a family member
   • "Are offenders usually strangers?" (No. Only about 10–15 percent of the time. Usually offenders are people who the child knows.)
   • "What are some good ways to say no to bad or disturbing touches?" (Elicit from students ways to say no assertively: speaking clearly and confidently, making eye contact with offender, repeating message if necessary, using body language that reinforces the message. Avoid giving a nonassertive response and smiling at the offender. Also avoid aggressive responses.)

- "Do you think it's hard or easy to say no? Why?" (It's hard for a child to say no to an adult. And if the adult offender is someone he or she knows well, it's doubly hard.)
- "Why is it important to tell an adult about the touching (or attempted touching?)" (Because then the offender can be stopped. Another reason: The offender needs help/treatment to stop this behavior.)
- "What if the boy or girl promised to keep the touching a secret?" (It's wrong for someone to ask you to keep bad secrets about wrong or uncomfortable touching. The only kinds of secrets we should keep are good secrets, for example, secrets about surprise parties or birthday presents.)
- "Why is it difficult to tell an adult about touching?" (Touching of private parts is embarrassing to talk about; the offender's threats may frighten the victim; maybe the victim is worried that the adult will blame him or her.)
- "What if the adult the victim tells about the abuse *doesn't* believe the child? Or just doesn't do anything to stop the abuse?" (The child should tell another adult and keep on telling until something is done.)
- "Who is to blame when disturbing or wrong touching takes place?" (The offender is always to blame; the boy or girl is never to blame. You may wish to explore this answer a bit further and explain that even if the victim didn't or couldn't stop the touching or didn't understand what the offender was doing or was afraid to report it right away, he or she is still not to blame. Sometimes offenders tell boys or girls that the touching is their fault, but it's not.)
- "Who are some people a child could tell about sexual abuse?" (Write suggestions on the board. Include: a parent or other family member, teacher, school counselor, pastor, church school teacher or youth group leader, police officer. Explain that the community also has people who work to prevent sexual abuse and who especially protect children and young people. Tell students about local organizations such as Council for the Prevention of Sexual Abuse, Children's Aid or Children's Protective Services. Have volunteers look up the telephone numbers of these organizations.)

4. End the class session with one of the following student activities:
   - Work in groups to make posters of personal safety rules or of good touches.
   - Write descriptions of favorite good touches or of how good touches influence feelings.
   - Write paragraphs telling what new things about personal safety students learned from this lesson.
   - Read stories from books in resource list or show an age-appropriate film on preventing sexual abuse. See Lesson Resources for suggestions.

● ● ● ● ● ● ● ● ● ● ● ● ● ● ● ● ● ● ● ● ● ● ● ● ● ● ● ● ● ● ● ● ● ● ● ● ● ● ● ● ● ● ● ● ● ● ● ● ● ● ● ● ● ● ●

## Related Activities

1. Give a short time for students to write down any questions that they would like answered or comments they would like to share. Collect the unsigned questions and comments. Those who don't have questions can write "no question today," but all should prepare a sheet of paper to turn in. Tell students that you may choose not to answer all the questions in a full-class session (some may not be of general interest and some may require a personal answer). Try to answer the questions at the beginning of the next health session.

2. Invite a member of the local council for the prevention of child abuse or from Children's Aid or Protective Services to speak to the class about their work.

3. Practice assertive self-protection skills (review of grade 5 lesson). Review definitions of *assertive, nonassertive,* and *aggressive.* Have role plays of all three responses in a variety of personal safety situations.

4. Broaden the discussion of abuse to include emotional abuse, physical abuse, and neglect.

# LESSON 4: DEAR FIRST AID EXPERT...

## Preparation/Materials
- Student workbook
- Be prepared to correctly demonstrate the Heimlich maneuver, or invite a resource person to demonstrate.
- Brush up on basic first aid procedures.
- Obtain student resources on first aid.

## Objective
- Students will review first aid procedures for common emergencies.

## Background
Prompt, efficient action in an emergency is significant in reducing the effects of an injury or sudden illness. The students should review how to activate the local emergency medical system, and they should become familiar with the basic procedures of first aid. Stress that the more they know about handling emergencies and providing first aid, the easier it will be for them to stay calm and give efficient help.

The first concern in first aid is to protect the person from further harm. The next priority is to take immediate steps to maintain life: Administer mouth-to-mouth resuscitation or stop serious bleeding. The third step is to obtain medical assistance. Students of this age cannot be expected to perform all these steps in every situation. However, they can get help, and with proper training they may be able to perform the first two steps in certain situations.

## Lesson

1. **Student workbook activity.** The worksheet gives students the opportunity to review first aid information covered in earlier grade levels. Have student reference books on first aid available for this activity. Follow these steps:
   - Each student is to imagine that he or she writes a newspaper column for a weekly paper. Give the column a title such as "The First with First Aid" or "Know Your First Aid."
   - Have students turn to the activity sheet containing a number of brief letters asking for first aid information. (F.A.E. stands for First Aid Expert.)
   - Have students compose answers to the letters. Stress that it is important that they give the correct advice—even for minor first aid problems—because minor problems can become major if they are not taken care of or treated correctly.
   - You may wish to assign letters to student groups or pairs to answer.

2. Use the letter answers to review basic first aid practices. Correct any misinformation. Use the following reference information as appropriate during the discussion.

**Nosebleeds.** Nosebleeds are usually more annoying than serious. A person with a nosebleed should sit up, and lean forward. Apply pressure on the part of the nose that is bleeding. Keep the pressure for a couple of minutes. If the bleeding continues, get medical help.

**Speck of dirt.** Avoid rubbing the eyes. Rubbing may scratch the eyes. Tears will usually take care of any small problem. They will wash away the dust, and also help prevent infection from germs. Blinking a few times helps spread tears over the eye. If tears don't clear up the problem, students should ask an adult for help.

**Knocked-out Tooth.** A dentist may be able to help you save a knocked-out tooth. Find the tooth (don't try to clean it). Place it in a clean glass or other small container of cool milk or water. Go to the dentist *immediately.*

**Choking and breathing problems.** When the windpipe or airway is blocked by a solid object, the person can't breathe. The most common cause of choking is a piece of food that didn't "go down the right way." Signs of choking: reaching for throat, inability to speak. If the object is not removed quickly, person's face begins to turn blue. Usually the obstruction can be dislodged by coughing. Sometimes a few hard slaps on the back will help to dislodge it.

In the Heimlich maneuver, abdominal thrusts are given to force air out of the lungs and move the obstruction. The Heimlich maneuver is only to be used on a conscious victim. It should not be used on young children. If the Heimlich maneuver doesn't work, the next step is mouth-to-mouth resuscitation to force air past the obstruction and permit breathing until further help comes.

**Shock.** Shock occurs when there is an insufficient supply of blood to parts of the body. It can occur several minutes to an hour after an accident. A person in shock has pale and clammy skin and feels very weak. Breathing may be shallow, irregular, and rapid. Sometimes a person in shock may feel sick and vomit. If shock is untreated, the person may become unconscious. Stress the importance of getting immediate medical help if a person is in shock.

Although treating the cause of shock (for example, bleeding), is the correct procedure, unless students are skilled enough to administer first aid they should concentrate on keeping the person lying down and calm and on maintaining normal body temperature. Because moving a person with a head or neck injury may cause further injury, stress not moving the person unless absolutely necessary for safety.

**Minor cuts.** A minor cut only needs to be thoroughly washed. Then cover it with an adhesive bandage to protect from infection.

**Burns.** The principle of first aid here is to cool the area as quickly as possible and to keep the area clean in order to prevent infection. Putting a mild burn under cool water for 10-20 minutes helps to reduce pain. It is important to flush chemical burns with water. Serious burns, of course, need medical treatment as soon as possible.

**Poisoning.** Since different poisons have different antidotes, it is important to find out what the poison is. Sixth grade students should probably not try to administer first aid, but should quickly find out what the substance is and call the local poison control center or emergency number. Since speed is very important, students should clearly say that this is a poisoning emergency and carefully follow directions.

**Bleeding.** Applying pressure on a wound helps to stop bleeding by flattening the blood vessels and giving time for blood clots to start forming. In severe bleeding, pressure should be applied continuously for five to ten minutes. Deep cuts may require stitches to ensure that the wound heals properly.

You may wish to review that although HIV cannot be transmitted through casual contact, it can be transmitted through body fluids such as blood. So if someone with a cut or other opening in the skin touches HIV-infected blood, it is possible to pass the virus.

**Fractures and sprains.** The main purpose of first aid is to keep the damaged part or parts immobile until the person can get medical help. Sometimes a splint or a sling can be fashioned in order to support a fractured limb. The signs of a fracture are swelling, bruising, pain, arm or leg angled where there is no joint, loss of movement. However, stress that the only way to know in some cases is by having an X-ray of the area. Also be on the lookout for symptoms of shock.

**Animal bites.** The wound of an animal bite should be washed with soap and water. If the bite is bleeding, place a clean cloth on it and exert pressure. Identify the animal. Be sure to tell an adult.

**Insect stings.** If possible, the insect's stinger should be carefully removed. The bite should be covered with a cold, wet cloth. Tell an adult.

3. Demonstrate (or have your invited health professional demonstrate) the Heimlich maneuver.

    Review the signs of choking: reaching for the throat, inability to speak. If the obstruction in the throat is not removed quickly, the person's face will begin to turn blue. Usually the obstruction can be dislodged by coughing.

The Heimlich maneuver is only to be used on a conscious victim. It should *not* be used on young children. If the Heimlich maneuver doesn't work, the next step is mouth-to-mouth-resuscitation to force air past the obstruction and to permit breathing until further help comes. Tell students that the next lesson will deal with helping people by giving artificial respiration.

● ● ● ● ● ● ● ● ● ● ● ● ● ● ● ● ● ● ● ● ● ● ● ● ● ● ● ● ● ● ● ● ● ● ● ● ● ● ● ● ● ● ● ● ● ● ● ● ● ● ● ● ● ● ● ●
## Related Activities

1.  Make a class first-aid book.

2.  Have the class develop a Babysitter's Safety Checklist. Make a list of ways to screen job requests, a sheet for recording safety information for each babysitting job (emergency telephone numbers or contacts, special family rules, bedtimes), and safety questions to ask before adults leave (Any special alarms in the house? How does the door lock? Are all doors locked?)

# LESSON 5: IT'S AN EMERGENCY!

## Preparation/Materials

- Invite a resource person to demonstrate how to give artificial respiration.
- Student workbook activities 1 and 2
- Optional: Obtain a poster on artificial respiration from the Red Cross or other local health agency.

## Objectives

- Students will identify mouth-to-mouth resuscitation as the procedure to use when breathing stops.
- Students will know how to administer mouth-to-mouth resuscitation.

## Background

If at all possible, have a person skilled in administering artificial respiration conduct this lesson. Your school may wish to have at least one staff member complete a CPR training program so that a certified "in house" resource person is available (for emergencies as well as for teaching artificial respiration). Your local Red Cross chapter most likely will also be able to provide a person trained in teaching artificial respiration.

Of course, for this lesson to be truly helpful, students need opportunity to practice artificial respiration. Again, tap local resources. Red Cross chapters and/or local emergency squads will most likely have mannikins for practice. However, currently inexpensive models with a plastic head attached to a disposable "lung" are also available (see Lesson Resources).

A copy of this lesson also appears at the grade 5 level. What you plan for the lesson will depend on students' experience in fifth grade. You may wish to build on their knowledge and provide a hands-on lesson or you may wish to make this a review.

## Lesson

1. Have students identify some type of accident in which a person might stop breathing (drowning, breathing in smoke or carbon monoxide, drug overdose, heart attack, stroke, choking on food or other object, electrical shock).

2. Elicit from students signs of breathing problems. Make a list of responses on the board. Add the following signs to complete the list.

   Breathing is a noisy, bubbly sound.
   Breathing is slow.
   Person is pale, grayish-blue.
   Person's chest is not moving up and down.
   No air is heard or felt at the nose or mouth.

3. Introduce the concept of artificial respiration. Ask if students have heard the term "artificial respiration." (Some Red Cross material uses the simpler term "rescue breathing"; CPR, which stands for cardiopulmonary resuscitation, is a combination of chest compressions and mouth-to-mouth resuscitation.) Explain or elicit from students that artificial respiration is used to help a person who has stopped breathing. Note that artificial respiration is a technique that requires special training.

4. **Student workbook activity 1.** Ask the resource person to explain and demonstrate the procedure. Have students turn to their workbook activity and follow along step by step. If no resource person is present, go over the handout with the students.

5. If possible, have one or more models available so that students can practice techniques of artificial respiration on the demonstrator. Only do this activity under the supervision of a trained resource person.

6. **Student workbook activity 2.** Reinforce the lesson by having students complete the activity sheet.

• • • • • • • • • • • • • • • • • • • • • • • • • • • • • • • • • • • • • • • • • • • • • • • • •

## Related Activity

• Review local emergency telephone numbers. What information is of utmost importance in making an emergency call? Stress staying on the line until told to hang up.

# LESSON 6: FROM ONE EXTREME TO THE OTHER

## Preparation/Materials
- Student books

## Objectives
- Students will be aware of the connection between weather conditions and safety.
- Students will know how to prevent health problems caused by extreme heat or cold.
- Students will know first aid treatment for some problems caused by heat and cold.

● ● ● ● ● ● ● ● ● ● ● ● ● ● ● ● ● ● ● ● ● ● ● ● ● ● ● ● ● ● ● ● ● ● ● ● ● ● ● ● ● ● ● ● ● ● ● ● ● ● ●

## Lesson

1. Ask students if they have ever experienced very, very cold weather or very, very hot weather. Perhaps try to establish the lowest and highest temperature that a member of the class has experienced. Have students describe how they felt in these temperature extremes. Note that extremes of temperature bring specific safety problems.

2. **Student book.** The student book section entitled "Weather: From One Extreme to the Other" covers safety in very cold and very hot weather. It deals with the dangers of frostbite, hypothermia, sunburn, heat exhaustion, and heatstroke.

   Consider having student groups read the information in the student book and then make presentations to the class on these subjects. Encourage creativity. They may wish to perform skits on their topic, find articles about real-life situations, or give a straightforward informational report.

3. After the presentations, fill in any important information that students may have omitted. Use the following material as appropriate during the discussion.

---

**Frostbite.** The purpose of first aid is to restore circulation to the frostbitten area. Although the folk remedy for frostbite is rubbing the affected area with snow or ice, that remedy is not recommended because of the danger of removing skin and further damaging tissue. Warming the frostbitten part in warm, but not hot, water is the recommended first aid treatment. The area may be very painful as circulation is being restored. Even after healing, the area may continue to be sensitive to cold. And serious cases of frostbite can have serious effects. Gangrene may set in and the toes or fingers may have to be removed.

**Hypothermia.** In hypothermia, the temperature of the body is below the normal level of 98.6° F. Although in this lesson, the stress is on outdoor exposure, hypothermia can occur in the elderly in cool indoor temperatures. Some elderly people seem unable to sense cold.

---

A person with hypothermia can die if the body temperature continues to drop. According to *World Book Encyclopedia*, "The heart rate and blood pressure decrease during mild to moderate hypothermia—95° to 82° F. Breathing is slower and shallower. From 86° to 82° the victim becomes unconscious. During deep hypothermia—64° to 59°—the action of the heart, the flow of the blood, and the electrical activity of the brain stop completely."

Students may be interested in knowing that sometimes doctors put patients in a state of hypothermia in order to perform brain or heart surgery.

**Sunburn.** Sand, snow, and water reflect the sun's rays, so in these environments chance of sunburn increases. A brown pigment in the skin, melanin, gives some protection from sunburn. However, because light-skinned people have only a small amount of melanin in the skin, they burn much more easily than dark-skinned people.

Stress that taking precautions can keep our skin from being permanently damaged by the sun's ultraviolet rays. A sun lotion can block the sun's invisible rays. According to one Harvard University study, regular use of a sunscreen with a Sun Protection Factor of 15 during the first 18 years of life can reduce a person's lifetime risk of developing skin cancer by 78 percent.

**Heat exhaustion and heatstroke.** Sunstroke is the folk term for any condition caused by overheating the body. More accurate terminology uses the specific terms heat prostration and heatstroke. Sunstroke is actually a form of heatstroke which results from exposure to the sun.

Heat exhaustion or heat prostration is not as serious a condition as heatstroke. In heat exhaustion the temperature drops below normal; the condition is similar to being in shock. In heatstroke, however, the body is unable to control body heat and the temperature of the body rises rapidly. In heat exhaustion, the victim perspires heavily, but in heatstroke the person sweats very little—if at all. Since sweating is one cooling mechanism of the body (evaporating sweat cools the body), when it stops the temperature of the body can rise to dangerous levels. Because high temperatures can cause brain damage, heatstroke is a medical emergency.

**Heat cramps.** Heat cramps result from loss of salt because of sweating. People who work in high temperature surroundings are most apt to get heat cramps. Of course, people engaged in any extended physical activity during hot weather may also get heat cramps.

4. Have students answer the "Think It Over Questions." You may wish to make this a written exercise.

   1. *Answers will vary, but students should show awareness of the importance of adequate warm clothing for the weather and for meeting emergencies.*

*2. Student answers should reflect the importance of being prepared to cope with possible rapid changes in weather conditions that are common in the mountains.*

*1. Answers will vary. Possible precautions are taking plenty of beverages along or planning the hike to include drinking stops; protection from sun—lotions, hats, long sleeved shirts; take a break during middle of day when sun is hottest or hike through woods during that time.*

*2. Heatstroke is more serious than heat exhaustion. A person with heatstroke has dry skin, but in heat exhaustion a person sweats heavily; in heatstroke a person has hot, red skin, but in heat exhaustion, clammy skin; both may feel dizzy; heatstroke is a dangerous condition needing immediate medical attention, but heat exhaustion can usually be treated by sponging down with cool water, drinking beverages, and getting out of the sun.*

• • • • • • • • • • • • • • • • • • • • • • • • • • • • • • • • • • • • • • • • • • • • •

## Related Activities

1. Ask a student volunteer to research the use of hypothermia during cryosurgery and report to the class.

2. Examine various sun lotions. Note the Sun Protection Factor (SPF) from 1 to 15 or higher that pegs the ability of the lotion to block out the sun. Check which ones appear to be the most effective and why.

3. Integrate with social studies, and study how various people living in very hot climates and very cold climates deal with the weather. For example, why do those who live in desert climates frequently wear white? What kind of clothing do they wear?

# LESSON 7: NATURAL DISASTERS AND SAFETY

## Preparation/Materials
- Student books
- Student workbook

## Objectives
- Students will know how to protect themselves from injury in specific natural disasters.
- Students will understand why there are natural disasters in God's creation.

• • • • • • • • • • • • • • • • • • • • • • • • • • • • • • • • • • • • • • • • • • • • • • • •

## Lesson

1. Write the words *natural disaster* on the board, and ask students to define what a natural disaster is. Ask students to share their experiences with such natural disasters as hurricanes, typhoons, tornadoes, earthquakes, or blizzards.

2. **Student book.** Read and discuss "Natural Disasters." Put a positive spin on the discussion, stressing what students can do to promote safety during emergencies. Answer the "Think It Over" questions.

   1. *Supplies such as drinking water, food, candles, batteries for flashlights.*
   2. *Hurricanes pack dangerous winds; their rains can cause floods.  Coastline areas are especially vulnerable.*
   3. *These all refer to the same kind of storm, the name depends on where the storm occurs.*
   4. *Answers will vary.*

   1. *Answers will vary.*
   2. *Answers will vary.*

3. Consider how natural disasters fit into a Christian view of the world. Hold a debate on one or more of the following questions:
   "Why do you think there are natural disasters in the world?"
   "Do you think that there will be natural disasters on the new earth?
      Why or why not?"
   Assign student groups time to prepare the "case" for their stand. After the debate have the class discuss the issue.

4. **Student workbook activity.** Have students complete the crossword puzzle (answer key on following page). As you check the completed puzzle, review safety concepts.

• • • • • • • • • • • • • • • • • • • • • • • • • • • • • • • • • • • • • • • • • • • • • • • •

## Related Activities

1. Have students find out how the community is organized to deal with natural disasters. What plans do hospitals, police and fire departments, and other local organizations have for mobilizing? Consider having class members work together to make a bulletin board showing local emergency management.

2. Class members can research provincial, state, or national organizations that provide assistance in disasters. Students may wish to contact organizations such as the Red Cross or Salvation Army for information. Also include denominational or other religious organizations in their research.

3. Health notebook: Ask students to find articles in newspapers and magazines reporting on natural disasters.

4. If a natural disaster has recently occurred, students could write letters of support to people in the area. Or they could have a fundraiser, and perhaps send money to the Red Cross or another organization providing relief.

5. Integrate with language arts, and have students write stories of experiences with natural disasters. These can be true or imaginary experiences. Be sure to have them include—in some way—how to promote safety.

6. Student volunteers can research and report on other types of disasters (floods, volcanic eruptions) and find out what specific types of health-related problems frequently follow disasters.

7. Interested students can find out how building materials and architectural design can cut down on injuries and deaths due to earthquakes.

8. Integrate with social studies. Research a few major natural disasters (for example, the eruption of Mount St. Helens or Vesuvius).

## Student workbook activity answer key:

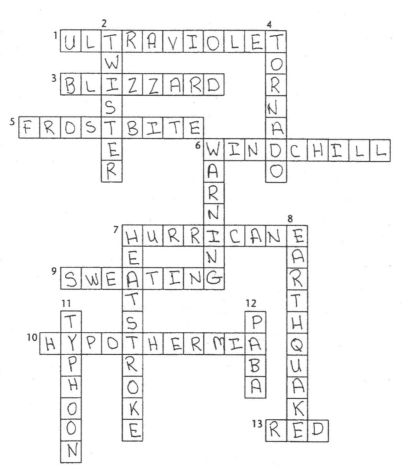

# LESSON 8: CULMINATING LESSON

## Preparation/Materials
- Student book
- Unit evaluation in student workbook
- Props to use for microphones and TV news desk, etc.

## Objectives
- Students will review safety concepts by writing skits.
- Students will decide to observe safety rules.

● ● ● ● ● ● ● ● ● ● ● ● ● ● ● ● ● ● ● ● ● ● ● ● ● ● ● ● ● ● ● ● ● ● ● ● ● ● ● ● ● ● ● ● ● ● ● ● ● ●

## Lesson

1. **Student book.** Read and discuss "And Now, the News..." in the student book. If desired, ask for volunteers or assign students to read the various parts of the skit. Be sure to follow the play by answering the last question posed by the commentator. Answer the "Think it Over" questions.

    1. *Answers will vary.*
    2. *Answers will vary. Encourage students to be open and honest when answering this question.*
    3. *Answers will vary.*

2. **Unit evaluation.** Use the worksheets in the student workbook to review and evaluate unit material.

    *Fill in the blanks:*
    *1. hypothermia; 2. Frostbite; 3. ultraviolet rays; 4. Artificial respiration; 5. hurricane, cyclone, typhoon; 6. Wind chill; 7. Shock; 8. minor or first-degree; cold water; 9. heat exhaustion; heatstroke; 10. PABA; 11. blizzard; 12. take cover*

    *Short Answer:*
    1. *Possible answers include using sun lotion with PABA to block out ultraviolet rays; avoiding prolonged exposure between 10 A.M. and 2 P.M. when rays are strongest; covering up when in the sun for a long time.*
    2. *Possible answers include avoiding being very active in extreme heat; getting medical help right away.*
    3. *Possible answers include storing these materials away from heat sources, out of the reach of children, and in metal cans.*
    4. *Possible answers include preparing to cope with rapidly changing weather conditions when planning a hike or camping trip, warming a person with hypothermia with blankets, dry clothes, hot drinks.*
    5. *Possible answers include drying hands before using electrical appliances; never operating appliances when in the tub or shower or when standing in water; keeping cords of appliances in good repair; grounding appliances as necessary; not overloading outlets.*

6.  *Possible answers include listening to weather reports when tornadoes are predicted, taking cover immediately if a tornado warning is given.*
7.  *Possible answers include having adequate clothing for cold weather, preparing for cold-weather outings wisely to avoid prolonged exposure to freezing temperatures, and warming up injured body part by placing it in warm water for 20–40 minutes.*
8.  *Possible answers include having medicines clearly labeled, storing medicines out of reach of small children, not taking prescription medicines belonging to others, and taking the correct dose.*
9.  *Possible answers include saying no to attempted inappropriate touch, getting away, and telling a trusted adult; not keeping a secret about sexual abuse; acting on feelings about confusing touches and telling an adult; saying no even if it's hard to say to an adult; being careful around strangers.*

*Short essay:*
1.  *Answers will vary.*
2.  *Answers will vary.*

2.  Do one or more of the following activities:
    *   Have students write short skits or plays about safety. Divide the class into groups, and have each group make up and give a play. To make the planning simpler, students can follow the interview format of the sample play (Student Activity) included with this lesson.

    *   Ask students to create presentations to give younger students about various aspects of safety. They could give the skits or play suggested previously. They could also make up a skit to demonstrate what to do in an emergency (who to call, how to call, etc.).

    *   Have students make coloring books about safety for students in a lower elementary class. Each page can be about a basic safety rule. Have each student contribute at least one page. Duplicate the completed pages to create the number of books you need.

● ● ● ● ● ● ● ● ● ● ● ● ● ● ● ● ● ● ● ● ● ● ● ● ● ● ● ● ● ● ● ● ● ● ● ● ● ● ● ● ● ● ● ● ● ● ● ●

## Related Activity
*   Show the class a film about safety to review unit concepts. See the Unit Resources for suggested titles.

# Teacher Resources – Reproducible Masters

# Muscular System

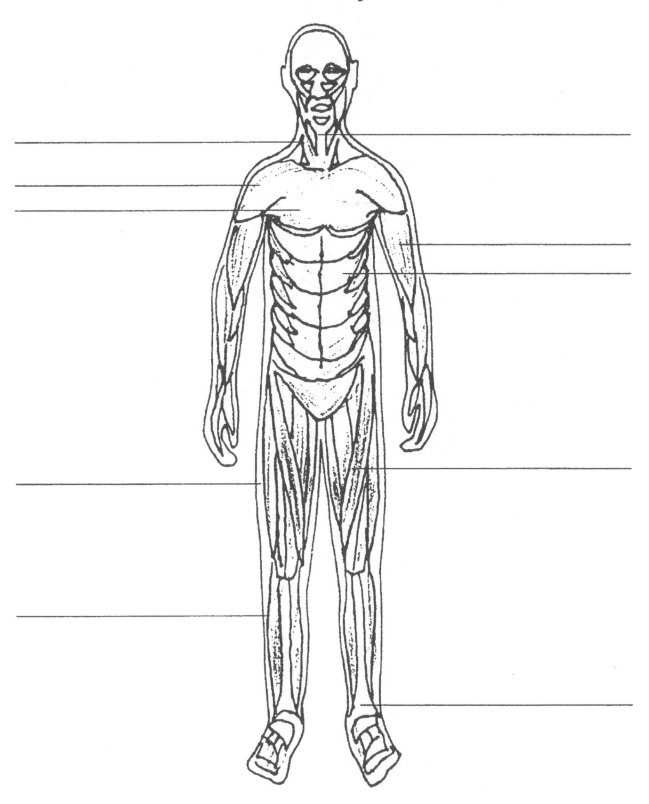

# Skeletal System

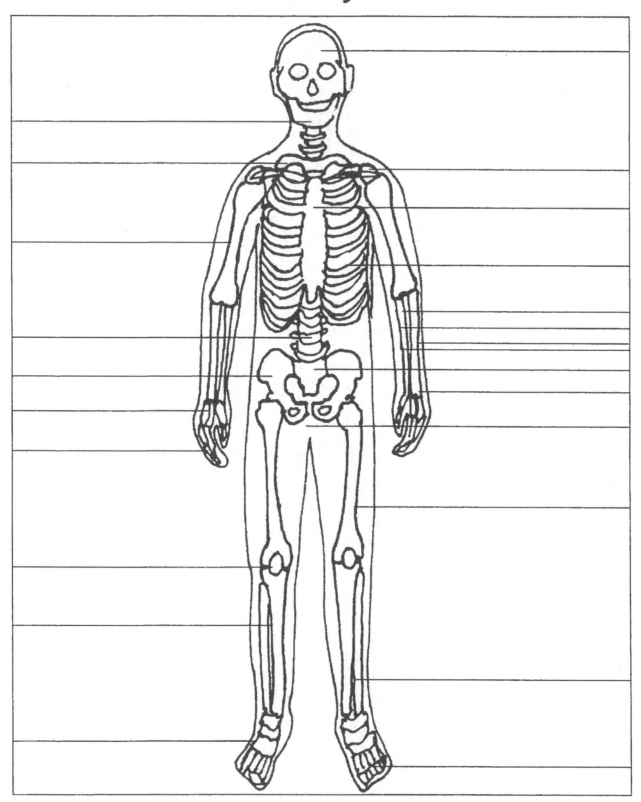

# Circulatory System

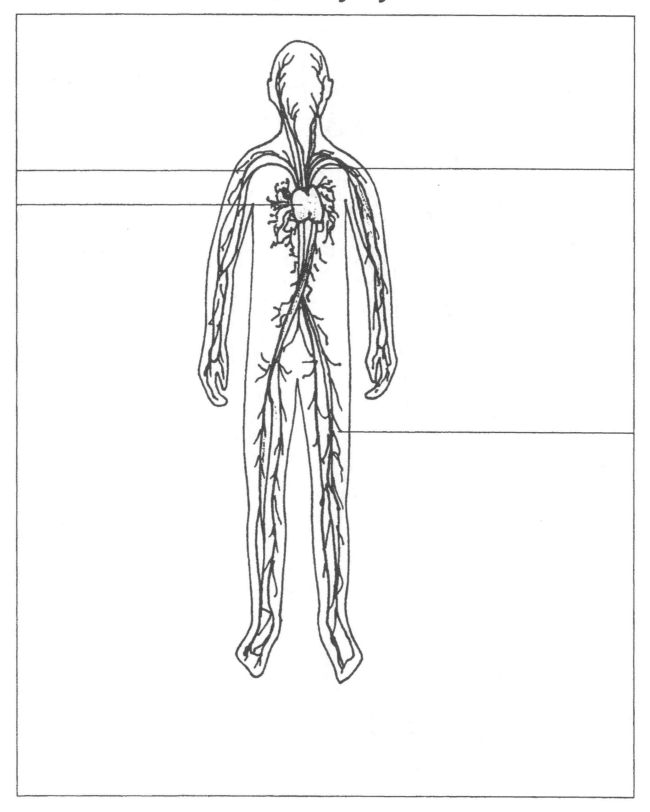

# Respiratory System

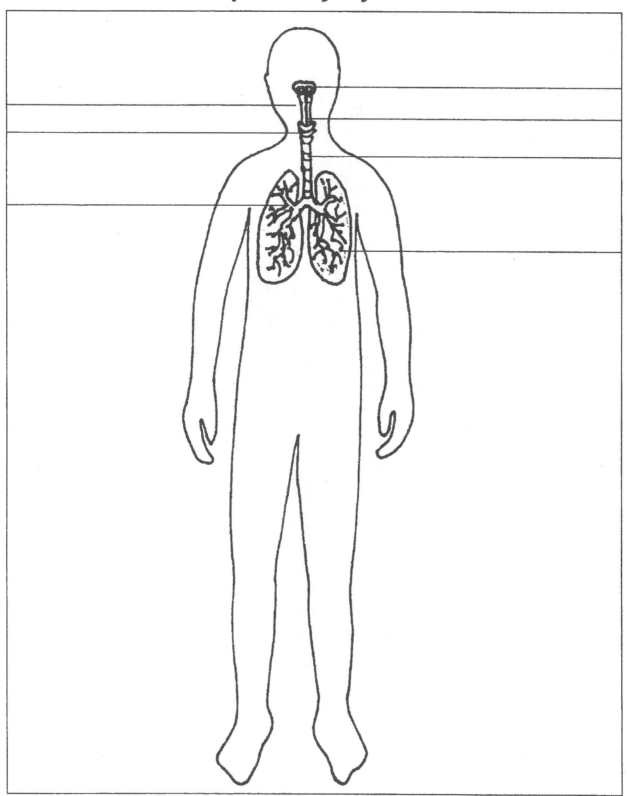

# Urinary System

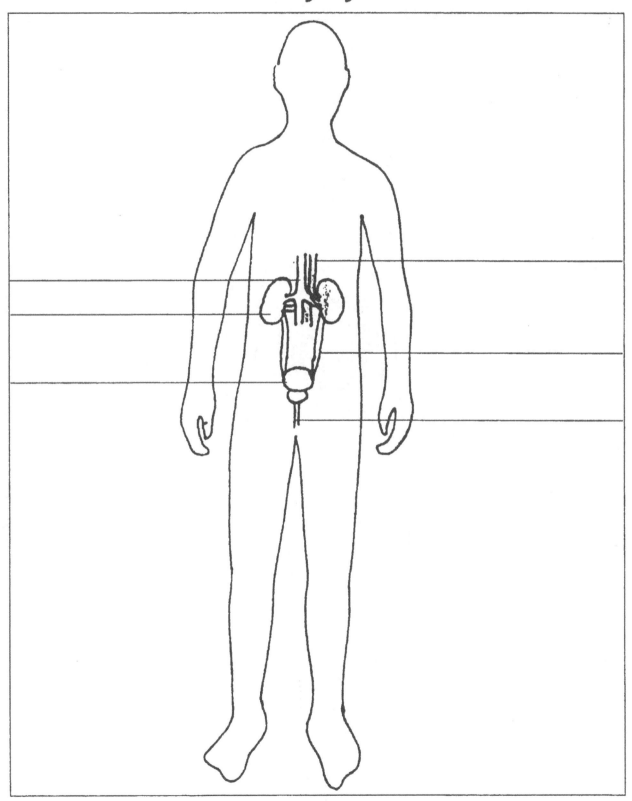

# Digestive System

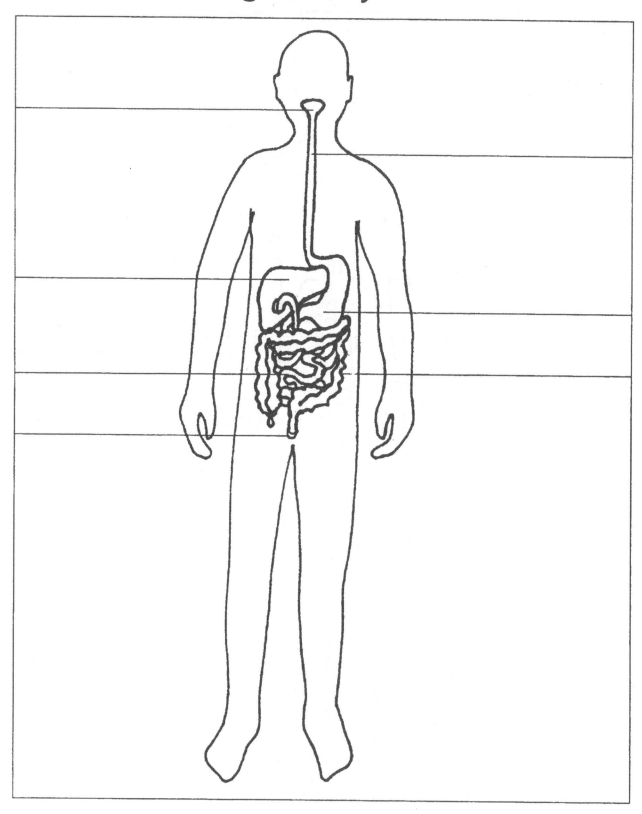

# Endocrine System

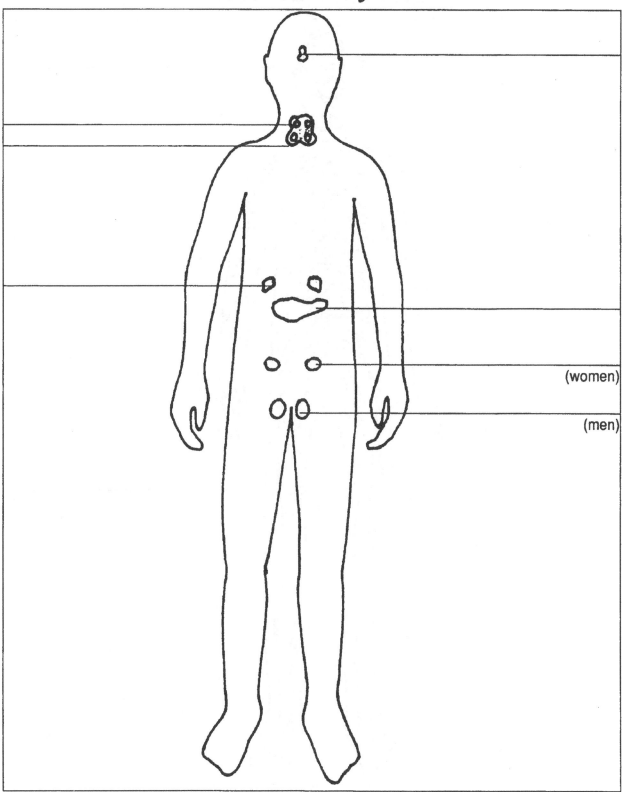

(women)

(men)

# Nervous System

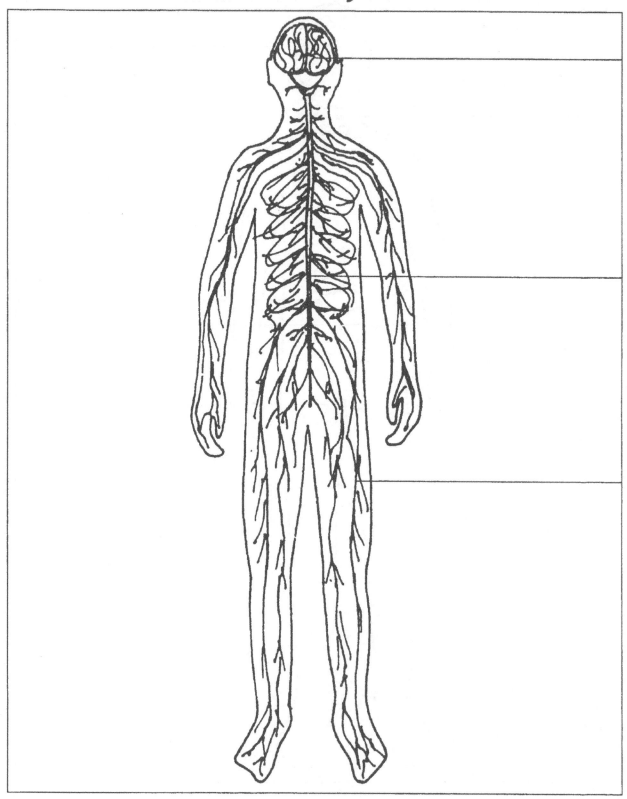

**Body Systems Jeopardy Game Cards:**

| | |
|---|---|
| **Respiratory system** – 50 points<br><br>The process of breathing in and out.<br><br>*(What is respiration?)* | **Circulatory system** – 50 points<br><br>One of the main jobs of the circulatory system.<br><br>*(What is transporting materials around the body or regulating body temperature?)* |
| **Respiratory system** – 40 points<br><br>When the muscles of the rib cage pull the ribs up and outward, and the diaphragm contracts and flattens downward to receive air.<br><br>*(What is inhaling?)* | **Circulatory system** – 40 points<br><br>Tiny blood vessels where cells receive their oxygen and get rid of carbon dioxide.<br><br>*(What are capillaries?)* |
| **Respiratory system** – 30 points<br><br>A waste gas that you breathe out through your lungs.<br><br>*(What is carbon dioxide?)* | **Circulatory system** – 30 points<br><br>They carry blood away from the heart.<br><br>*(What are arteries?)* |
| **Respiratory system** – 20 points<br><br>Tiny air sacs in the lungs where the exchange of oxygen and carbon dioxide takes place.<br><br>*(What are the alveoli?)* | **Circulatory system** – 20 points<br><br>The substance that delivers oxygen and nutrients to the cells.<br><br>*(What is blood?)* |
| **Respiratory system** – 10 points<br><br>It is a dome-shaped muscle that moves to cause air to enter or leave the body.<br><br>*(What is the diaphragm?)* | **Circulatory system** – 10 points<br><br>A muscle that contracts regularly every minute of every day of your life.<br><br>*(What is the heart?)* |

| | |
|---|---|
| **Digestive system** – 50 points<br><br>Wave-like muscular contractions that push food down the food tube.<br><br>*(What is peristalsis?)* | **Urinary system** – 50 points<br><br>Blood enters the kidney through this artery.<br><br>*(What is the renal artery?)* |
| **Digestive system** – 40 points<br><br>The process of breaking down food into nutrients that can be used by the cells of the body.<br><br>*(What is digestion?)* | **Urinary system** – 40 points<br><br>Tiny filtering units in the kidneys that remove unwanted materials from the blood.<br><br>*(What are the nephrons?)* |
| **Digestive system** – 30 points<br><br>A bag that holds our food for four hours while hydrochloric acid and digestive juices continue to break down the food.<br><br>*(What is the stomach?)* | **Urinary system** – 30 points<br><br>These organs clean your blood by filtering it.<br><br>*(What are the kidneys?)* |
| **Digestive system** – 20 points<br><br>Tiny, finger-like structures in the small intestine where food is absorbed into the blood.<br><br>*(What are the villi?)* | **Urinary system** – 20 points<br><br>An organ that holds liquid waste material.<br><br>*(What is the bladder?)* |
| **Digestive system** – 10 points<br><br>The liquid in your mouth that contains an enzyme that begins to break down carbohydrates.<br><br>*(What is saliva?)* | **Urinary system** – 10 points<br><br>A liquid waste produced by the kidneys.<br><br>*(What is urine?)* |

| | |
|---|---|
| **Endocrine system** – 50 points<br><br>Substance produced by the pancreas that controls the level of sugar in blood.<br><br>*(What is insulin?)* | **Nervous system** – 50 points<br><br>The parts of the central nervous system.<br><br>*(What are the brain and spinal cord?)* |
| **Endocrine system** – 40 points<br><br>Chemicals that are secreted into the bloodstream and affect the activities of certain organs in the body.<br><br>*(What are hormones?)* | **Nervous system** – 40 points<br><br>The name of the body's communication network.<br><br>*(What is the nervous system?)* |
| **Endocrine system** – 30 points<br><br>A gland that is sometimes called the master gland.<br><br>*(What is the pituitary gland?)* | **Nervous system** – 30 points<br><br>These carry the messages from both inside and outside the body to the brain.<br><br>*(What are nerves or nerve fibers?)* |
| **Endocrine system** – 20 points<br><br>Glands on top of the kidneys that produce a chemical that makes your heart beat faster.<br><br>*(What are the adrenal glands?)* | **Nervous system** – 20 points<br><br>Name of nerve tissue linking the brain to lower parts of the body.<br><br>*(What is the spinal cord?)* |
| **Endocrine system** – 10 points<br><br>A gland in the throat that controls the rate at which cells use food.<br><br>*(What is the thyroid?)* | **Nervous system** – 10 points<br><br>This controls—among other things—a person's thinking and creativity.<br><br>*(What is the brain?)* |

| | |
|---|---|
| **Endocrine system** – 50 points<br><br>Substance produced by the pancreas that controls the level of sugar in blood.<br><br>*(What is insulin?)* | **Nervous system** – 50 points<br><br>The parts of the central nervous system.<br><br>*(What are the brain and spinal cord?)* |
| **Endocrine system** – 40 points<br><br>Chemicals that are secreted into the bloodstream and affect the activities of certain organs in the body.<br><br>*(What are hormones?)* | **Nervous system** – 40 points<br><br>The name of the body's communication network.<br><br>*(What is the nervous system?)* |
| **Endocrine system** – 30 points<br><br>A gland that is sometimes called the master gland.<br><br>*(What is the pituitary gland?)* | **Nervous system** – 30 points<br><br>These carry the messages from both inside and outside the body to the brain.<br><br>*(What are nerves or nerve fibers?)* |
| **Endocrine system** – 20 points<br><br>Glands on top of the kidneys that produce a chemical that makes your heart beat faster.<br><br>*(What are the adrenal glands?)* | **Nervous system** – 20 points<br><br>Name of nerve tissue linking the brain to lower parts of the body.<br><br>*(What is the spinal cord?)* |
| **Endocrine system** – 10 points<br><br>A gland in the throat that controls the rate at which cells use food.<br><br>*(What is the thyroid?)* | **Nervous system** – 10 points<br><br>This controls—among other things—a person's thinking and creativity.<br><br>*(What is the brain?)* |

| **Muscular system** – 50 points | **Skeletal system** – 50 points |
|---|---|
| Another name for skeletal muscles. | Bones store this kind of nutrient. |
| *(What are voluntary muscles?)* | *(What minerals or calcium and phosphorus?)* |
| **Muscular system** – 40 points | **Skeletal system** – 40 points |
| The name for muscles that work without your control. | Bones must have this substance to provide the nutrients and oxygen they need. |
| *(What are involuntary muscles?)* | *(What is blood?)* |
| **Muscular system** – 30 points | **Skeletal system** – 30 points |
| The name of the involuntary muscle that helps you to breathe. | Some bones manufacture these in their marrow. |
| *(What is the diaphragm?)* | *(What are blood cells?)* |
| **Muscular system** – 20 points | **Skeletal system** – 20 points |
| The body has over 400 of this type of muscle. | One purpose of the skeletal system is to protect some of these. |
| *(What are skeletal muscles?)* | *(What are body organs [or vital organs], such as the brain and heart?)* |
| **Muscular system** – 10 points | **Skeletal system** – 10 points |
| Names of two muscles of the upper arm. | The "straps" that hold two bones together. |
| *(What are the biceps and triceps?)* | *(What are ligaments?)* |

# Dissecting a Heart

**Looking at the outside of the heart:**

1.  The size of the heart depends on the size of the animal. A larger animal has a larger heart. A human being's heart is about the size of a fist.

    • What kind of heart are you examining? _____

    • Make a fist and place it over the top of the animal heart. Is the animal heart larger or smaller than that of a human being? _____

2.  The heart is made up of smooth muscle tissue. The heart is an involuntary muscle, which means that the muscle works without conscious control. Examples of other smooth muscles are the stomach and intestines.

    • Touch and feel the reddish-brown muscle tissue on the heart. How does it feel?

3.  All hearts have a small amount of fat around the top edge right above the muscle tissue. A small amount of fat is normal and healthy. However if the muscle of the heart is completely covered with fat, the muscle cells can't work as they should.

    • Find the fat tissue around the top edge of the heart. How does the fat tissue feel? Does it feel different from the muscle tissue? _____

4.  The arteries and veins around the outside of the heart bring food and oxygen to the heart itself.

    • Look at the lines all over the outside of the heart. Push the liquid inside the lines with your finger. With a probe, follow along inside one of the bigger lines. Are the cells of this heart receiving food and oxygen right now? _____

5.  The veins and arteries attached to the top section of the heart are the largest in the body.  Find these tubes on the top of the heart. Feel them and then describe what you think they are like.

6.  The thin outer covering of the heart is called the pericardium.

    • Take your fingernail or the point of the probe and peel off a small section of the pericardium near the bottom tip of the heart. Take a close look at the pericardium. Describe what this tissue is like.

    • Now find the pulmonary artery in the heart. With the open side of the heart faring you, poke the second finger of your right hand into the back of the right ventricle to find the opening that leads out of the heart. As you take your finger out, put a straw in the opening.

**Looking at the inside of the heart:**

7. Now you will cut open the heart and identify its parts and trace how blood flows through it.

    • Have one person pick up the heart and hold it in both hands. Hold it with the top of the heart up and the bottom pointing down.

8. The right side of the heart is the soft, thinner side. This is the side where blood loaded with carbon dioxide comes in from all parts of the body.

    • Squeeze the sides of the heart until you can identify a soft, thinner side and a hard, firmer side. When you have found the firmer side, hold it in the palm of your left hand.

9. On the right side of the top of the heart is a flap with a scalloped edge. The flap has an opening on the top. When you look through this opening, you are looking at the upper chamber of the heart, called the atrium. Right below the right atrium is the right ventricle.

    • Use your second finger (or your right hand) to find the opening that leads into the right atrium and push down. If your finger goes all the way, you are in the right place. Next, take your finger out and put a straw where your finger was. Then put the heart down. Push the straw until you can see a bulge on the bottom that shows where the end of the straw is.

    • Insert the point of your scissors through the bulge. Then cut the side open all the way up to the top following the straw. Pull the whole side of the heart open. Now remove the straw and you can look at the inside of the heart.

    • In the heart may be clotted blood, which is a black jelly-like substance. Pull it out so you can clearly see the right atrium and ventricle.

10. The tricuspid valve separates the right atrium and right ventricle. Blood comes into the heart and flows from the atrium into the ventricle. The valve closes at the right time to keep the blood from flowing backward.

    • Put your finger under the strings or strands that look like threads. You should be able to see the transparent membrane that is the valve.

11. The pulmonary artery is the blood vessel that carries blood loaded with carbon dioxide from the heart to the lungs. Like all the other arteries, this artery carries blood away from the heart. But this is the only artery in the body that carries blood containing carbon dioxide. Other arteries all carry oxygen-rich blood.

- Now find the pulmonary artery in the heart. With the open side of the heart facing you, poke the second finger of your right hand into the back of the right ventricle to find the opening that leads out of the heart. As you take your finger out, put a straw in the opening.

12. When the blood arrives at the lungs it unloads the carbon dioxide and picks up oxygen. It comes back to the heart through the pulmonary vein. Like all the other veins, this vein carries blood 'o the heart. But this is the only vein in the body that carries oxygen-rich blood. Other veins all carry blood loaded with carbon dioxide. The blood in the pulmonary vein enters the left atrium of the heart. From there it passes into the left ventricle.

   - Pick up the heart again. With the firmer, harder side in the left palm of your hand. Find the opening on top of the left atrium. Use the same procedure you used on the right side. First poke your finger into the left atrium. Take out your finger and put in a straw. Push the straw all the way down to the bottom of the heart. Next, insert the point of the scissors where the end of the straw is. Then cut the left side of the heart open, so that you can see both the left atrium and ventricle.

   - Is the left side of the heart you are working with thicker and heavier? What do you think might cause this?

13. On the left side of the heart, the mitral valve separates the atrium and ventricle.

   - Look at the strands of the mitral valve. Are they the same or different from the strands of the valve on the right side? _____

14. The blood leaves the left ventricle through the aorta. From here the blood is pumped to all parts of the body.

   - Towards the middle of the heart find the opening in the left ventricle that leads to the aorta. Put a straw in the opening. If the arch of the aorta has not been cut, three openings may be present. One leads to the upper part of the body, one to the arms, and one to the lower part of the body.

15. The semilunar valve is inside the aorta. The valve has little half moons called cusps. This valve covers the opening that leads to the coronary arteries.

   - Cut the aorta from the top down and examine the semilunar valve. Pull down one of the cusps in order to see the opening leading to the coronary arteries. What is the job of the coronary arteries?

# Normal Age Range for Physical Changes in Girls

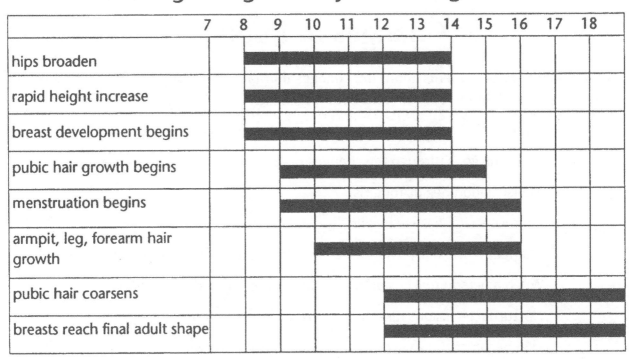

# Normal Age Range for Physical Changes in Boys

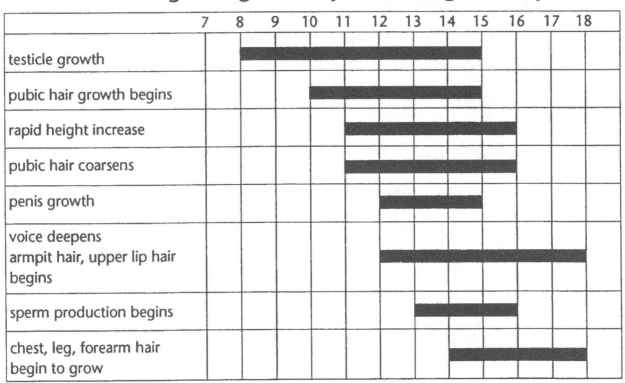

# Changes of Puberty

**Are the following statements about the changes that take place during puberty true or false? Write T or F in the blank before each statement?**

_____ 1. Glands release hormones that trigger the beginning of puberty.

_____ 2. Everyone goes through the changes of puberty at exactly the same time.

_____ 3. Menstruation begins for girls.

_____ 4. There is an increase in height.

_____ 5. Changes in the body's hormone levels may cause frequent changes in mood.

_____ 6. When a person reaches puberty is partly determined by heredity.

_____ 7. Nocturnal emissions take place for boys.

_____ 8. Skin becomes dry as sweat glands become less active.

_____ 9. The changes of puberty follow a pattern.

_____10. Reproductive organs develop and begin to function.

_____11. The age at which puberty starts will affect what a person will be like as an adult.

_____12. Body hair begins to grow.

_____13. The body changes shape during puberty, but the face changes little.

_____14. Voice changes occur.

_____15. Girls' hips become wider.

_____16. There is a stronger desire to be independent.

# Male Reproductive Organs

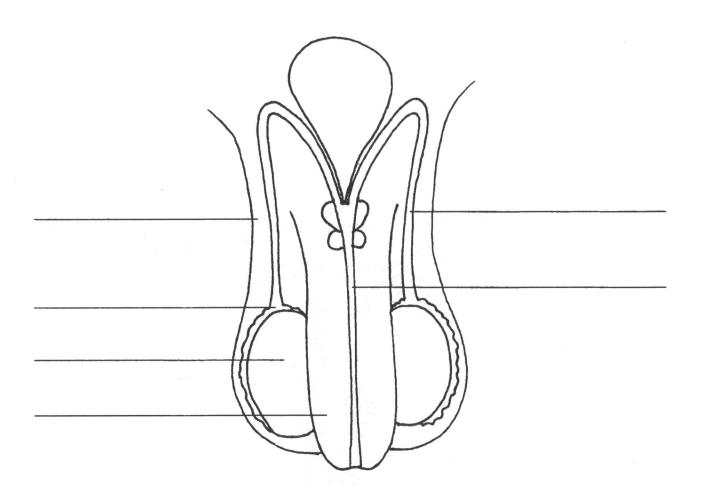

# Female Reproductive Organs

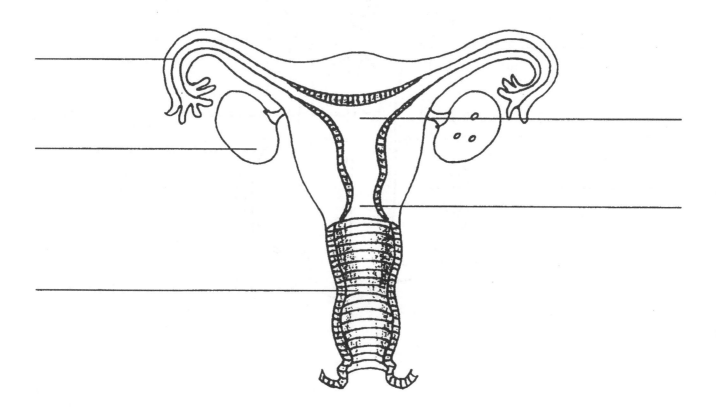

# Stages of Labor

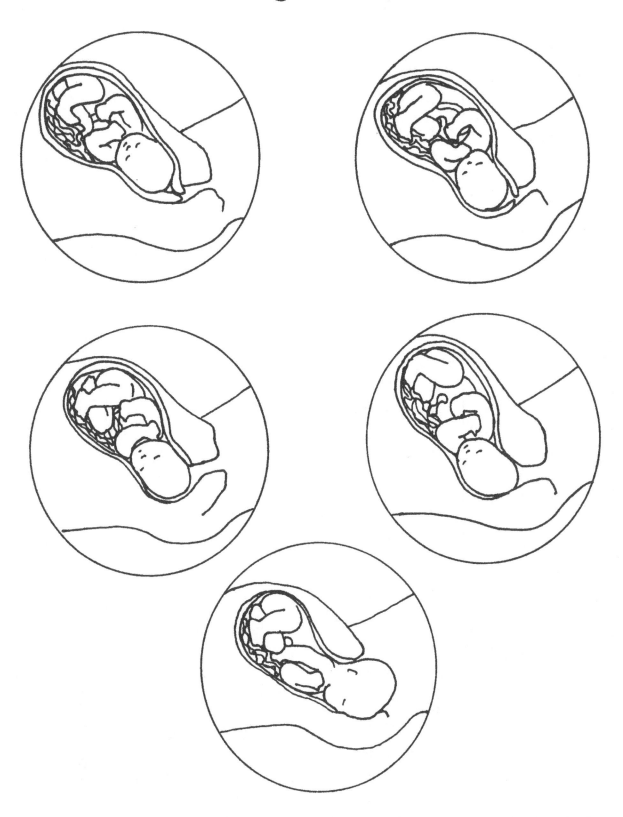

# Family Group Chart

Father _____

Born _____ Place _____

Married _____

Father's Father _____

Father's Mother _____

Mother _____

Born _____ Place _____

Place _____

Mother's Father _____

Mother's Mother _____

## Children

Last Name, First Name
Middle Name, Nickname or Other

| | When Born Day/Month/Year | Where Born Town/County/State | Date of Marriage To Whom | When Died Day/Month/Year |
|---|---|---|---|---|
| 1. | | | | |
| 2. | | | | |
| 3. | | | | |
| 4. | | | | |
| 5. | | | | |

## Religious Rituals

_____

_____

## Sources of Information

_____

_____

# Family Tree

_(My name)_

Born:

Place:

Family of God:

Married:

_(Mother)_

Born:

Place:

Family of God:

_(Father)_

Born:

Place:

Family of God:

_(Grandmother)_

Born:

Place:

Family of God:

_(Grandfather)_

Born:

Place:

Family of God:

_(Grandmother)_

Born:

Place:

Family of God:

_(Grandfather)_

Born:

Place:

Family of God:

_(Great grandmother)_

Born:

Place:

Died:

Family of God:

_(Great grandfather)_

Born:

Place:

Died:

Family of God:

_(Great grandmother)_

Born:

Place:

Died:

Family of God:

_(Great grandfather)_

Born:

Place:

Died:

Family of God:

_(Great grandmother)_

Born:

Place:

Died:

Family of God:

_(Great grandfather)_

Born:

Place:

Died:

Family of God:

_(Great grandmother)_

Born:

Place:

Died:

Family of God:

_(Great grandfather)_

Born:

Place:

Died:

Family of God:

# Some Sources of Help

People who have a terminal (incurable) illness know that they are going to die. Some terminal illnesses last a long time. Hospice is a program that provides special care for people who are dying. The specific services available through hospice vary from place to place. Often, hospice nurses visit homes to help both those who are ill and their families. In some areas hospice also provides a place where people who have a terminal illness can be cared for until they die. Here hospice provides a home-like atmosphere. The staff works not to cure the illness, but to keep those who are dying as comfortable as possible. They are concerned with more than the physical needs of people. They also attend to spiritual, emotional, and social needs. Hospice workers are experienced in helping people with terminal illness and their families to face and accept the fact of death.

## Support Groups

A support group consists of a group of people who meet to help each other. The people in the group have all gone through a similar problem. For example, parents who have children with certain illnesses may form a support group. Many people find it a great help to talk to others who have gone through the same experience.

## Christian Counselors

Counselors are trained professionals who understand the grieving process. They are available to talk with families or individuals who are having rough times. Counselors may be needed to help people make the difficult adjustments that follow the death of a family member. It is important that the counselor be a Christian. Then he or she can talk about problems of faith and about the Christian hope.

## Pastors

Pastors are prepared to provide comfort and guidance to people who are facing death or are grieving. As the shepherd of God's flock (1 Peter 5:2), a pastor is called to care for God's people. Sometimes people who are angry or depressed have a hard time praying. The prayers of the pastor (and of the elders and other church members) support them in a special way. Many people have felt the power of prayer supporting them during times of grief.

# Nerve Cell and Parts

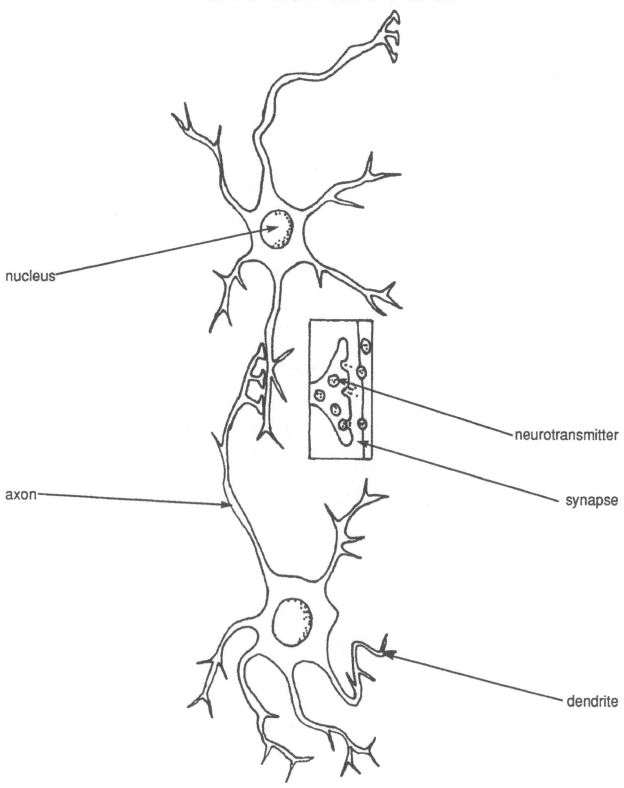

nucleus

neurotransmitter

synapse

axon

dendrite

# Where Drugs Harm the Human Body

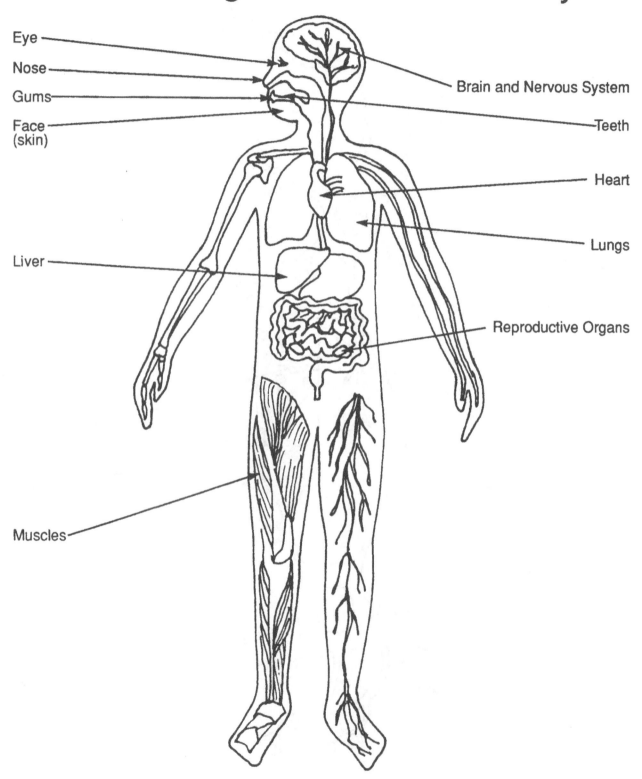

Eye

Nose

Gums

Face
(skin)

Brain and Nervous System

Teeth

Heart

Lungs

Liver

Reproductive Organs

Muscles

# Where Drugs Harm the Human Body

Eye                                    alcohol

Nose                                   inhalants
                                       cocaine

Gums                                   tobacco

Liver                                  alcohol
                                       inhalants

Face (skin)                            tobacco
                                       steroids

Muscles                                alcohol
                                       inhalants

Brain and Nervous System               alcohol
                                       inhalants
                                       marijuana
                                       stimulants: amphetamines, crank, ice, cocaine,
                                         crack, freebase
                                       designer drugs
                                       depressants: tranquilizers, barbiturates, sleeping
                                         pills
                                       narcotics: codeine, morphine, heroin
                                       hallucinogens: LSD, PDP, peyote, mescaline

Teeth                                  tobacco

Heart                                  tobacco
                                       marijuana
                                       alcohol
                                       inhalants
                                       steroids
                                       stimulants: amphetamines, crank, ice, cocaine,
                                       crack, freebase
                                       depressants